Education and Psychology of the Gifted Series

James H. Borland, Editor

Planning and Implementing
Programs for the Gifted

James H. Borland

Patterns of Influence on Gifted Learners:
The Home, the Self, and the School

Joyce L. VanTassel-Baska and Paula Olszewski-Kubilius, Editors

Reaching the Gifted Underachiever:
Program Strategy and Design

Patricia L. Supplee

Reaching the
Gifted Underachiever
Program Strategy and Design

PATRICIA L. SUPPLEE

Teachers College, Columbia University
New York and London

Published by Teachers College Press, 1234 Amsterdam Avenue
New York, NY 10027

Library of Congress Cataloging-in-Publication Data

Supplee, Patricia L.
  Reaching the gifted underachiever: program strategy and design / Patricia L. Supplee.
     p. cm. —(Education and psychology of the gifted series)
  Includes bibliographical references.
  ISBN 0-8077-3020-3 (alk. paper). —ISBN 0-8077-3019-X (pbk. : alk. paper)
  1. Exceptional children—United States. 2. Underachievers—United States. 3. Gifted
children—Education—United States. 4. Special education—United States—Curricula. I. Title. II. Series.
LC3981.S87 1990
371.95'6—dc20   90-10772
                                    CIP

Printed on acid-free paper

Manufactured in the United States of America

96 95 94 93 92 91 90   8 7 6 5 4 3 2 1

To all the children and educators from whom I have learned so much, especially Robert, who first made me aware of the special problems gifted underachievers face.

The research cited in this work was supported in part by a grant from the New Jersey State Department of Education, Division of General Academic Education.

I gratefully acknowledge the assistance of Hope Van den Heuvel, Lorraine Weingast, Elaine Pace, George Johnson, Alan Markowitz, and an anonymous reviewer for their comments on earlier drafts of this book.

Contents

Foreword

In some ways, the motto of the United Negro College Fund—"A Mind Is a Terrible Thing to Waste"—is the theme of this helpful book by Patricia Supplee, for the book is about how to reach underachievers, children who have indicated by some means that they have potential for achievement at a much higher level than their performance. By not achieving at or near a predicted level, these youngsters are wasting their potential.

My colleagues and I wrote in a report of a three-year, mostly unsuccessful, effort to reverse the pattern of underachievement among a group of gifted high school boys:

> The intellectually gifted underachiever is an ubiquitous phenomenon, identifiable in all schools at all academic levels; but he appears a most significant challenge at the secondary school level. He may appear in many guises—lazy, disinterested in school, bored, rebellious, unable to relate to teachers, or having difficulty with one or more subjects. Nonetheless, no matter what the appearance, he is generally a youngster who is not using his intellectual potential in meeting the academic demands of the school. As generally defined, the high ability underachiever not only fails to reach the academic excellence which his outstanding ability suggests he is able to attain, but also is found lagging behind the achievement level of students of average ability, or, at best, only managing to hold his own with them. (Ralph, Goldberg, & Passow, 1966, p. 1)

We used the male pronoun "he" because that was the writing convention at the time, but underachievers are found among students of either sex. I found EQUAL numbers of boys and girls—a first in the field, but a phenomenon that has persisted over 5 years. I should do another study—but not right now!

In Supplee's case, it was with Robert that she felt profound "failure" and it was his behavior—ending up in prison—that started her on the search for ways that she and her colleagues could avoid other Roberts. As she tried to teach Robert and felt constant dissatisfaction and frustration, she kept thinking: "Somewhere, someone knows something that somehow has to be effective enough to keep kids from getting to the point that Robert reached." This book is the result of Supplee's search and, while it does not contain the final answers to the complex problem we call "underachievement," it clearly provides readers with a better understanding of the nature of this phenomenon and some solid insights into what practitioners can do to reverse it.

The author has designed and tested a curriculum with differentiated instructional practices and a heavy affective component. Writing often from the student's perspective, Dr. Supplee gives us a description of the program in sufficient detail that readers will recognize what she was up to, what the program was that she designed and tested, how it worked for her and her colleagues, and how it can be adapted by other teachers who are confronted by this phenomenon in their classes. Her presentation is a fine blend of practice and program, soundly based on research and theory. She does not have recipes, but she certainly provides practical direction for all of us concerned with reversing underachievement among gifted students.

To be sure that readers understand where she is coming from, the author provides us with a clear definition of both *gifted* and *underachievement*. She then provides us with case studies of eight students in her school to illustrate what they actually look like and how they behave, putting them in a theoretical context as the basis for designing interventions.

A rather thorough and perceptive review of the theory and research literature helps the reader understand the phenomenon better, what program interventions have been tried with what degrees of success, and the basis for the program Pat Supplee designed and implemented.

The bulk of the book is a detailed description of the UAG (Underachieving Gifted) program design—its philosophy and rationale, goals, differentiated instruction, restructured environment, and parent involvement. Pat Supplee knows that change is not easy in schools and so she draws on what research says about implementing change, combines it with her own experiences in bringing about programmatic change, and provides guidance for readers who want to make changes in their efforts to deal with underachievement among gifted students.

The UAG program encompasses all aspects of the curriculum. The author's suggestions and guidelines are clear, concise, practical, and integrated in the sense that all chapters in Part 3, "Curriculum," are related to an overall plan and not simply a collection of isolated pieces of the curriculum and instruction for an underachieving population.

Although this book will not resolve all the issues and questions surrounding underachievement among gifted students, readers will find it useful and insightful. There is no question that Supplee has helped us to understand the nature of underachievement and provided us with sound, practical guidance as to how to reverse it in our gifted students, with the result of not wasting good minds and the potential for outstanding performance.

A. Harry Passow
Jacob H. Schiff Professor of Education
Teachers College, Columbia University

Preface

Sometimes there are children who haunt us. We have done our very best as their teachers, but our best wasn't enough. They needed more. So it was with Robert. When he let outsiders glimpse the workings of his mind, it was sharply evident that he was gifted. The world could be his, and the world could be a better place because he had lived. But it wouldn't be. Robert was a rebel, tracked in the lowest classes. He walked around with a sullen expression on his face and took little care with his personal appearance. He cut classes often, failed most tests—no wonder his teachers had given up hope. He dropped out of school, which wasn't surprising, but the greater tragedy was that he wound up in prison at a very young age.

I knew Robert; I tried to teach him. Only occasionally did I know that I had reached him at all, but those occasions had a profound impact on me. This book is in your hands because I needed to quell the dissatisfaction and frustration I felt when I didn't know enough to be able to help him. I kept thinking, "Somewhere, someone knows something that somehow has to be effective enough to keep kids from getting to the point that Robert reached." I kept reading and kept hoping that I'd find the perfect answer.

In the course of looking and learning, I met Joanne Whitmore, Sylvia Rimm, and Priscilla Vail, first through their writings, then in person. They had asked many of the same questions and suggested some solutions, but I continued to feel that theirs were only partial answers, and not practical for me. I had to come up with my own answers, answers that would also address how underachievement meshes with current ideas about what giftedness really is.

This book is the result of that search. The program for gifted underachievers that is described was developed as part of an initiative by the State Department of Education, Division of General Academics, State of New Jersey. Exemplary programs were funded for a one-year period, renewable for a second year. I taught the program during the initial year. During the second year, Sherry Gooen taught the identified underachievers and after three years, a third teacher, Maryann Meyer, took over the responsibility for teaching our underachieving gifted (UAG) students. Sherry and Maryann were successful using the very earliest scribblings that eventually became this book. If you hope to implement a similar program, you should also find this volume practical.

While focusing on the day-to-day challenges of implementing and teaching an adaptive program, the UAG design was conceived within a theoretical framework. Part 1, therefore, opens by establishing a common framework and a definition of underachievement among the gifted that matches today's theories of giftedness. You will meet some of our students through case studies. By considering their histories in light of Tannenbaum's conception of the necessary elements for giftedness, we see that underachievement in our students is the absence of at least one of those elements, sometimes more. Chapter 2 shares the historical insights that a search of the literature revealed. We see what has been tried, what didn't work, and what was at least partially successful.

This book is intended to be first and foremost practical. Part 2 presents the program design, providing the philosophy, rationale, and program goals for Chapter 3. In Chapter 3, also, the differentiated instructional practices that were effective in changing students' behaviors are presented from the students' point of view. We see why the affective curriculum always came before the cognitive, how journal writing bridged the gap between the two, and how individualization, acceleration, enrichment, and remediation fit into the UAG classroom. Because the environment itself was restructured, what was done to modify the classroom surroundings, the class management strategies used, and scheduling variations are also described.

Chapter 4 takes you step-by-step through implementing a program in your own school. Possible pitfalls are discussed to prevent dooming an innovation before it can prove itself. Chapter 5 explains the process used to identify gifted underachievers, a process that screens the student population with minimal effort on the teacher's part, and that maximizes teacher awareness of these children's characteristics. The identification process is followed by a description of start-up tasks, such as developing case histories, preparing for the change in teacher responsibilities, and orienting students. A way of providing for students who are screened for, but not admitted to, the underachievers' program is also delineated.

Part 3 offers help in the day-to-day practice of a teacher in a UAG program. The curriculum used for each content area is thoroughly detailed. Chapter 6 describes the results of current research on reading instruction for the gifted and provides strategies that teachers can use in the classroom to implement an exciting reading-writing curriculum that is based on sound theory. Actual lesson plans, annotated bibliographies of works used by the children, issues of scope and sequence of skills, record keeping, readability levels, and scheduling of individualized instruction are presented.

Chapter 7 discusses current research in effective teaching of mathematics to gifted students. The theory is then translated into practice. A differentiated scope and sequence for UAG math instruction is provided. The kinds of instructional decisions important for effective math teaching, issues in the assessment of the students, and requisite teacher competencies are included. I detail record-keeping strategies, provide sample lesson plans, and discuss teaching basic facts, the use of calculators, and the importance of manipulative materials for students of all ages.

Chapter 8 describes the affective curricula. There are five parts to this curricula, group self-direction skills, work-study skills, cooperative sports and games, pro-social skills, and stress-reduction skills. Each one is explained thoroughly and a rationale for its inclusion is provided. Sample lesson plans for each subcurriculum are provided, along with anecdotes that support the extraordinary impact these curricula had on the students.

In our concern for students, we must not forget their parents. In Chapter 9, I describe the curriculum used to help the parents understand and support the changes their children were undergoing. Again, this curriculum is not presented in isolation; I discuss the previous work on which this curriculum is based.

Chapter 10 includes some of the changes the program underwent as it developed. Understanding what happens when students are ready to exit the group and managing the entrance of new students are discussed. Some of the unresolved issues, as well, are presented for consideration.

The ideas presented in this book worked for me as I designed and implemented the program and curricula, for the teachers who took over the classes for me as I continued my research, and for the gifted, underachieving children that we met through the established program. The ideas are too important to keep under wraps; they provide at least partial answers to questions about how to help the most neglected of our gifted children. More important, by sharing the practical, step-by-step approach used to implement the UAG program, I hope to give you the courage to try the same. It can be done. You will learn much more than any one book can tell you as you work with the enigmatic, underachieving gifted. May you be encouraged to share what you learn with the rest of us.

I don't believe teachers or schools can be or should be expected to be the solution to all the problems of the world, but I do believe our job is to educate. As educators, we make a quiet pact with our society that we will pass on a body of cultural knowledge and prepare students to use that knowledge for their own futures and the betterment of society. With children like Robert, until only recently, I did not succeed. Now, I do. My deepest hope is that you will be able to learn from my discoveries to help all the students you know like Robert.

Acknowledgments

There are so many people who have contributed to my general knowledge of gifted education over the past decade. My deepest thanks to all the professionals in the field whose work I read voraciously hoping to find a miracle cure for these children, and to A. Harry Passow, Heidi Hayes Jacobs, and Joanne Whitmore, who helped me see that it was my turn to add to what was known.

It is proper to recognize the contributions of many others as well, including the children in the classes for gifted underachievers and their parents who wholeheartedly supported them and me while we learned together. Sherry Gooen and Maryann Meyer, the two teachers who took over the underachievers' program and proved that it was not just a one-teacher phenomenon, deserve my deep appreciation. Thanks are due as well to Jeanne Carlson, gifted education specialist in the New Jersey State Department of Education for her assistance through the grant-supported days and to Stanley K. Robinson, my former chief school administrator. Without his vision and encouragement, it is not likely that any of this work would have occurred.

Most of all, I wish to thank my family who put up with my preoccupation so often during the researching and writing of this book. I could not have completed it without their patience and help and the encouragement I received from their pride in my success. Ron, Lauren, and Mark, I love you all very, very much.

PART ONE

OVERVIEW

CHAPTER 1

Who Is the Gifted Underachiever?

"Robert is a gifted child . . ."

Most people who hear those words imagine a child superior in many, if not all, areas of development. Most people expect that children like Robert will mature earlier, that they will be more adept socially, more emotionally stable, and highly creative. They expect the Roberts of the world to be involved in many extracurricular activities and to produce excellent work in all intellectual and academic areas. Indeed, many of the gifted fit this image as children. Robert does not.

Robert is an underachiever. As an adolescent, he demonstrated in English class that he understood the motivations of the four men in Stephen Crane's "The Open Boat." He appreciated and could imitate the satire in Charles Lamb's "Dissertation Upon a Roast Pig." He could decipher the symbolism in Robert Frost's poetry and could write exquisite poetry of his own. Robert also was tracked homogeneously with the "losers" because of his habit of cutting classes, his rebellious attitude towards teachers, and his lack of concern about passing tests. Robert began to escape through drugs, dropped out of school at age 16, joined the Army, and went AWOL three weeks later. He committed armed robbery on his way home, and from his jail cell, he wrote beautifully and sensitively about how deeply he cared about people and about life.

Robert *was* gifted, but he obviously would never have "made it" into a gifted program. And he certainly didn't "make it" in life—at least not through his early adult years. It is people like Robert that make us question what giftedness really is. What makes promise go awry, and what might help such students reach their potential? They seem to need so much more than their more typical gifted counterparts. Can we give them what they need? I maintain that the answer is yes. Teachers have experienced success in identifying and intervening in the lives of underachieving gifted children. Through case studies you will meet actual children who were helped. These children will share what they felt was most instrumental in reversing their patterns of underachievement.

The program for gifted underachievers in Green Township, New Jersey, was based on sound theory, but it was not purely theoretical. It was practical and taught by several teachers over a period of five years, each of whom found it easy to implement and effective for the children served. This book will offer you guidelines to set up a similar alternative program. Ultimately, many other gifted, underachieving students may come closer to realizing their hidden talents.

ESTABLISHING A COMMON DEFINITION

There are many gifted children who never reach their potential, though they appear to be capable of outstanding achievement in socially desirable fields. Most professionals in our schools are able to identify children, like Robert, who are gifted underachievers. These children hint at exceptional ability but do not achieve excellence. They find school an uncomfortable, stressful experience. They may fail, or they may exhibit learning or emotional problems that interfere substantially with their own success and sometimes with the total class environment. These children experience frustration and become a burden to themselves and to others. But who, exactly, are they? Can we define *gifted underachiever* so that we have a clear conception of whom we are looking for?

Giftedness in adults has been described as outstanding achievement in a socially desirable field. For children, giftedness is recognized most often as general intellectual ability or as a specific academic aptitude in one or more distinct disciplines such as math, language, science, and art. This type of childhood giftedness is most often identified by high IQ and achievement test scores, sometimes by teacher recommendation. PL 97-35, the Education Consolidation and Improvement Act passed by Congress in 1981, defined school-age, gifted children as "children who give evidence of high perform-ance capability in areas such as intellectual, creative, artistic, leadership ca-pacity, or specific academic fields, and who require services or activities not ordinarily provided by the school in order to fully develop such capabilities" (Sec. 582). This definition of childhood giftedness expands the areas in which we might look for special abilities. It also implies potential that may or may not be indicated by IQ and achievement tests. Evidence of "capability" may result from observation of high interest in and knowledge of a specialized area, from talent demonstrated in an extracurricular area, or from student products other than tests. While giftedness can exist in areas such as creative thinking or psychomotor ability, we will focus our attention on the academic areas. Success or lack of it in school has an enormous impact on students' future choices.

Underachievement, on the other hand, generally refers to children who appear to have high academic potential (if IQ and/or achievement tests are to be trusted as predictors) but who are not functioning successfully in school, either in a general or specific discipline. Underachievement can exist in areas of giftedness other than the academic. Occasionally in schools we hear reference to "negative leadership ability," i.e., the ability to lead, but the use of that ability in a nonproductive or counterproductive manner. This, too, is a form of underachievement, but rarely is much concern expressed about, or effort given to reversing this type of underachievement. Never do we hear about a student's lack of creative thinking ability, or poor performance in the psychomotor areas or the visual or performing arts, though here, also, it is possible to underachieve. This lack of attention probably reflects the fact that few repercussions arise for students in our schools if they do not live up to their potential in these areas.

Academic underachievement is not clear-cut. In the case of nearly every student we identified, creative or productive thinking and/or creativity in the visual or performing arts emerged before any increase in academic performance that was measurable on standardized achievement tests or report cards. Perhaps the lack of validation of the creative aspects of our students' identities has a significant impact on their development in other areas.

In this book I define the gifted underachiever as an elementary student with high academic *ability* (as indicated by one standard) and low academic *achievement* (as indicated by a second measure). The academic ability was assessed through an IQ score or through achievement test scores at the eighth or ninth stanine. (Later, one student was included through teacher ratings only.) The low academic achievement was indicated by low achievement test scores (a difference of two or more stanines from the IQ score) or by teacher ratings or school grades showing a marked discrepancy from expected achievement based on IQ or achievement tests.

A VIEW OF OUR GIFTED UNDERACHIEVERS

The children identified for the special program to help them reverse their underachievement all displayed high potential and low achievement. But that is where their similarity to one another ended. The sixteen individuals differed in age, race, gender, socioeconomic status, personality traits, and family patterns and cultural background. I shall discuss eight of the students here, as examples of the effect of the Underachieving Gifted (UAG) program. The students' names and insignificant details of their lives have been changed to protect their identities, but each case is real.

Our first clue that Marcia, a nine-year-old third grader, might be gifted came when she scored over 130 on the group IQ test that was administered routinely to all the students in her class as part of the screening for the gifted program. When we first met her, neither her parents nor her teachers could name any particular area in which Marcia had special talent. Her achievement test scores were average for her grade. Marcia was achieving on a low-average level in class. The only hint that she might be different from other children, according to her mother, was that Marcia asked hard questions that were unusual for a third grader: "If the sky is blue because of the sun, is it blue when it gets close to the stars?" "Why do some people who are white have dark skin and some people who are black have light skin so it looks like they're the same color?" She is an identical twin; her twin sister was classified as educable/mentally retarded. Her other siblings, one older brother and an older sister, had also been classified for special education services. In most screening processes for gifted programs, Marcia's IQ score would appear to be an anomaly, and she would be passed over. We, however, felt we needed to know Marcia better and looked more closely at her school history and her potential. Was she being allowed to underachieve in school because of low parental and teacher expectations based on family background?

Jamal entered our district as a second grader. Prior to that time, he had lived in a series of foster home placements where he had been malnourished and physically abused. Jamal was afflicted with severe asthma and was hyperkinetic. He was medicated for both but, due to side effects, was eventually withdrawn from the medication for hyperactivity. His adoptive mother had him retained a year when he entered our school. It was hoped this would help him gain some academic time—and it did—but Jamal's social and emotional skills were also severely delayed. One year was not enough to help him surmount all his difficulties. His academic, social, and emotional problems led to classification by the child study team. Jamal received special services to help him overcome his handicaps. His teachers, though, felt he needed more help. He frequently flew into a rage, and he often was physically abusive to others, causing him to spend much time in the office to "cool off." When he wasn't acting out, Jamal was seldom on task; he found it difficult to concentrate or to discipline himself to do anything he did not want to do. In short, he was not successful in a regular classroom setting. Given all these difficulties, it is remarkable that his classroom teachers still saw in him the sparks of giftedness. They often remarked on his exceptional artistic ability, which deeply involved him for long stretches of time (defying the idea that he couldn't attend to a task). His extraordinarily broad and precise oral vocabulary was totally out of keeping with his IQ of 87 as measured on the WISC-R.

Mike came to our attention during first grade. He was a very handsome youth who appeared to be very bright, learning quickly and easily. He read fluently, well beyond his peers in first grade. Yet his social and emotional needs were overwhelming. He was unable to make friends. He frequently exploded in tremendous frustration at his teachers and refused to do what they asked. Mike was referred to the child study team but not classified because his emotional problems were not causing him to fail to learn; in fact, his achievement test scores were well above average. His emotional control did not improve, however, and by second grade, the school psychologist was asked to intervene. Because Mike was still achieving well beyond grade level and so was not eligible for special services, the psychologist was asked to suggest changes in the classroom that might help him. Mike was given instruction in relaxation techniques and a place where he could go for time out when he needed to vent his anger and frustration. Mike took advantage of these interventions, but still exploded regularly. He became the victim of other children who goaded him to see when the fuse would ignite. When Mike moved to third grade in another building, all intervention stopped. He often infuriated his teacher, and other students still made him the butt of their torment. By fourth grade it was evident that something else needed to be done to help him as he could not function successfully in a group. While his reading achievement and IQ score indicated superior ability, Mike was now having enough difficulty in math to be a low-average student.

Vicki was a student who almost qualified for the gifted program from the time she entered our school in second grade. Her IQ was 123; her achievement was very good, but not excellent. She was highly dramatic and would use her voice and body with artistry to emphasize her ideas. She wrote very well, although she had trouble with spelling. She loved to read and chose to read Shakespeare in fifth grade when her peers were reading Judy Blume. Despite her high-average IQ, her grades slipped by sixth grade. She was earning C's and D's, rather than the A's and B's she should have earned. Her mother was distraught and believed that punishment was the way to bring about achievement. Her classroom teachers recommended that we consider Vicki for UAG because they felt that, as she entered adolescence, her emotional difficulties were increasing and exaggerating her academic problems.

Ned's test scores and recommendations qualified him for the regular gifted program in third grade. His ideas were always unique; his products were always excellent; his sense of humor was droll and adult-like from the earliest years. He was an actor in a local, semiprofessional community theater. As he progressed through school, however, he experienced more and more difficulty with time management, assignment completion, and tests. His achievement test scores, which had been high in the primary years, began to slide. By fifth grade, he scored at the 37th percentile in reading; when retested in an untimed situation on an alternate form, he achieved at the 98th percentile. By the end of sixth grade, an informal reading assessment revealed that Ned couldn't read. He could decode individual words and complete workbook pages with their fill-in-the-blank format. When given unlimited time and strong motivation to do well on achievement tests, he struggled word-by-word through the paragraphs and questions, making the best sense he could from the text and filling in with his broad experiential background. But in real life, when he needed to read books quickly and effectively, he made substitutions and reversals that destroyed the meaning. Not surprisingly, he had tremendous difficulty with math word problems and with social studies and science textbooks, and this difficulty was reflected in his grades.

Juliet qualified for the regular gifted program each year from third through sixth grade but chose not to participate. She was highly sensitive, very artistic, and wrote stories and poetry that were exceptionally sophisticated in the use of metaphor. Juliet was also a highly independent thinker, an atypical student for our school. As she entered adolescence, a death occurred in her family. Deeply affected, she made a conscious choice to stop doing her schoolwork. Her grades took a steep dive and never came up again; a former A student, she now earned D's and F's and didn't care.

Marty was screened in seventh grade for UAG. He was bright; his former grades, achievement test scores, and IQ score supported that. Though not technically truant, he was absent excessively, often two or three days a week. He found it impossible to make sense of the new work when he was in school and to catch up with the work he had missed. He had no long-term goals in school. His religious beliefs strongly discouraged education beyond high school. His religion also prohibited participation in interscholastic sports, which isolated him from opportunities to make friends. He found this latter restriction particularly hard to accept because he loved to play basketball. Marty was emotionally immature and frequently cried in class and on the playground when he was teased by his peers (the teasings, of course, became more frequent as the students learned they had a victim). Marty had no friends, no study skills, and as time went on, no sense of pride in himself or his schoolwork. A bright child began to fail.

Ricardo was easily identified as gifted from the day he entered kindergarten. His ability to read fluently when he entered school, his encyclopedic store of general knowledge, his particular interest in science and technology with advanced skills in both areas, and his fascination with computers before computers were generally available quickly distinguished him. Ricardo, though, didn't do anything he didn't want to do. He was also completely disorganized. Very early in his school life he was dubbed the "absent-minded professor" because of his total inattention to routine expectations such as getting to school on time and doing his assignments. His academic ability continued to grow as he grew, but so did his concomitant negative habits. Although his achievement test scores remained above the 97th percentile every year, Ricardo did as little as he could to get by, a habit that eventually earned him very poor grades, disciplinary actions, and personal conflict.

These eight children were referred to the UAG program through many avenues. Some were recognized during routine screening for our regular pull-out program. Others were referred to us by school administrators or their secretaries who were responsible for reviewing and entering standardized test information into permanent record cards. Many students were brought to our attention by other interested people: parents, peers, siblings, the school nurse, and classroom teachers. They were all children in serious need: Eleven of the sixteen had been referred earlier for child study team services, but only two had received services. The achievement of the other students was too high; they had to wait until they were two full years below grade level before being eligible for help. The slide to that point was far greater for these children than for average children. The problems causing the slide in achievement were magnified, too, by the time someone stepped in to help.

FITTING THE ACTUAL INTO THE THEORY

How do people become underachievers? Theories about the origin of giftedness vary considerably but generally fall into two categories. One school of thought believes that giftedness in a given area is an innate quality, that genetics determines who is gifted (Nichols, 1965; Terman, 1924). This point of view supports the belief that a high IQ is a clear indication of giftedness. Effort, to adherents of this position, has little or no relationship to giftedness. Giftedness exists regardless of whether the gifted person puts forth the effort to be successful. Underachievement results if someone with a high IQ is not successful in school or in life.

A second point of view is that giftedness is a behavior (Phenix, 1964; Renzulli, 1978; Witty, 1958); it is learned, and it can be practiced like any other behavior. Those who adhere strictly to this thinking often believe that everyone has some gift, something they can do very well. Thus, "giftedness" is something earned through extraordinary efforts. Those who exert the needed effort to do exceptional things in a special field are gifted and receive recognition and rewards for their efforts. From this perspective, there are no gifted underachievers; people are only gifted if they exert sufficient effort. No effort, no giftedness.

Tannenbaum's Conception of Giftedness

Tannenbaum (1983) suggested that giftedness is a quality that emerges when five broad conditions, encompassing both innate and environmental factors, are present. Thus, he integrated these two polar positions into a single paradigm. The five necessary conditions are as follows:

1. The *g* factor or general intellectual ability
2. Special abilities in a distinct area
3. Special non-intellective traits appropriate for the area of special abilities
4. A challenging, appropriate environment for the nurturance of those abilities
5. Chance factors—being in the right place at the right time

Tannenbaum (1983) defined the *g* factor as superior, but not necessarily extraordinary, intellect. He believed there was a threshold of general intelligence needed for giftedness to emerge. The cutoff point was not fixed but varied according to the form of special ability in which excellence showed itself. Other research (Sternberg, 1984) suggests the *g* factor is probably a composite of several abilities including reasoning ability, speed of learning, method of information input and retention (memory and perception), and degree of automaticity of intellectual skills. Usually this general intelligence is measured by an IQ test. The *g* factor allows a gifted person to grasp and organize quickly the fundamentals in his or her field of special interest. With this foundation, the gifted person is able to become the producer of new ideas in that field.

According to Tannenbaum (1983), general intelligence is meaningless until it is applied to a field for which a person has a special capacity, the second condition necessary for giftedness to emerge. The existence of special abilities is more easily apparent to an untrained eye, and thus less controversial, than is the existence of a general ability factor. But our understanding of special abilities becomes clouded after this. We do know that different special abilities become apparent at different points in time. In some cases, special abilities have appeared very early in life: take the case of Mozart, who began composing music before the age of 5 and gave concerts at the court of the Empress Maria Theresa when he was six. More recently, Yehudi Menuhin in music and Norbert Wiener in mathematics have attracted attention as child prodigies. In other fields of accomplishment, politics, for example, or science or writing, giftedness may not emerge so early. In most cases, differentiation in ability is evident by adolescence, but not all. We don't know whether such talents are innate and always present in a given person, needing only specific stimuli to bring them to the fore. We don't know if there are developmental points of readiness at which they emerge. There is a clear need for research in this area.

Tannenbaum was not the first or the only person to suggest different kinds of specific talents. Notable earlier work in the field of special intelligences was conducted by Guilford (1967). His definition of the structure of the intellect is probably the best-known multifactor theory of intelligence in the field of gifted education. Guilford identified 150 special factors. These factors, he believed, result from varying combinations of the ways a person recognizes data, mentally processes that data, and produces something using that data. Different combinations of these "contents," "operations," and "products" yield different strengths and weaknesses in individuals with equal IQ scores.

More recently, Howard Gardner (1983) proposed that multiple intelligences exist, each one being relatively unique. According to Gardner, an intelligence can be considered autonomous if it can be found in near-isolation in special populations (e.g., idiot savants) or be absent in someone otherwise normal (e.g., those with localized brain damage). We must also be able to find the talent highly developed in specific individuals or specific cultures. Gardner's final qualification is that core abilities for each intelligence (e.g., recognizing pitch in music or comprehending numeric symbols in mathematics) can be proposed and measured. Gardner has delineated the following intelligences as separate, unique special abilities: linguistic intelligence, musical intelligence, logical-mathematical intelligence, spatial intelligence, bodily-kinesthetic intelligence, and the personal (inter- and intra-) intelligences. Gardner's work suggests that special abilities are always present but that they demand a supportive environment to reach fruition. Educational efforts, based on knowledge of the individual's talents from observation and experimentation, can build talent.

Tannenbaum's (1983) first two conditions (the *g* factor and special abilities) are the qualities that "nature" proponents believe characterize giftedness, while the third (non-intellective factors) and the fourth (because a supportive environment may be needed for the innate special ability to develop) and are qualities the "nurture" proponents espouse. Tannenbaum believed that certain non-intellective factors facilitate accomplishment. Without a belief in oneself, task commitment, self-sacrifice, and other personality factors, a person has little hope for great achievement. Talent that is obscured will never be acknowledged. Therefore, a non-intellective trait also necessary for giftedness to emerge is the ability to showcase the particular talent so it has a maximum impact on appropriate audiences. Knowing how to "play the game," whether in school as a child, or in the business world, the university, or the arts as an adult, is an essential non-intellective trait for those gifted in a corresponding area of special ability. Persistence, motivation, independence, mental health, and originality also contribute to giftedness.

Recently, the field of neurobiology has contributed to our understanding of activity in regions of the brain that affects our mental ability. The thalamus acts as a gatekeeper allowing us to process and store information more or less effectively depending on our emotional state (Ojemann, 1985). It is now generally acknowledged that the limbic system in the brain, which controls our emotional life, actually shuts down higher centers of the human brain when stress or a threat is perceived by a person, as reported by Krech (1969); Lozanov (1977); Martindale (1975); Restak (1979) (all cited in Clark, 1986). These understandings about the way our minds work make knowing how to manage stress an important non-intellective trait that can increase the likelihood that giftedness will emerge.

Tannenbaum (1983) went beyond the innate-effort debate by including a fourth and fifth factor necessary for giftedness to emerge. Environmental factors, Tannenbaum's fourth condition necessary for the emergence of giftedness, include parental and peer group influences, school, religious, and community influences. The encouragement or discouragement students feel from any one of these groups can serve as a catalyst for or inhibitor of talent. Tannenbaum believed that some people succeed despite, or even because of, the adversity they need to overcome to reach their peak, but few actually "beat the odds." Most people need a nurturing environment provided by those closest to them in order to excel.

Societal and cultural influences have an impact as well. During the Renaissance, an age that valued music and the arts, the broader social context, including family, friends, church, and fellow scholars, encouraged these talents. During our own times, when money, sports, and entertainment are so highly valued in America, different talents are recognized and encouraged than would have been supported during the Age of Exploration. Ability in shipbuilding goes unrecognized today because this talent is no longer valued. Different values promote a different view of necessary talents. Subcultures within the larger culture, e.g., our own minority cultures in America, may value talents that differ from those of the dominant culture. Lack of recognition of special abilities that are important within a subculture leads to lack of encouragement of those abilities by the dominant culture. Conversely, children in a minority culture who have talents valued by the dominant culture often remain unnurtured if the minority subculture holds conflicting values.

Tannenbaum's conception of giftedness supports both "nature" and "nurture" positions but adds another critical factor: chance. The "market" for people with particular talents, for example, medical credentials, can become flooded. An obstetrician who can deliver a breech baby by caesarean section would have been a "gifted" physician at the turn of the century. Today the same talent is overlooked because the doctor is only one of many with equal skills. Personal events such as a marriage, a birth, or an accident or illness can interfere with the fulfillment of potential at crucial points in a person's career. We can increase the likelihood of success by being prepared to take advantage of chance when it comes our way and by making efforts to be at the right place at the right time with the right people. But good fortune cannot always be managed; there are some things simply beyond our control.

While not listing it as a separate condition, Tannenbaum (personal communication, July 1985) also believed that creativity was a necessary, pervasive quality that influenced giftedness. A person's creative ability affected the way he or she might utilize abilities, non-intellective traits, the environment, and chance situations. Someone who is highly creative would be more likely to evidence more giftedness in any particular society or time because of the uniqueness of his contributions.

Passow (1985), in discussing Tannenbaum's view of giftedness, stated that each of the five factors was necessary, but insufficient on its own, for the achievement of excellence in any area. No combination of four was adequate to compensate for the absence or the inadequacy of the fifth. And it is the Tannenbaum five-factor conception of giftedness that underlies the work described in this book. If we accept that all five conditions are needed before giftedness emerges, the gifted underachiever can be viewed as a student who is probably relatively creative, but who is completely or partially lacking in one or more of the five main conditions necessary for giftedness. With even one condition lacking, it becomes difficult or impossible for academic giftedness to emerge in the school setting. The inadequacies or absent conditions have an impact on the intellective factors, making it appear that the child is not reaching his or her potential.

Do Our Students Confirm Tannenbaum's Concept?

Tannenbaum (1983) used a five-pointed star to portray the five necessary conditions for giftedness (see Figure 1.1). Our underachievers appear more like a group of starfish, the spiny-skinned echinoderms whose spines and small pincers scattered over their surfaces protect them from enemies and whose tubular suckers on their undersides allow them to hang on in hostile conditions that would destroy other species. Starfish are also able to regenerate, just as our underachievers were. Our underachievers each had arms, the conditions needed for giftedness to emerge, missing. Given the right combination of circumstances and time, regeneration replaced these missing arms, allowing the students to fulfill their potential. Some of our underachievers had small arms, an indication that parts of that condition needed for giftedness to emerge were present. But none were whole. And no two were exactly alike.

All but one of our "starfish" children appeared to have general intellectual ability. The child without that arm was the child who scored 87 on the WISC-R, yet had such highly developed special abilities that it seemed unlikely the IQ was accurate. All but one child appeared to have special abilities; no special abilities were expected from this child by anyone in her environment, so none emerged. Six students had learning disabilities of one type or

Figure 1.1: Starfish.

A normal starfish would have no damaged arms. If each arm represented one needed condition for giftedness, it would look like this:

general ability

special talent

chance

non-intellective traits

environment support

Our gifted underachievers had missing one or more of the conditions needed for giftedness to emerge.

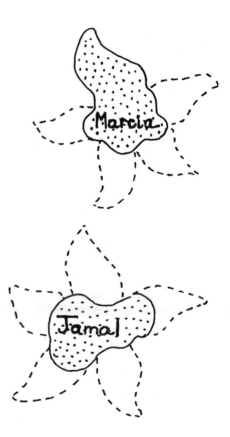

Ned

Marcia

Jamal

another that were only diagnosed after they were included in the underachievers' program. These disabilities could easily have masked or depressed their general ability scores or the recognition of their special abilities.

Some children appear to have buds emerging from their "chance" arm. The bud in one instance was the adoption of that child who had been malnourished and abused for seven years in various foster homes. Other chance buds indicate the children's eligibility for the traditional gifted and talented program, which might have nurtured their gifts. Most of these students, however, could not benefit from this program because their needs were so different and so great. Too often, the characteristics and events that fell under the chance condition were negative. One child was deserted by her mother at age 14 and had an emotionally disturbed sibling. The father of another was imprisoned. One child lived in an alcoholic family, another with an abusive father and unsupportive mother, and yet another with an emotionally abusive grandmother. Another had two physical disabilities, one a birth defect and the other due to unintended neglect. One child suffered from frequent illness, and another from severe allergies. Two children had to learn to deal with the death of a close relative.

For two children, environmental support was strong. Both home and school recognized and encouraged the giftedness that was manifested in easily recognized special abilities. In other situations, however, children had to deal with cultural expectations that differed from the dominant culture and religious regulations that made them appear radically different from their peers, a devastating occurrence during adolescence. Overly high or exceptionally low expectations from parents and teachers, sexual bias in the family, poor or nonexistent role models, and neglect of basic physical, psychological, or social needs plagued others. Others endured parental or intergenerational conflict and sibling conflicts so severe that they interfered with normal routine living. One suffered too much freedom and too much responsibility for his age.

Without exception, the underachieving gifted students were missing at least some non-intellective skills. Many, but not all, had very low self-esteem. Many had poor work study skills or lacked time-management skills. Many lacked social skills or "playing the game" skills for school success. Several exhibited inappropriate risk-taking behavior. Some were unwilling to take any risks, preferring to fail because they chose to do so rather than risk actually failing and destroying their carefully nurtured sense of self. Others took unreasonable risks for their physical safety and well-being, resulting in injuries that kept them from school. Three children were emotionally immature. In others, tremendous anger was unresolved, stress was overwhelming, trust was impossible, rebellion and perfectionism were incapacitating. In one extreme case, suicidal tendencies became evident.

Do these children fit the model? Without question. Would their gifted-ness ever appear without intervention? Very unlikely.

SUMMARY

The conception of underachievement among the gifted has been placed within a paradigm that tries to explain the occurrence of giftedness. Because the paradigm lends structure to our insights on giftedness and on under-achievement, we can proceed to design interventions with a greater likelihood of working. The children discussed here are not from the inner city, although they could be; they lived in a semirural area. They had good teachers who cared about their students and gave much of themselves to help those in trouble. But it wasn't enough. Children like these exist everywhere, and each child deserves the help that the standard school environment cannot give. And that is what this book is all about—what can be done for them.

CHAPTER 2

Historical Insights

The first researchers to consider the problem of underachievement tended to look only at the intellectual factors. Early work in the field offered conflicting information about the phenomenon of bright students who did not perform (Raph & Tannenbaum, 1961). Because of the inconsistencies in research results about gifted students who did not achieve, Thorndike (1963) expressed the view that underachievement might not even exist. He argued that what researchers may have called underachievement was more likely caused by a measurement problem, with overprediction on one assessment making us think the child was not performing competently on another. Thorndike urged researchers to look for other factors that might more accurately predict successful achievement. Subsequent efforts to study the problem began to consider other possible causes, including personality characteristics, psychological determinants, familial causes, sociological factors, and school-related factors (Gallagher, 1975; Heinemann, 1977; Raph, Goldberg & Passow, 1966; Shaw & McCuen, 1960; Wellington & Wellington, 1965 [all cited in Whitmore, 1980]; Clark, 1983a, 1983b; Clemens & Mullis, 1981; Daniels, 1983) (French & Carden, 1968; Goldberg, 1959; Gough, 1955; Haggard, 1957; McCandless & Evans, 1973; McGillivray, 1964; Morrow & Wilson, 1961; O'Shea, 1970; Perkins, 1965; Shaw, 1961; Shaw & Dutton, 1962; Strodtbeck, 1958; Walsh, 1956; Williams, 1962 [all cited in Pirozzo, 1982]). In each of these cases, the factors were considered in isolation. Multiple conditions and the interactive nature of those conditions necessary for giftedness to emerge were not studied.

A MEDICAL ANALOGY

An analogy may help clarify the historical, predictable steps taken in the study of underachievement. Let's compare researchers' efforts to those of doctors, and the underachievers are analogous to patients who come to the doctors complaining of heartburn; in our case, the complaint is underachieve-

17

ment. In the 1950s, if patients were uncomfortable because of heartburn, doctors prescribed an antacid. When the distress was temporary and mild, this treatment was enough, and the patients recovered in short order. However, the distress did not disappear in all patients. If the doctors were consulted again, their thoughts were probably, "Maybe this isn't heartburn after all. Maybe our patients are just calling it heartburn, while it's really something else." At that point, doctors looked for another cause, thinking if the real cause could be determined, the discomfort could be eliminated.

There are strong parallels in this scenario, so far, to our historical work with the gifted underachiever. The conflicting evidence in early work may be the result of some early, temporary, or minor "case" of underachievement being treated with short-term remediation that happened to be successful. Other underachievers, whose habits were more ingrained or whose situation was less supportive, were not affected by simple treatment. The suggestion that the description of the symptoms might be incorrect can be compared to Thorndike's idea that perhaps underachievement was really something else, a measurement problem. His idea spurred research that considered psychological, social, and environmental causes. Despite such research and growing sophistication in educational measurement, underachievement didn't go away. It wasn't explained or cured despite researchers' efforts to delineate and eliminate a single underlying cause in each case.

Returning to our medical analogy, today physicians recognize that a minor surface symptom, like heartburn, can imply a medical condition that is far more serious, say, an impending heart attack resulting from many years of poor personal health habits. The more numerous and the more interrelated the factors affecting heart disease, the greater the threat of a heart attack. In someone at risk because of physical, personality, sociological, and familial factors, the likelihood of a heart attack is greater than for someone at risk only because of a sedentary life-style. Many deaths that could not have been prevented in the 1950s can now be avoided because of more accurate recognition of the warning signs of heart disease. Doctors, as part of their training, learn what the risk factors are, who is most at risk, and how patients can control those factors before the heart disease does permanent damage. A wide-ranging public relations effort for adults and health education for children now make average citizens aware of life-style habits that affect their hearts. If a person can be convinced to cooperate, the risk of heart disease may be substantially reduced.

We need to recognize that, with gifted underachievers, as with sufferers from heart disease, numerous interacting factors appear to affect an observable trait. Reversing underachievement with a single strategy—whether that strategy be diagnosis-remediation or parent and/or student counseling—is only going to be effective with "minor" cases. Complex or long-term cases will take much more effort, even perhaps the simultaneous restructuring of many parts of the students' lives. We will never completely eliminate underachievement, just as we cannot completely eliminate heart disease, because some students will choose not to change even when they know the consequences and the alternatives available to them. But we can make great strides if we launch a broad public information campaign that promotes "healthful" parenting skills, skills that will develop children's potential from birth on. We, as the professional community, can make great inroads into the problem if we teach our teachers how to locate at-risk children early enough to intervene. The students and their parents and teachers have to be taught to take control of the risk factors that often lead to underachievement just as those at risk of heart disease need to learn to manage their risk factors.

WHAT DOESN'T WORK

Tannenbaum's (1983) paradigm makes it easier to see why typical provisions for the gifted, which are designed to identify and address students with superior ability, are appropriate for children who have the other conditions for giftedness met through out-of-school experiences. Some, but not all, gifted programs provide students with opportunities to take risks, to showcase or share their abilities, and to meet others who can help them develop more fully. Most gifted programs, however, are not appropriate for children who are very bright, yet lacking the affective traits required for success. Most gifted programs are designed to be effective with students who have supportive, nurturing home environments. This design often leads to charges of elitism in gifted education, as it is the already favored who receive gifted education programming. Few gifted programs take it upon themselves to ensure that the student has an appropriate, consistently available, challenging, supportive environment for the development of his or her gifts.

Many of the non-intellective traits needed for giftedness can be taught. An effective curriculum can help students learn to value and use their intellectual and creative abilities. The appropriate, challenging environment needed to nurture the child's gifts can be created either to supplant or supplement a home environment.

Schools have an obligation to help intellectually capable children who do not achieve. We can learn to identify them, and we can provide a more appropriate environment for them. Schools can serve as one of Tannenbaum's (1983) chance factors, "the smile of good fortune at crucial periods of life" (Passow, 1985, p. 25) that can allow gifted underachievers to develop the necessary non-intellective traits for success. Without intervention, a pattern of underachievement is unlikely to change. If we do not identify and serve such children as early as possible, they may live lives filled with frustration. Society may well lose the future Woodrow Wilsons, George S. Pattons, Auguste Rodins, and Thomas Edisons. These men, in retrospect, can be identified as gifted underachievers, whose successes can be attributed to intervention by caring parents (Thompson, 1971), not to their schools. And just as schools of that time failed to help these men—and almost completely neglected gifted women—they seldom help similar students today. We have a responsibility to bring schools closer to the ideal of providing both excellence and equality in education.

RECENT EFFORTS THAT WERE MORE HELPFUL

The Cupertino Project

In 1970, Joanne Whitmore (1980) took a giant step towards meeting the needs of gifted underachievers by initiating the Cupertino Project. Whitmore believed many school-based problems contributed to the vulnerability of gifted underachievers. Such problems included:

1. A textbook-oriented curriculum, stressing only the basics and lacking social studies, science, and the arts.
2. Classroom instruction that stressed only the low-level thinking skills of recall and comprehension.
3. Work that was too easy, therefore requiring too little effort for success, enabling gifted students to develop poor study habits.
4. Teaching that permitted children to bluff through curricular concepts with their advanced verbal ability.

According to Whitmore, children who spent the early years of their schooling in this type of setting were lost when truly challenged. Early identification was thus critical if any intervention was to be successful. Continuing intervention with stimulating, appropriate curricula and instruction was needed to sustain the motivation and positive attitudes developed from this early-intervention plan.

In *Giftedness, Conflict, and Underachievement* (1980), Whitmore outlined her design for a self-contained class for primary-age, highly gifted students "who evidenced need of an intensive program of social and emotional rehabilitation as well as academic remediation" (p. 206). The program goals were

1. To change the behavior pattern of the child . . .
2. To increase the emotional adjustment and maturity of the child . . .

3. To accelerate the socialization of the child . . .
4. To reduce the academic gap between aptitude and achievement. (pp. 212–213)

The basic methodology of the class was a student-centered, individualized approach. An important component of the program, however, was the development of a supportive peer group that provided a sense of community.

Whitmore's (1980) program was in place long before Tannenbaum (1983) defined his necessary conditions for giftedness to emerge. She seemed to anticipate his thinking. Whitmore recognized the *g* factor and found special abilities in the children with whom she worked. She provided an appropriate school environment that nurtured the gifts these children had and helped reduce the academic lags and gaps that many of the children experienced. She also recognized that gifted children underachieve for a variety of reasons, including learning disabilities, mental health problems, neurological handicaps, and perfectionism. She created curricula with activities that addressed the need to build self-esteem and that developed the social skills and school survival skills many of the students lacked. Based on the research that provided the foundation for her work, Whitmore did not recommend individual or family counseling. She believed that counseling programs were only minimally effective and that little transfer occurred between the counseling sessions and the classroom or playground. Individual or small-group counseling within the full-time classroom was more influential in changing children's inappropriate behaviors. The environment could be modified to meet the students' needs and the peer group could provide needed support.

Parents in the Cupertino Project were involved in several ways. They participated in the initial team study of their child's needs, and they agreed to cooperate and participate as requested. The request usually consisted of two monthly activities: (1) a parent–teacher–child conference to evaluate the child's progress, and (2) a parents' meeting during which the teacher would share information about the characteristics of gifted underachievers, curriculum and instruction in the classroom, ways of improving relationships at home, and ways of providing assistance to the child or class.

The Cupertino Project was a masterly piece of craftsmanship. It was a student-centered classroom with an emphasis on motivation and mental health. The follow-up study conducted by Whitmore in 1972, two years after the inception of the project, and again in 1975, found that there were lasting program effects that resulted in improved attitudes and behavior throughout the elementary years. Less consistent were the effects on academic achievement of the students once they left the UAG class.

The only major drawback to Whitmore's (1980) design is its cost. Large districts may find it possible to identify a classroom full of underachieving gifted students in the second and third grades and to provide them with a full-time teacher. But there are many areas of our nation where the entire district instructs only a few hundred children with widely varying abilities in grades K–12. Such districts may not even have a full-time teacher for the achieving gifted. Underachievers are still found in such small districts, should still be served, and can be served, but not in a design such as Whitmore described.

A second problem, one that perhaps explains the varying long-term academic achievement of the students in Whitmore's follow-up study, relates as much to philosophical commitment as to program design. Is a design that keeps gifted, underachieving students totally segregated from other students the wisest? Are their needs so great that isolation can be justified on the same grounds that it is justified for seriously disturbed children whose achievement is average or below? Are gifted underachievers' needs similar to those of children with severe physical handicaps? Or is mainstreaming important for gifted underachievers? I think it is. I worry that the children in the Cupertino Project had difficulty in making the transition to the "real world" despite the careful planning described by Whitmore. Moving to a totally new class, and in some cases a totally new school, is a "sink or swim" experience for many children. For students who had previously experienced difficulty in a regular classroom, the move must have been very stressful. The fact that, for many, a specially selected site was needed and that the transition was achieved more successfully over the natural summer break indicates that all was not fine. Whitmore's children appear to be like hothouse flowers, flourishing in a climate-controlled environment, but withering in less than ideal conditions. We need to be sure that once underachieving children reverse self-destructive patterns, they can make it in the "real" world of traditional classrooms, a temperate climate that blows both hot and cold, good and bad. The opportunity to practice newly acquired social, school-survival, and work-study skills in the mainstream with immediate feedback and support by the peer group in the UAG class is more effective. Students learn to deal better with the chance factors that enter their lives when they are mainstreamed. With support, they are gradually "hardened off," just as plants are, actually surviving better in natural surroundings without intervention, and achieving at an appropriate level.

The Family Achievement Clinic

Sylvia Rimm (1983) believed a very fine line existed between the behaviors that encouraged giftedness and those that encouraged underachievement. The lack of clear messages received by the gifted, she felt, were a possible cause of the problem. Rimm believed that caregivers had to remind themselves they were dealing with a child rather than a short adult, the child's giftedness creating a false impression of maturity. Caregivers had to teach right from wrong, had to emphasize the need to behave responsibly and reach closure, had to establish routines to permit time for creativity, and had to help students prepare for a real career in a highly competitive world. In other words, the gifted underachiever needed a supportive environment. Rimm stated that children had to develop a sense of control over desirable attributes and a sense of self-esteem, or they would learn to control their lives in whatever way worked. Rimm affirmed the need for non-intellective factors and approached the problem of underachievement through counseling.

Rimm's (1983) approach is reasonable for those students who lack only factors three and four: a challenging, appropriate environment for the nurturance of those non-intellective abilities that allow giftedness to emerge. Her approach would be particularly effective when only the home environment, not the school and not cultural values, need alteration. Rimm's dedication to the students and the families with whom she worked is admirable. She reported exceptional success in her clinic. But some questions remain unanswered. I worry about the children whose parents do not realize they themselves might be part of the problem and those who would be unwilling to enter counseling. I worry about the children whose parents do not have the money to participate in private counseling. I worry about the children whose parents are not the problem, whose underachievement is more deeply ingrained than short-term counseling can touch. I worry about those who may be missing many non-intellective traits, who may be blocked by cultural barriers, who may be learning disabled. These children are unlikely candidates for success through the Family Achievement Clinic.

Special Efforts for the Gifted/Learning Disabled

Learning disabled children who are also gifted are usually unable to demonstrate their giftedness in school due to a chance factor—a minimal brain dysfunction that affects school success, often in only one subject area. Learning disabilities may affect a child's memory, perception, or retention ability in reading, math, writing, or speaking. But such disabilities do not necessarily inhibit lifetime success and may, in fact, allow for highly creative responses to ordinary situations due to altered perceptions.

Paul Daniels (1983) was among the first to recognize that some of the many learning disabled students at the Kennedy School of Johns Hopkins University were especially bright and learned differently from the others. Because his first allegiance was to the learning disabled, he was concerned that these children tended to operate at or below grade level, with their giftedness masking their disability. Daniels felt that because they were gifted, students' disabilities often went unrecognized and unserved. He emphasized the

school's responsibility to identify these children early in their school careers
so that appropriate help could be offered for their learning problems. He also
knew that learning disabled, gifted children needed to have their gifts recognized, to be successful, and to maintain a positive sense of self-esteem, conditions that were unlikely to be met when the combination of giftedness and
learning disabilities existed simultaneously.

Based on his work with children who had severe reading and learning
disabilities, Daniels (1983) wrote *Teaching the Gifted/Learning Disabled Child.*
This is a practical, rather than scholarly treatment of the subject. Daniels
discussed recognition and diagnosis of these children, special abilities and
disabilities that he identified in them, and specific teaching techniques that
he found helpful. In the final section of his book, Daniels discussed the supportive aspects, including the roles that teachers, administrators, counselors,
and parents played in the children's lives.

In *Smart Kids with School Problems* (1987), another practical approach to
the problems of learning disabled/gifted children, Priscilla Vail offered specific ways to find the roots of gifted children's academic problems. She suggested field-tested interventions for circumventing or surmounting difficulties in each learning system that may have broken down: visual, motor,
auditory, and language. She also briefly explored children's psychological
availability for learning.

Using a more theoretical approach, Fox, Brody and Tobin (1983) collected a series of monographs that addressed issues connected with learning
disabilities in gifted students. Among other topics, Tannenbaum and Baldwin (1983) addressed the paradoxical combination of the two qualities. Fox
and Brody (1983) described a model for identifying giftedness in the learning
disabled, and Senf (1983) described the nature and identification of learning
disabilities and their relationships to the gifted child. Rosner and Seymour
(1983) presented clinical evidence describing such children. Udall and Maker
(1983) described a pilot program for elementary-age learning disabled/gifted
students.

Also theoretical, the research of Baum and Kirschenbaum (1984) dealt
with identification of the learning disabled/gifted child. Susan Baum (1984)
then further described some of the ways the special needs of learning disabled/gifted students' needs could be met.

None of these publications considered the holistic, interactive nature of
multiple factors affecting giftedness. Each author except for Vail (1987) approached the problem from the diagnostic/remediation perspective of how to
deal with learning disabilities when the child is also gifted. Giftedness was a
secondary focus. The modus operandi was how do we "fix" what is wrong
academically, that is, emphasizing the weaknesses rather than capitalizing on

the strengths of the gifted child. Little attention was given to any of the other conditions necessary for the emergence of giftedness.

SUMMARY

This chapter traced the growth in understanding of underachievement among the gifted. Researchers in the field progressed from wondering if the problem existed at all to recognizing that it does. At first viewing the problem as a relatively simplistic, single cause–effect relationship, researchers came to recognize that underachievement results from complex, interactive dynamics. The contributions of the practical work of Whitmore (1980) in the Cupertino Project, Rimm (1983) in the Family Achievement Clinic, Daniels (1983) at the Kennedy School, and Vail (1987) in her independent school classroom was discussed. The theoretical insights, and their role in improving our understanding of the phenomenon, lent by Baum (1984) and by Fox, Brody, and Tobin (1983) were also discussed.

Underachievement is a problem that will not solve itself. Research has shown (Raph, Goldberg & Passow, 1966) that if not reversed by high school, established, self-defeating patterns of behavior have little hope of changing. These conditions are as handicapping to our able youth as those meriting special education classifications. There is a practical way to help these children. It is possible to restructure a small corner of our schools so these children have a better chance of reaching their potential. It appears that, if implemented before ninth grade, the type of intervention we describe is capable of reversing the school problems experienced by some of our brightest students. Relatively little investment of time and money, especially compared to the cost of the personal and societal consequences if schools do not intervene, is needed. What is stopping us?

PART TWO

PROGRAM DESCRIPTION

CHAPTER 3

Program Design

Often when people first learn of a program for gifted underachievers, they ask challenging questions. Why not just let these children be average? Why not put such children into the already existing remedial classes if they are failing? Shouldn't students have the "right to fail" if they so choose?

PHILOSOPHY AND RATIONALE

Some children are content being average. But more frequently children with high IQs or high achievement test scores and failing grades know they should be doing better—often without anyone telling them. This causes their sense of self-esteem to drop, leading to more difficulty and frequently more failure. Allowing gifted students to "be average" doesn't last; without help, these children often fall below average. We have found that many of these children were learning disabled or were undereducated or lacked motivation. These problems can be helped, but special techniques are necessary.

Remedial Programs Won't Work

At first glance, it would seem that the existing programs in a school could suffice. Resource room teachers are generally good teachers with extra training in the specific methods of remediation that help children with special needs. Normal resource rooms, however, function with a rationale that works best for children with normal to below-average ability. Repetition and highly structured approaches have been proven effective for typical students with various learning problems. But gifted children are not typical learners. Repetition and high structure are counterproductive for gifted students. These children learn exceptionally well in a classroom using varied, novel approaches that capitalize on their high reasoning ability and creativity. Placing gifted children in the regular resource room would impossibly tax the teacher's ability to help either group of students effectively, as opposing strategies are needed.

Students Who Choose to Fail

Do children have the right to choose to fail? Perhaps the question should be viewed from an adult vantage point. How often have you, as an adult, deliberately chosen to fail at something just because you wanted to fail? I venture to guess never. Such a choice would affect your self-image and others' perceptions of you. Once we, as adults, learn how to make intelligent choices, it is far too threatening to the ego to deliberately *choose* to fail in public without explaining to others why we are doing so. If the question is changed slightly, and you are asked if you have ever been willing to *risk* failure, most likely you will answer yes. When successful, productive adults feel there is a reasonable chance of success in a new venture, and when that success would be personally rewarding, the possibility—not probability—of failure can be tolerated. Reasonable tension generated by a small possibility of failure (with the emphasis on reasonable and small) can serve to make us even more determined not to fail and thus enhance our chances of success.

Now think in terms of children and adolescents. What choices do they have when it comes to school? By law, they must attend. Once there, they must take a prescribed course of study with teacher-designed experiences that may or may not be appropriate for their ability. They can only determine to a certain extent, their mental presence and their behavior in that school and during those activities. If they, like adults, feel successful and productive, and if there is a high probability of success in what is asked of them, they may be willing to risk occasional failure, especially during their early years. But if students meet with frequent failure, either in their own eyes or in the eyes of parents and teachers, can we honestly believe they begin to choose failure? Do children and adolescents choose to have their self-esteem threatened by public awareness of their failures? Isn't it more likely that the "choice" to fail is a protection of the ego? By choosing not to work (which is different from choosing to fail), students can avoid confronting the more threatening issue of being unable to do what is asked. The consequent damage to their self-esteem is lessened because no one can tell if they *can't* do something, only that they *won't* do so.

School philosophies often reflect an intention to provide all children with experiences that help them reach the school's goals and their own potential. Special programming exists by law (PL 94–142, the Education for All Handicapped Children Act of 1975) for handicapped students so that they, too, are helped to reach their potential and the school's goals. Differentiated education is recommended, but not mandated, for the gifted so that they, too, can reach their potential (PL 97–35, the Education Consolidation and Improvement Act of 1981). For gifted underachievers, who tend to show neither their gifts nor their handicaps clearly, something more is needed. "If a student has emotional, social, environmental, [or physical] blocks that have eliminated his freedom to develop, have destroyed his motivation to achieve, or have tied him to compulsive behaviors that interfere with achievement, then the educational institution has a responsibility to help the child become free from those handicapping conditions" (Whitmore, 1980, p. 167). Schools must address underachievement among their gifted if they hope to live up to a philosophy that espouses equal opportunity to achieve. The UAG program can help them do so.

PROGRAM GOALS

To help underachievers reach their potential, program goals were established. The goals of the UAG program are:

1. To improve students' self-esteem
2. To improve attitudes that inhibit students' success
3. To improve school behaviors
4. To promote academic growth at an appropriate pace for these students.

Goal four is more specifically defined as:

a. Improving achievement test scores at 1.5 times the expected rate of growth for students of average ability
b. Overcoming specific academic weaknesses as defined by criterion-referenced tests
c. Bringing report card grades to above-average levels as might be expected from objective indicators.

DIFFERENTIATED CURRICULUM AND INSTRUCTION

Helping gifted underachievers bring their school achievement in line with their potential is a challenge. Achievement gains are unlikely without the development of a strong sense of self-worth, an "I am lovable and capable" attitude. The UAG program has an affective curriculum designed to build self-esteem and to promote the students' acceptance by their peers and teachers. Success in school and demonstrable gains in achievement can make students feel good about themselves. Therefore, the program also has a cognitive component, structured for the teacher, that allows quick student success while remaining open-ended to increase students' motivation. Lastly, a parent education program is part of the package. When changes occur in any person's life, others who live and work with that person feel the impact. Changes in the students demand changes in long-established patterns of interaction with parents and siblings. In order to provide a supportive environment for the children who are changing and for their families, we have devised a six-point curriculum for parents. Parents are helped to:

1. Develop an understanding of some of the possible causes of under-achievement in school
2. Examine their expectations for their child to determine the appropriateness of the expectations
3. Explore their personal family structure and dynamics
4. Practice positive communication skills
5. Develop an understanding of the problems that require intervention and find the sources of such help
6. Have the opportunity to discuss problems with a support group and develop self-help systems.

Each of these objectives will be described at length in Part 3 of this book and actual lesson plans are provided.

INSTRUCTIONAL PRACTICES THAT SUPPORT CURRICULA

Instruction needs to be orchestrated carefully. New skills, both cognitive and affective, are taught and then practiced in the resource room, with planned "bridging" activities to encourage transfer to the larger, more realistic life experiences in the regular classroom and at home.

Affective Before Cognitive

Self-concept and academic achievement appear to be very closely related, particularly in gifted students who underachieve. It is important to include both if we are to be successful. But both goals are not stressed equally at all times. It is essential that the children first learn that *this* classroom is a safe place, *this* classroom is a supportive arena where it is okay to practice new things because nobody is allowed to make another person feel badly. It is a place, also, to analyze how new skills might help in the real world and to choose the one place and time that a new skill will be tried in a bridging activity. It is a place to share successes and be cheered on when new behaviors work. It is a place to cry without fear and to get a hug when the real world falls apart. It is a place to be encouraged to try again after more practice in the safety of the small group. In short, it is a second home and surrogate family. The children need to bond to one another quickly.

Instruction is both planned and spontaneous. The planned affective curriculum for students includes direct instruction in pro-social skills, school-survival skills, group self-direction skills, conflict-resolution skills, and stress-reduction skills. Pro-social skills emphasize socialization, communication, cooperative sports and games, trust building, and reasonable risk taking. School-survival skills include instruction in time management and in how to meet classroom expectations without violating one's own needs. Work-study skills also help students manage their day-to-day expectations more effectively. Group self-direction skills allow students to (1) recognize the need for rules; (2) determine those rules to be used in the resource room; and (3) resolve conflicts arising there through an agreed-upon process. Stress-reduction skills are also taught. They include learning to use relaxation techniques, fantasy, and creative imagery, and learning to use physical and artistic outlets as personal stress-management tools. Students also learn when the various affective skills are needed, how to choose which one to try, and what to do if the first try fails.

The spontaneous part of the affective curriculum occurs as students demonstrate particularly desirable skills in the UAG class. The children are immediately reinforced for appropriate, new behaviors that occur.

As time passes, the focus shifts. The academic portions of the program assume greater priority, but never are the affective components ignored. Special time slots are designated for activities that promote good self-esteem every day of the school year. The program's more academic components, built around the students' identified interests and preferred learning styles, are emphasized. Remediation of the gaps in their skills, continued growth in the basic skills areas, and development of their creative and advanced thinking skills become as important as the affective program.

The cognitive curricula are differentiated in several ways. Guidelines were developed with the help of four students who were unserved, gifted underachievers in our school and who graduated before our pilot program was established. In discussions with them about what would have made school a better place for them, what would have encouraged them to achieve, they suggested the following changes:

1. No lectures—learning should take place through games, movies, computer work, plays, and field trips.

2. Positive reinforcement—students should know what to expect and know at once when they have done something well and have their friends know, too.
3. Flexible time schedules—students should be able to really "get into" something they like (although all agreed some routine would help them adjust to real life).
4. Food and other interesting breaks—students should be involved in social activities and have responsibilities, such as animals to watch and care for.
5. Learning centers—students should be able to pursue *their* interests, not the teachers' (emphasis theirs).

Did placing the affective before the cognitive have any impact on the students? In *Listen to the Children* (Supplee, 1987/1988), UAG students reported the effects various parts of the UAG program had on them. Completing a personal characteristics checklist, in response to the question, "Can you think of any reasons for the changes [in you]?" Karen said, "In U.A.G., I found the good points in me and before I only knew of the bad points" (p. 121).

Most of the successful students who took part in the study chose cooperative games, part of the affective curriculum, as one of the subjects having the greatest impact on them. Marty expressed the thoughts of many others well by saying, "They [games] helped me to trust and got me to help others" (p. 70). Having another person trust and depend, really depend, on you has a powerful influence on self-perception. It makes you feel valued as an individual. All of the students in this study noted that the pro-social skills lessons had been important to them. Most of the successful students also chose the group process skills and the creative activities (p. 71).

In the evaluation study of the program (Krantz, 1986), students were asked what made this class different for them. They cited such examples as:

"You get a chance to express your feelings."
"You're not always in the wrong when you don't do what the others are doing."
"There's no pressure."
"She [the teacher] cares about you."
"You learn to get rid of tension."
"We play games, but they are related to how we feel and what we learn."
"The teacher and people in class encourage me, instead of making a big deal when I'm not prepared."
"I can talk about my feelings; when I'm upset, she [the teacher] lets [sic] me alone until I can talk about it." (p. 6)

These are exactly the aims of the affective curriculum: improving students' self-esteem and attitude towards school. There were comments about cognitive areas, too, but the affective comments far outnumbered them. While the students never said which should come first, it appears that the affective area presented the greatest differences in their school experiences and deserved immediate attention when they enrolled.

Journal Writing

One technique that blurs the boundaries between cognitive and affective strategies deserves mention. Students are required to keep a daily journal as one of their standing assignments. The teacher can thus diagnose which instructional needs of individuals should be addressed through mini-lessons during the writing workshop. However, journal writing is much more.

The communication between student and teacher in the journal is absolutely private (except in life-threatening situations). Only the teacher and student (co-writers) read the journal unless they both agree to share it with another. The student must write a minimum of three sentences each day, even if the sentences are stilted and noncommunicative. In every student's case, beginning entries are routine and noncommittal. Regardless of the blandness of the student entry, the teacher responds by giving positive feedback about specific things she sees in the child or that she admires in the child's actions or work that day. Soon she shares some of her own successes and some of her worries. Occasionally, the teacher will make a suggestion for an activity the student might enjoy or will share a cartoon. Over time, these journals encourage a caring, special kind of communication between teacher and student.

Student journals over the past five years give evidence of the turning point in the life of each student who participated in UAG. The point at which each student started to take control and responsibility for his or her own life and well-being is obvious. Sometimes it takes only a few weeks to reach this point, sometimes it takes a year; but one day the student begins to talk through the writing. Often, the first real communication is anger. When a student realizes from the teacher's response that anger is an acceptable feeling, that it is okay to express anger in an acceptable way, and that the response she or he gets is not angry in return, a pathway opens. The journal then becomes a way of sharing many emotions—sometimes triumph at signs of growth, sometimes hurt with a plea for help with a big problem. Always it records a journey.

Students can reread their own words and see where they have been and how they have changed. For many students, journals are their first real experience with purposeful writing. The journal becomes a daily log, documenting the steps students take in their own behalf to develop their potential.

Many students continue their journal writing or begin letter writing to their teachers after "graduating" from UAG because they find such value in it.

Individualization

The journal is only one of several standing assignments. In each subject area, each student has a separate composition-type notebook. During class time, when the teacher is working one-on-one with other students, class members are obliged to complete their notebook assignments. These assignments are short and may do one of several things. Some assignments provide reinforcement for previously learned skills. Others are reminders about long-term assignments the student planned with the teacher and now must carry out. Still others ask students to consider several possible assignments, think of the consequences of each, and decide which they prefer and why.

There are other ways the curriculum is individualized as well. The language arts curriculum, including reading, writing, listening and speaking, is based on student purposes and on interests the children have, rather than on the interests of district curriculum writers or basal textbook designers. Curriculum goals and objectives are still met, but in a different way. Vocabulary development, comprehension instruction, word-attack skills, and writing skills are improved through student- and teacher-designed activities using topics and materials chosen by the students. Many learning activities are issue-based, focusing on what is happening in the world; others capitalize on students' creativity and incorporate the visual and performing arts.

The mathematics curriculum is adapted to meet students' strengths and weaknesses. By reorganizing content to eliminate repetition of skills (important for average students but unnecessary for gifted ones) and by maximizing time use, students are able to meet their personal math objectives more efficiently. Their personal math objectives are also fewer than they would be in a regular class because pre-testing eliminates the need to teach already mastered concepts. Students are more highly motivated to learn the math concepts they need because they see the real-life application of the skills before they are taught the concept.

The UAG students meet with the teacher daily for a short math lesson in an individual or a small group setting. Manipulative materials are used to make learning as concrete as possible. Students may sit in on the lessons of other students either to advance or reinforce their own understanding. Regular, incremental practice activities are scheduled for all students to maintain newly learned skills.

In a study of students' perceptions of effective components of UAG (Supplee, 1987/1988), all of the then-successful students selected math, as it was taught in the adaptive class, as one of the three subjects most helpful in

Table 3.1 Attribution of Success on Mathematical Task

	POINTS ATTRIBUTED TO*	
Group	Helplessness	Mastery
Success; out of UAG	11	21
Not yet successful; in UAG	16	16
Never in UAG	21	10

*Out of 32 possible

making them better students. This was supported by their performance in a task designed to determine why students thought they were successful in mathematics. Students were asked to perform a computation activity at their current achievement level. When they completed the task correctly, the researcher asked students to use colored chips to represent why they thought they were successful in the task. The four most common reasons (effort, ability, ease of task, and luck) identified by Diener and Dweck (1980) were each represented by a different colored chip. A drawing of a straight-sided container that looked like a chemistry flask filled with eight empty circles could be filled with the colored chips that represented why the students believed they had been successful. They could use all the same color or any combination of colors that they felt represented their reasons.

The students' responses were divided into three groups to see if any distinction would be evident among responses from students not enrolled in the UAG class, those enrolled but not yet "graduates of," and those who had been in the UAG class, but had "graduated" and were now back in mainstream classrooms full-time. The attributions for success in the different groups showed a fairly distinct pattern (see Table 3.1). Students in the group not included in the program showed the greatest sense of helplessness in this task. They attributed their right responses to luck or an easy task (although the tasks were not easy). The students who were still in the UAG program felt an increased sense of mastery (i.e., that their intelligence or their effort caused their success), and the mainstreamed students—those who had "graduated from" the UAG—possessed the greatest sense of mastery.

The researcher questioned the UAG students about the differences they perceived between the math instruction in the adaptive classes and in their regular classes. Students volunteered that "giving them other chances" and "going back over" when the student was "stuck" was important to them. All the students, without suggestion on the part of the researcher, volunteered that they had all of *their*, not the teacher's, questions answered in the adaptive class. This process contrasts quite sharply with the process students described in their regular classrooms. The typical class routine included checking homework, getting classwork, doing it, checking classwork, getting homework and sometimes beginning it in class. The regular math teacher was perceived to be an assignment giver and work checker, not an explainer and facilitator of understanding.

Specific instructional strategies that students believed differentiated their experiences and were important in helping them achieve were the following:

1. The individualized learning plan
2. The choice and control they were allowed to exercise over their goals and objectives
3. The use of talk-aloud to help determine where their thought processes were breaking down
4. Ten-minute lessons to develop new concepts and small-group instruction to reinforce concepts learned earlier
5. The use of hands-on math materials to develop a concrete representation in their minds of the processes they learned
6. The use of notebooks to record and work individual assignments instead of commercial workbooks
7. Learning how learning in general occurs so they could plan effective strategies for themselves to remember concepts.

Comments in the students' journals and anecdotal notes recording what the students considered the "bests" and "worsts" of each day also suggest that the students felt a greater sense of mastery in math. Often students began to comment on their success in math. Later, they viewed math lessons as the best part of their day. One student was quoted as saying, "[We] don't use . . . books, workbooks, and we don't do the same math problems over and over." Others said, "You work hard, maybe harder than other classes, but you want to," and "[There are] more things to choose" (Krantz, 1986, p. 8).

Acceleration

Both the language arts and mathematics curricula, particularly the latter, provided for acceleration as rapidly as possible through the standard curriculum skills. Regular brief reviews of skills and reinforcement of previously learned concepts took place at scheduled interviews throughout the year. The curricula were organized topically with a designated period of time allotted during the school year for each topic. In reading/language arts, the organizational topics were types of literature, including fiction, nonfiction, poetry, and drama. Writing as process was an integral part of this curriculum. In mathematics, topics included number theory, computation, measurement, geometry, pre-algebra, statistics, and probability. Estimation and problem-solving skills were consistently sharpened throughout this curriculum.

Objectives taught in particular topics (e.g., in geometry) in the time allotted (e.g., four weeks) often spanned several years of standard curriculum objectives. If children demonstrated mastery of the objectives in one topic at one grade level, they were moved on through new content objectives at more advanced grade levels.

Mike is a good example of this system. In fourth grade, he had great difficulty mastering multiplication facts, a third-grade objective. Mike willingly devoted time to remedy this problem during the portion of the year devoted to computation skills. He did so because earlier, when studying geometry, he advanced to the point of understanding the relationship between the volume of a cone and the volume of a cylinder, and between the volume of a pyramid and the volume of a cube. Using a calculator, Mike learned how to compute the volume of each geometric solid. He knew this was an objective normally taught in high school and he was very proud of his achievement. He also knew he wouldn't always have a calculator handy and that he would need to know his multiplication facts. Mike felt that if he could master high school math, he could learn third-grade math facts—and he did.

Vicki provides another case in point. The seventh-grade social studies curriculum, a world regions course, was reorganized with the teacher's help to consider themes that reappeared as each area was introduced. The reorganization provided extra time to explore questions Vicki posed about the best place and time to live. Over the year, she selected one nation from each region to study in depth. She learned how each nation had developed and how it functioned to help its citizens meet their basic physical and social needs. By the close of the year, she used the generalizations she had formed to compare the course of her parents' native land, an Iron Curtain country, to that of her country, the United States. She argued persuasively for the benefits of American citizenship and became a resource person for the social studies teacher in our school. Vicki learned far more than the seventh-grade curriculum. She was well on her way to honors courses in high school.

Enrichment

Enrichment in topics not normally part of the regular curriculum was also provided. In math, students worked "brain busters" (mathematical problems without numbers) and learned about unique subjects such as tessellations, a topic that tapped their artistic as well as their academic interest. They learned to measure precisely during an archaeological dig in their school yard and to record carefully the data collected. In language arts, students wrote for publications, entered nationwide contests, and rewrote their favorite authors in an alternate genre. They published their own bound books. They learned to create databases using the plot, characters, settings, themes, and stylistic techniques of the authors they read. They used a modem to communicate with others who shared their interests via a local computer bulletin board.

Remediation

In many cases, when students entered the UAG class, they had gaps in their academic skills. One of the aims of the program was to identify and remedy these gaps. In some cases, as described above, remediation was approached by demonstrating the need for absent skills in more advanced work and proving to the students that they were capable of the more advanced work. In other cases, for example, in writing skills, students' remedial needs were addressed through mini-lessons. When editing, students used an editing checklist designed with their personal objectives in mind. A student with remedial writing needs could complete writing projects that demanded high-level thinking, but focus on lower-level mechanical skills, such as using commas in a series or using too/to/two correctly, in the editing process.

Students with remedial needs in reading were often scheduled for special work with the reading specialist, while continuing to participate in the whole-language approach used in the resource room. The specialist coordinated her work with the resource-room projects the students were completing. When Ned's disability was discovered, for example, the reading specialist, the media specialist, and the resource-room teacher worked together. Ned was preparing for a debate in the resource room on the advisability of banning all nuclear weapons. The media specialist found an article by Carl Sagan that appeared in the Sunday magazine supplement of many papers and several articles in *Reader's Digest, Time,* and *Newsweek* that were appropriate for Ned's reading level and skills. Using these articles as instructional materials, the reading specialist helped Ned practice comprehension skills, such as summarizing and finding supporting details for a major premise: Ned learned to separate fact from opinion, while completing a project of great interest to him. As his project progressed, he also learned how to use the abridged *Readers' Guide* to locate such information for himself in the future. The written material was supplemented with videotapes from the county library, interviews with local residents and faculty members, and a fictionalized TV special on the effects of nuclear war. Ned's analysis of the broad range of materials enabled him to present an effective defense for the position he drew: abolishing nuclear weapons. He was equally well-prepared to have defended the opposing point of view. And his reading skills were improving.

A RESTRUCTURED ENVIRONMENT

The UAG students met in a part-time, multi-age, cross-graded group that included students from third through eighth grade. It was similar to a large, old-fashioned family. Such an age span also encouraged peer teaching, though not at the outset of the program. When first entering UAG, most students lacked the social skills needed to be effective in a peer teaching/learning situation.

The Classroom

One of the differences between UAG and the typical school program was that ours capitalized on children's successes. Our students were more successful outside of school than in. We arranged our environment, therefore, to look as if it were not a classroom. An especially good description of the type of environment we felt was important for our children is described by Clark (1986). Her book *Optimizing Learning* is worth reading as it offers additional suggestions to those we present here for making a classroom a more effective learning environment.

Our room itself, while very small, was homelike (see Figure 3.1). Couches and chairs made discussions about books and great ideas as natural as a family get-together. Normal classroom desks and chairs were pushed together to make larger, flat, working surfaces for projects, while separate desks and a computer area were designated for privacy or specific types of work. Students had assigned storage areas for their own supplies and works in progress. A mini-kitchen (sink and small refrigerator) and cloth-covered table provided an area for breakfast, snacks, and quiet socialization. Students often used this area to reward themselves for reaching goals they had set. Artwork, both student-produced and borrowed from local libraries and museums, graced the room.

Organizing a homelike environment need not be an expensive venture. It was fun to scrounge. Garage sales and want ads were excellent sources. We spent almost no money. Instead, we explained what we were looking for and why. Most of the needed items were donated. For larger items, we offered to supply a form signed by the principal or superintendent and typed on school stationery. This indicated the value of the donation for income-tax purposes. We were able to equip our room with a comfortable couch and chairs, a stool (which became a favorite of the students as they "rose to great heights"), with lamps, bookcases, end tables, and an eating area equipped with a small table and two chairs. We were offered a rug as well, and would have taken it, but were concerned about keeping it clean in a busy (and often messy) project-

Figure 3.1: Floor plan of the UAG classroom.

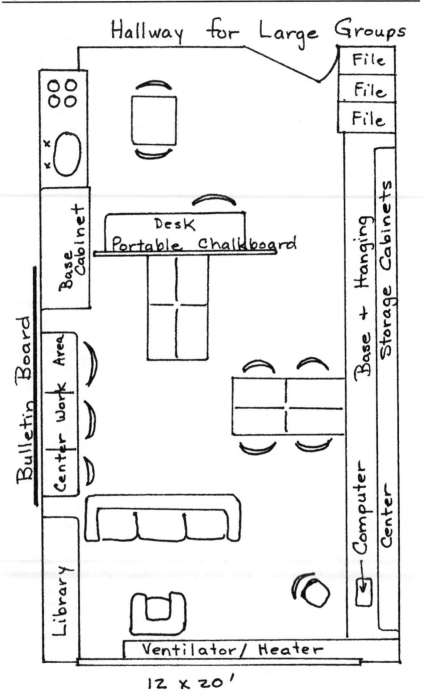

centered room. People are amazingly generous when asked. We got everything we needed for less than $100.

It is worth mentioning that space was a serious problem for us. The small room we shared with another teacher was considered substandard, yet we were able to adapt it to our purposes successfully. At regular intervals, the students were encouraged to rearrange the furniture and storage areas to better meet the class's needs. Using graph paper and measuring each piece in the room provided a practical exercise in mathematics and scale drawing. Social skills were also practiced. As the room was shared with the regular gifted classes and with a basic skills class, the students asked those groups to review their proposed rearrangement. Our students modified their original plans to meet the requirements of others, a practical exercise in pro-social skills. After several changes, the students learned to analyze task requirements carefully, create several alternatives, share these with the affected parties, consider the consequences of each alternative, and evaluate which alternative was the best, a practical exercise in creative problem solving.

When asked about the regular classroom environment, all the groups interviewed in *Listen to the Children* (Supplee, 1987/1988) agreed that their favorite places in their regular classrooms were their own desks and the back of the room. At least three-fourths of the students in each group chose these. The least favorite areas were the teacher's desk and the front of the room. The reasons given by students for their choices were similar. Students' sense of ownership and territory caused them to select their desks. Students' reluctance to be singled out for problems or spotlighted for achievement (for fear of embarrassment) led them to dislike the front and like the back of the regular classroom. Punishment and embarrassment were associated with the teacher's desk.

In contrast, the adaptive classroom had no clearly defined areas that were "front" and "back" of the room and no assigned desks. There were storage cubicles that were assigned to the children for their supplies, but they were free to choose where they wanted to do their assigned work each day. Centers encouraged them to use several areas of the room depending on their plans. There was no "teacher's desk." There was a homelike desk, but students were encouraged to use it. The teacher frequently used students' desks as the work and preparation area. Lessons were just as frequently held on the couch as they were at the chalkboard or at a child's desk. Reprimands never occurred at the "teacher's desk." Compliments and reprimands (except on the few occasions when safety was at stake) occurred privately in many places in the room and were only shared with the student's permission. These observations may support the students' claims that the teacher's responses to student error were an important feature in helping students become successful (Supplee, 1987/1988, 146–147).

Class Management

Students in the class were asked an open-ended question about what made the class a pleasant place to be. All the students mentioned the home-like room arrangement, meeting early in the day, the small number of students in the room, clear and appropriate expectations, and varied learning materials as important and helpful to them. Three-fourths of the students also mentioned the management routines in place in the classroom as one of the three most important parts of class climate in the adaptive classroom. These management routines included a sign-out sheet for bathroom and out-of-classroom trips, free access to needed school materials, daily chores, and a debriefing period during which students told the teacher and other students the best and worst parts of that day. The students also liked the fact that they had a place to store their work and a say in designing classroom, kitchen, and computer agreements. Such routines allowed the students to feel comfortable and in control of their classroom. Several students also mentioned the few rules (four in all) that were easy to live by and reported discipline in the class as "you couldn't get to do something good later."

Scheduling

We hypothesized that meeting the class during the first hours of the day might encourage better attendance at school and punctuality. Our school routinely used the Joplin plan for grouping students according to achievement in reading, language arts, and mathematics. Students in third through sixth grades normally began their day with reading and math instruction. In regular classes, under the Joplin plan, students could have as many as four different teachers for a single subject over the course of a year. This arrangement, while apparently effective for most students, particularly gifted students, presented disruptions in the lives of underachievers. Just as the students figured out what one teacher expected, the teacher could change and the students, who lacked school-survival skills, were back at square one trying to determine and live up to new expectations. In the UAG class, the same teacher was the teacher for reading, for math, and for language arts as long as the students needed the intervention. The UAG classroom was self-contained for the first two 50-minute periods of the school day every day of the week, every week of the year. This 100-minute assigned time period at the start of the day with the same teacher provided consistency and continuity. Every day the students knew to expect safety and encouragement with the same group of children when they reached school. They knew if they had a problem, it would be handled immediately. They knew they might need to support someone else who was having a problem, and their confidence grew as they learned they were effective at helping other students. Coming to school was like waking up to the best world they could make, a world attuned to them and their friends.

The seventh- and eighth-grade students' schedules differed slightly and presented special challenges. These students missed a "special" and either a science or social studies class during the first two periods. Since physical education is required by law in our state, the seventh and eighth graders needed to attend this "special" rather than our class two times weekly. We scheduled the students' instructional meetings with the resource-room teacher around the physical education time during the second 50-minute period with little difficulty. We kept students during the first 50-minute period to maintain the importance of the first contact of the day being with others in the resource room. To alleviate conflicts with social studies and science classes, we rescheduled students' mainstream classes to have them learn social studies rather than science in the resource room. This allowed students to continue to have the advantage of science with a lab, which we could not offer in the resource room. It also eliminated excessive planning for the resource-room teacher.

Time was restructured, as well, within that 100 minutes. Our "day" was segmented for planning purposes into ten-minute time blocks (see Figure 3.2). For individualized instruction, ten minutes was long enough to teach one concept and short enough to maintain the attention of any student. The limited time forced a businesslike atmosphere when it came to lessons. No time could be wasted, so instructional techniques were precisely planned. With ten-minute modules, we found it easy to use multiples flexibly to arrange instructional time for small and larger group work. The affective portions of the curriculum, which often involved games or role-playing, and the free computer time the children decided upon as a reward for work accomplished were easily organized using 20-minute blocks. A planbook, *The Special Education Plan and Record Book* (Basile, 1980), published by Teachers College Press, was very helpful in keeping track of "who's on first."

With ten-minute modules, every student was able to have a math and reading meeting every day. The seventh- and eighth-grade students who missed social studies were able to have lessons four times per week. Each day there was at least one affective lesson. The sample page (see Figure 3.3) shows how a typical week was organized in the planbook.

The instructional schedule was posted on the chalkboard at the start of the day so the children were aware of the times they needed to be prepared to meet alone with the teacher and together with the group. It was their responsibility to be in the right place and ready to start when their time slot came up. Therefore, they were taught to begin to prepare a few minutes earlier. They learned to come on time with their notebooks and writing tools.

Figure 3.2: Sample teachers' planning schedule.

	MONDAY	TUESDAY	WEDNESDAY	THURSD
9:10-9:20	Class	*Ed. + computer* / *Phys. Ricardo* — Helen (math)	*computer* / *Ed.* *Karen Phys.* — Helen (math)	*computer*
9:20-9:30	Meeting	Marcia (math)	Marcia (math)	*Doug*
9:30-9:40	*computer* — Karen (math)	*Marty and Doug* — Karen (math)	*computer* *Helen and Marty* — Karen (math)	Kar (ma
9:40-9:50	*Marcia +* — Helen (math)	Ricardo (alg.)	Ricardo (alg.)	Ric (
9:50-10:00 / 10:00-10:10	Interactive --- Reading	Interactive --- Reading	Reading --- Mini-groups	I
10:10-10:20	*computer* Marcia (math)	Marty + Doug (soc. st.)	Marty + Doug (soc. st.)	M
10:20-10:30	*Marty –* Ricardo (alg.)	School Survival	Cooperative	
10:30-10:40	Marty + Doug (soc. st.)	Skills	Games	
-10:60	Care of the environment + debriefing			

Figure 3.3: Page in planbook of week's typical plans.

MONDAY	TUESDAY	WEDNESDAY	THURS/

<u>Class Meeting</u>
run: Ned
record: Jamal
new business:
   class
   decor
Problem of week:
"Toothpick Trick"
	<u>Pro-Social</u>
	• Define skill
	  introducing
	  others
	• Define im-
	  portance of
	  skill
	• Practice
		<u>Coop Games</u>
		p. 28
		  Jigsaw
		    Animals
		p. 31
		  Partner
		  Pull-ups
			<u>Sch</u>
			<u>Sur</u>
			• Giv
			  tea
			an
			int
			me

<u>Ned</u> - soc. st.
• Compare econ.,
  polit., religious
  maps —
• Make inferences
	<u>Ned</u> - soc. st.
	• Intro. use of
	  atlas
	• Show value
	  of using
	  atlas well
	  when playing
		<u>Ned</u> - soc. st.
		• Use atlas
		• Use ° latit.
		  + longitude
		  to locate.
			<u>Ned</u>
			• Gai
			  usin
			  ° lat
			  + lon

<u>Inter. Reading</u>
? What feeling
  does this
  part of book
  make you feel
 	
• Summarize
• Discuss
  thoughts
	"Where in the
	World is Carmen
	San Diego"
	
	<u>Read - mini-
	groups</u>
	J- teach "rule
	of thumb" to
	choose a book
		<u>Inter Reading</u>
		? What if you
		  grew up in
		  the slums.
		  Would you
		  get different
		  feelings in
		  book?
		• Summarize
		• Discuss
			<u>Mike</u>
			• Ta
			  gr
			  ac

<u>Writer's
Workshop</u>
• Mini-lesson
  "How to con-
  duct a peer
  conference"
• Writing
	M- know "trait"
	apply to main
	character in
	his book
	R- use dia-
	critical
	marks to
	pronounce
	words
	<u>Mike</u> - math
	• Determine
	  area of
	  triangle
		<u>Writer's
		Workshop</u>
		• Mini-lesson
		  "Using an
		  editor's
		  checklist"
		• Writing	

Phys. Ed. (Ned to) — Phys. Ed. (Ned to)

PARENTS' PROGRAM

An important component of the pilot program was parent education. Each parent was sent a copy of a small pamphlet titled, "What Parents Often Ask About the Special Class for Gifted Underachievers." This gave answers to some of the most frequently asked questions (see Appendix E). Parent education did not stop there, however. Parents were invited (though not obligated) to attend weekly evening sessions. These sessions focused on helping parents understand their children's stages of development and needs at each stage as well as their own needs at the stage of life they found themselves. The intent was to establish a parent-support network and to share effective techniques of parenting and communication between parents and children. Several parents initiated individual meetings with a psychologist as a result of participation in the parents' program.

Parents are critical in effecting the kind of change that gifted underachievers need. Many parents did recognize that their children were having difficulty, but until the adaptive program began, did not know what the problems really were or how to make changes that would help their children. The school provided them as well as their children with an education. Parents were delighted with their newfound understanding of how to deal with and help their children, the happiness and reduction of stress that followed and their children's achievement gains.

SUMMARY

Gifted underachievers and our society are not well served by allowing bright students to "be average" or to fail if they so choose. Remedial programs, however, are not the answer. In this chapter, I outlined a program designed to improve gifted students' self-esteem, attitudes towards school, school behaviors, and academic achievement. The children's giftedness was the primary concern. Differentiated curricula, both cognitive and affective, and appropriate instructional strategies required to meet these goals were suggested. Acceleration, enrichment, and remediation were woven together to provide an alternative for these children. Changes in the classroom environment, classroom-management techniques, and scheduling were offered. Ways of involving parents to help them learn to support the changes their children were making rounded out the information provided.

The results of the study *Listen to the Children* (Supplee, 1987/1988) confirm the importance of the specialized curricula and instructional strategies as perceived by the enrolled students. Teachers, as well, recognized the positive effect the specialized strategies had on the students. As part of the regularly occurring evaluation of the overall gifted and talented program, the teachers were asked to rank in order (in terms of importance to the children) the five options for gifted students currently operating in the district. (These included a pullout program for grades 3–8, a primary enrichment program for grades K–3, an independent study program, a publishers' workshop, and the UAG program.) The adaptive class for underachievers ranked first.

CHAPTER 4

Politics and Practicalities

Implementing a new program of any type involves changing an existing system. Much has been written about ways to bring about effective, long-term change in schools. The more familiar change agents are with what *should* happen and what *can* happen, the better prepared they will be to deal with what *does* happen. Change is not easy. When trying to adjust the everyday operation of a school system, the more knowledgeable a person is about the change process, the more smoothly the process should proceed.

WHAT RESEARCH SAYS ABOUT CHANGE IN SCHOOLS

One of the most widely cited and respected studies of effective organizational change is the Rand study. Results of this study were reported by Lieberman and Miller (1979). The Rand study found that effective change efforts had the motivation and commitment of the entire institution. There was a better chance of effective change if all of the people who would eventually be involved in implementing the change helped in planning and creating the change. The best efforts resulted from ideas that originated from the bottom up, not the top down. When the participants felt a sense of personal power and believed they had the ability to achieve the ultimate aims of the organization, they were effective in implementing the change. The commitment of the building principal was the single most important factor if change was to be successful.

The Rand study (Lieberman & Miller, 1979) also defined factors that had a negative impact on change or no impact at all. Organizations that had participants with more years of experience and greater age were less successful at implementing change. The way people described or talked about the change seemed to have little or no relationship to whether the change was implemented effectively.

Knowing what facilitates change, what can or should the change agent do? What if the change agent is not a "bottom" person trying to bring about change? Or, what if the change agent does not have the agreement of all the people in the institution? Miller and Wolf (1978) suggested strategies that could help the lone person with a good idea. Presented here in a slightly modified form are their ideas.

1. *Deal with the immediate, close concerns of the people who will be touched by the change.* A change has to be perceived as important by those who will be involved—the community, the Board of Education, the administration, other staff, parents and students—not just the change agent. Work on them all. Try to imagine them looking at the new idea through their eyes. How does the problem of the gifted underachiever look from their perspective? What will make people perceive the problem as important to them?

2. *Take small steps.* Segment plans and then do so again. Take plenty of time and encourage involvement in the decision-making process by those who will feel the impact of the decisions. This always takes longer than individual decision making, but results in more commitment from those involved, particularly if consensus seeking rather than voting is used to arrive at decisions.

3. *Allow for the development of small working subgroups.* Then pull these subgroups together for determination of the final form of change. Capitalize on people's strengths. Different people from each of the affected groups may be experts in many things: teaching reading, budgeting funds effectively, communicating with the public, etc. Involve as many subgroups as possible in your planning, expand the feeling of ownership of, and thus commitment to, the change. Bring them all together when drafting final recommendations to reinforce the idea that there is support for the change in many places, not just their own small group.

4. *Allow time for extended periods of adjustment to the segmented changes.* The underachieving gifted program described in this book was developed in three phases and further modified as more input was received. "Stretch-out periods" were needed by the staff at several points. Initially it took time to have many recognize the need for such a program. Then it took time for classroom teachers to address the questions the program raised about their personal images as successful teachers. It took time for them to adjust to "losing" their kids. Those who "adjusted" in the beginning to the recommended change by assuming the program was too ambitious and could never be successful needed time later to talk about and to learn to deal with its evident success—success they had not been able to achieve with the children prior to the program's inception.

5. *Use a multi-path approach.* Have a map rather than an itinerary to help guide the process of change. Know what the final destination is, and don't be fearful of taking detours that will eventually get you there. The suggestions regarding the underachieving gifted program made in this book are for your

consideration. They have been tested and found workable in one context. But each situation is different. You may be faced with a larger or a smaller school building with more or less space available, a city location or suburb rather than a rural area, 4000 rather than 400 students in a district. Because of these differences, certain problems will have to be approached in new ways and solutions will be found that would never have worked in the original context. Differences are fine, as long as gifted students who underachieve are found and helped to change self-defeating patterns of behavior. That's the destination; the route is unimportant.

6. *Allow for acceleration.* If the change process seems to be speeding up and no danger is apparent, permit it to continue. But keep a wary eye open for signs of stress that may signal the need to slow down again.

7. *Provide for cushioning.* Not everyone will be happy with the change you propose. Plan ways to support those who are very uncomfortable, and plan an escape for those who truly need it; everyone will benefit. For example, a teacher may simply be unable to accept the paradoxical concept of gifted underachievers. It will be kinder to that teacher and the students if they are not placed together in their mainstream classes. An administrator is best able to plan for this kind of cushioning. She or he will need input and support in return for the adjustments requested for the students. The change agent, too, will need cushioning at times. A good friend, who can be accepting and supportive during difficult times, particularly one who can be a "friendly critic" because he or she is knowledgeable about the field, is invaluable. A chance to network at conferences and workshops with others in the field can also be a welcome hiatus.

8. *Allow for institutional spillover.* Any change in one part of a system, however loosely the parts are connected, will affect other parts of the system. Expect it. Permit it. Positive growth will be seen when a new program with new teaching strategies or curriculum is implemented. Don't become overly possessive of effective ideas. Just quietly and humbly rejoice when those ideas spread. It's the highest form of flattery.

9. *Prevent regression.* Provide for a low-level, lock-in device. This may be as simple as routinely distributing a checklist asking for new referrals. Or, it can be more complex, such as requesting a quarterly work sample as evidence that a student's educational goals and objectives are being addressed in the regular classroom as well as in the adaptive program. Whatever is chosen should be just enough to remind other people in the system at regularly scheduled intervals that the change is not going away. Whatever is required should not be overly taxing, though, or it will generate negative feelings towards the change.

Readers who are interested in broadening their awareness of the factors involved in successful and unsuccessful change in school settings are referred to Baldridge and Deal (1983), Gross, Giaquinta and Bernstein (1971), Lewin (1958), Sarason (1971), Smith and Keith (1971), and Weick (1978) in addition to the authors previously cited.

MAKING THE CHANGE STEP-BY-STEP

In the novel *To Kill a Mockingbird* is a statement wise and powerful. Atticus, a lawyer, tells his daughter that, before she makes a decision about anything, she should walk a mile in the other person's moccasins. While applicable to many situations in daily life, it is essential for those who are trying to bring about change. By scrupulously thinking about who might feel the impact of a recommendation, by looking at plans through their eyes, problems can be anticipated and solutions or responses prepared—most of the time. When these steps are forgotten, there are problems. Can a person take the research on change and apply it in a real-life situation? Here are the steps that were taken as the underachiever's program was first implemented and what was learned as a result.

Start From the Bottom Up

As the change literature notes, broad-based support is important if a new program is to be implemented successfully. The first steps, planning from the bottom up (Lieberman & Miller, 1979) and dealing with immediate, close concerns (Miller & Wolf, 1978), were to ask classroom teachers whether they saw the problem that existed. Were there apparently bright kids who were not doing well in school?

A resounding "Yes" was the response. Undoubtedly there are in any system at least a few students who fit this description. Classroom teachers saw a few of them daily. Gifted coordinators knew of them. Some of the students were in a gifted program and caused the teacher of the gifted to deal with questions like, "How can so-and-so be gifted when his grades are abominable?" The district coordinator had to deal with the ethical issue of excluding a child with an IQ exceeding 130 from the gifted program because the identification system required meeting a minimum on several criteria. There were children that teachers believed were gifted, not because of a measurably high intelligence, but because of the child's accomplishments outside of the school setting. Yet these students were not in the gifted program because their test scores were too low.

These are the kind of children to look for with the staff's help to build a rationale for an adaptive program. Finding them is a relatively easy task. It only takes one or two classic underachievers who have been labeled "lazy" or "emotionally troubled" to provide support for the idea.

Involve the Administration

After establishing the presence of the problem, the next person approached was the chief school administrator who also served as building principal. Because of his dual role, he was very pressed for time. We therefore tried to save him work by ourselves assuming the responsibility for preparing the proposal for the Board of Education. The superintendent's need was thoroughly researched, well-thought-out plans that were defensible and that could be communicated clearly.

To meet that need, data were compiled about the classic cases of bright underachievers in the school, all of whom were in fifth grade or higher. It was clear that probably there were more students, in particular younger students, who would become like these five unless something or someone intervened. The research that was available at that time (see Chapter 2) about successful school interventions was shared along with a proposal for the less costly plan, the UAG program. Anticipated cost factors (primarily salary, child-study team services, and start-up materials) were derived, and longer range costs (involving continued salary and replacement materials) were projected. A comparison between the UAG plan (on a cost-per-student basis) and the comparable costs for special education students and compensatory education students was figured (also on a cost-per-student basis to the district, excluding funds available from state and federal aid, as ours is a state that provides no funding specifically for the gifted). The number of personnel available to serve students with special needs at each end of the bell curve was also compared.

Possible concerns that might lead to rejection of the idea before it had a fair trial were brainstormed. Because classroom space was at a premium, space needs were analyzed. The building was scoured for possible locations to house such a program or to relocate another program that could be flexible in its placement. Again, spaces utilized for special-needs children at both ends of the bell curve were compared. Recommendations were readied.

One apparently logical route to follow if these children had special needs such as emotional problems or learning problems was to place them in regular special education or compensatory education classes. By checking with the child-study team to determine which of our "classic cases" had been referred, if any, and for what reasons, a startling discovery was made. *All five* had been referred, but not classified. There was no classification for them because they were too intelligent. Extraordinary scatter on the WISC-R was evident, but what did it mean? Large discrepancies between their measured IQs and achievement test scores existed, but their standardized test scores were still too high to qualify them for special classes. The team was reluctant to classify these children as emotionally disturbed (E.D.) because of the inappropriateness of the available placement and curriculum given the ability of the students. For gifted underachievers, the E.D. class would not be the least restrictive environment. E.D. students needed to be sent out of the district and would be grouped with others who were far more seriously disturbed than the gifted underachievers were. The underachieving students were in a Catch-22.

The data were supplanted with examples suggesting that the problem is not a new one. Einstein, for example, was 4 years old before he could speak and 7 before he could read. Isaac Newton did poorly in school. When Thomas Edison was a boy, his teacher told him he was too stupid to learn anything. Leo Tolstoy flunked out of college. Werner von Braun flunked ninth-grade algebra. Winston Churchill failed the sixth grade (Thompson, 1971). These were probably unidentified gifted children who were underachievers. They made it in spite of the system, but the question to be asked is, "How many might have been missed? How many didn't make it?" No one can promise to create such people of eminence, but the opportunity should be there to give children who had similar school experiences a chance at a better life for themselves and perhaps, eventually, for society.

Thoroughness is important. Take time to analyze and plan carefully, and there may be little difficulty obtaining the support of the administrator. What for some may be one step, for others may be several. There may be a few more middle administrators, each of whom should be approached in rank order. In every case, look through the administrator's eyes and see the problem from her or his perspective.

Gain Board of Education Support

The next step is the Board of Education. Generally, the board members are deeply concerned about education and about doing the right thing for the children of today. They are also responsible for a great deal of money, even when a district is small. It is their obligation to find the most reasonable balance between the educational needs of the community's children and the pocketbooks of the voters. Even in districts where board members are appointed and paid, the basic responsibilities remain the same.

According to the National School Boards Association, it is the job of school boards to see that schools are well run, but not to run them. Boards that are effective operate by setting policy, then designating an administrator to implement the board's policies. In public schools, board policies are public information. Generally, board policies are guided by a statement of philosophy that appears at the front of their policy book. The statement of philosophy can be an ally in addressing the needs of this special population. Look at the philosophy and at the sections of the policy book that deal with student services and curriculum. When a district's policy statements emphasize meeting the individual needs of students, the case is wrapped up. Quotes from their own policy book attesting to their intent to meet the needs of individual students are very powerful in convincing board members of the legitimacy of a request. The information that there is a gap between intended policy and actual practice is compelling.

Board members also have a fiscal responsibility. They are elected to see that the schools are well run, but the taxpayers who elect them are also watching what is done with the money from their pockets. Expenses for new programs have to be very clearly justified and supported with solid information. The research base and rationale developed should be available to board members who may be challenged for approving anything a taxpayer feels is unneeded. Board members should have information to support their decisions so they can share their reasons with the voters. Look at the idea through their eyes. Give them answers to questions they may be asked.

Competitive grant funds were available for innovative programs designed to meet the needs of gifted underachievers when the UAG program was begun. The superintendent felt confident that the resource-room idea had merit and recommended submitting a grant application. With funding available, the UAG program, risky because of the then-unknown outcomes, was approved relatively easily by the Board of Education. The board only needed to approve the grant application, which signified approval of the idea with a very small commitment of local funds until evaluation of the program proved its success. Approval may be somewhat more challenging if all funds must come directly from local budget funds. It may be worth looking for a funding source for start-up costs.

The gifted underachievers program suggested here is actually inexpensive as school programs go. One hundred minutes of teaching time and 50 minutes of planning time (based on New Jersey's $18,500 minimum salary at the time) equalled roughly $8,000 annually—approximately $1,000 per student enrolled per year. Put in a school context, where the telephone bill for the same year for equipment and service exceeded $10,000—or $1,000 per month that school was in session—it seemed reasonable. Once the approximate cost to start up a program for gifted underachievers is determined, find examples of things your school spends equal amounts on by looking at Board of Education minutes or by speaking with the school business administrator or Board of Education secretary. If items of equal cost but less direct value to the children in your district can be found that the board funds without question, it may be easier to engender more support for the expenditure needed.

Remember to walk a mile in their shoes. Board members often choose to serve because they want to make a difference in the educational opportunities available to the children in their district. Frequently, they get bogged down in committee work, in legal suits, and complaints. Give them a sense of purpose; appeal to their sense of efficacy. Show them a cost-effective program that is educationally sound and encourage them to do what is right. It might also help to point out the cost of a jail term for a year or two—the final cost to society of Robert's education. That, too, comes from the taxpayers' pockets. The cost was $16,425 per year per person (1986 figures from the Keogh-Dwyer Correctional Facility, Sussex County, New Jersey). At that rate, $1,000 per student per year is the bargain of the century.

Generally, it is the chief school administrator or a designee of that person who presents proposals to the board. All of the work done up to this point should be available to that person. It goes without saying that this is *not* an adversarial situation. You are working as a team to bring about something that is good for children. It is now known that the UAG program is not risky. It has the impact hoped for, and it is not teacher specific (Supplee, 1986). If the administrator can present the amassed data in a cogent manner, the board's questions will probably be mostly points of clarification.

Return to the Faculty

Once approval is granted, go back to the people who helped and say thank you. There is still much to be done, but savor the achievement of the first milestone.

At this point it is also essential to see through the eyes of other teachers. When the UAG program was first implemented, this point was forgotten. Think about who else could have used that money. Is there a staff member who believes any amount would be better put into salary or benefits packages for the entire staff? Is there someone currently working part-time who would like to be a full-time employee? Is there someone who lives in the district and whose child was not eligible for the gifted program for achievers, but whose child could have been served if a wider identification net were available? How will these folks view a decision to put district funds into a program to help students that seem lazy or unmotivated, but bright? More importantly, what reaction to their views is appropriate?

One stance that was helpful when the UAG was being planned was humility. It was important to recognize and to try to solve or circumvent the problems created by the needs of others as often as possible. There were times, and this was one of them, when solving the problems of others for them was simply not possible. Not every problem can be solved, nor should be solved, by one person for another. Straightforwardly communicating that fact with kindness and sincerity helped. Maintaining a sense of humor and a sense of the absurd allowed problems to be put into perspective. During the months between board approval and implementation, encourage a sense of guarded, let's-wait-and-see, optimism.

Co-workers need to be kept informed. They should know what is planned, what timelines are expected, how they are to be involved, and how the program will be evaluated. Their support is important and should be built. This may be more difficult to do during the identification phase, easier to do only after the students are enrolled. Obvious changes in the students occur very quickly once they are in the adaptive class, and then the changes persist.

There are teachers who will be constant critics. It is easy to feel defensive. It is wiser to make positive use of their criticisms. Use their voices to consider possible weaknesses in the design, their criticisms to adjust the program for new contexts. Try not to react defensively. Let the critics know their questions are helpful and hope that you are building bridges by doing so.

There are teachers who will be constant supporters. Find them, appreciate them, and use their talents. They probably have networks with some of the "middle-of-the-roaders" who are neither exceptionally supportive nor exceptionally critical. The supporters are the people who can begin the subgroups. Determine what their strengths are and let them know they are needed. Being asked to share expertise is a positive, encouraging statement to a teacher. It clearly states they are valued. It can reduce the sense of isolation many teachers feel when they are able to work with others who have similar goals. Be sure any teachers who help receive written commendation for their assistance.

The more specific the requests, the more success is likely in involving others. An effective approach is, "You are so good at . . . [enriching your reading program through the use of bibliotherapy, for example]. I'm particularly interested in . . . [finding books that deal with children who have overcome problems]. Do you have time to help me by . . . [recommending some of your favorite books and writing up cards that follow this format for our students' use]? Do you know of anyone else in the district that I might ask to help you because they have another excellent technique for . . . [enriching their reading instruction]? Do you think you might enjoy working together?"

Be sure to keep requests reasonable in terms of the personal time required of a teacher for a task or arrange for release time from present duties for such work. Other suggestions and effective recommendations may spill over from this initial request. Specific requests were much more likely to elicit a positive, truly helpful, response than, "I need help setting up the reading. What do you recommend?" Such a broadly stated request may elicit a speech about the teacher's favorite idea, but encourage no active participation from that teacher. No active participation equals no ownership. Another problem with the general approach was that if the idea offered is not used, the teacher may feel rebuffed.

Inform the Community

A public-relations effort is appropriate and necessary. People who pay taxes need to understand the problem that their money, poured into this new program, is supposed to solve. And they, like the Board of Education, need to understand the relatively inexpensive nature of this solution. Enlist the cooperation of the person who normally handles school public relations. If there is no one, find a good writer on the staff and start a public-relations subgroup.

Local newspapers are glad to announce awards, and that includes grants. Provide press release copy and a photograph to the paper. Ask the paper to follow up by having a feature writer prepare a human interest story for an education page. School-district newsletters are another vehicle to inform the community. An article, written as a series of commonly asked questions and answers about the program, can deal with issues that might arise in people's minds before the rumor mill is activated. Provide a phone number for answers to questions that aren't anticipated. Encourage members of the community to contact a spokesperson if they have questions. Also ask them to propose the names of children they know who fit the description of a bright child who was underachieving. Keep the community informed in subsequent newsletters about the progress and eventually the results of the different phases of the program. Pride is engendered in the community when their schools are recognized for unique accomplishments.

Meet With the Affected Students and Their Parents

The last group to be informed on an intensive basis about the program design and proposed results are those whom it touches most closely, the parents and students. Specifics of this effort are more thoroughly described in Chapter 5.

SUMMARY

The process of bringing about one specific change in schools, namely the implementation of a program for gifted underachievers, has been described in a detailed, step-by-step manner. These steps are grounded in sound theory, specifically the work of Lieberman and Miller (1979) and Miller and Wolf (1978), which is summarized in the text. Throughout the change process, those responsible for the success of the project must consider their decisions and procedures as they affect all who will feel the effects.

CHAPTER 5

Getting Started Yourself

The children to look for when beginning a program for underachievers are not those who fit the myths that surround the gifted. They are not good at everything they try. They may not demonstrate advanced language ability. They are not mature, independent, and self-directed children. They are not all easy to find. Gifted underachievers may be children who are unmotivated or lazy. They may be mildly to severely handicapped. They may be culturally different. They may hate to read and write. They may be immature, dependent children who are constantly in need of teacher direction. By looking hard enough, though, you can find them.

IDENTIFYING STUDENTS FOR THE PROGRAM

It is essential that every child in a district be evaluated during the start-up screening. Excuse no one: not special education resource-room children, not older children, and not those who are already in the gifted and talented program. Some interesting surprises may appear! This initial identification process will be the most lengthy, but the most crucial. Not only will the process serve to identify children for the start-up program, but it can begin to sensitize teachers to the types of students who may be in trouble.

The Process

Gather cumulative record files, identification matrices, and behavioral characteristic checklists for the screening process. Have enough behavioral characteristic checklists for each teacher to have five. (Copies of these check-lists are in Appendix A for your convenience.) Age, grade, and percentile equivalents should not be used because they have unequal units. Stanines that use standard deviation units to express an individual's performance relative to a group are the preferred statistical measure (Borg & Gall, 1983, p. 362). If stanines were not reported on the achievement test and/or IQ student record forms, obtain the test administrator's and norms manuals for analysis of the test results your district uses. Determine the equivalent stanines for the scaled scores and have this information available for the staff so they can record results in stanines.

Involve the entire faculty at an in-service day or extended faculty meeting. To predict how much time will be needed and to work out any bugs in the system, complete the screening of at least one student, preferably more. Then multiply the time it takes to do one student by the average number of homeroom students each teacher has. Estimate whether the teachers will need an afternoon or an hour for the task, then schedule the screening day.

At the initial screening meeting, give each teacher the cumulative records for his or her homeroom and one identification matrix (see Figure 5.1). Ask the teachers to write the names of the students in their classes on the matrix in alphabetical order. Then, under the guidance of the person responsible for the initial screening, have the teachers survey the cumulative folder of each student for the following records:

1. *IQ, if given.* This should be entered in the appropriate column on the matrix. The stanine score should be noted.
2. *Achievement test scores over the last three years.* Again, have teachers look at the stanine scores in reading, mathematics, and for the total battery. They should note, by putting a check in the appropriate matrix column, any child whose scores have been erratic and/or any scores that have declined during the past three years by more than one stanine (e.g., from the seventh to the fifth). They should put a second checkmark in that column if the original score was at the eighth or ninth stanine. There are separate columns, one each for reading, for math, and for total battery. Ask teachers to observe whether, in the primary grades, the phonics and word analysis subtests were lower than the vocabulary and/or reading comprehension. Have them notice any large discrepancy between reading and math scores. If such conditions are present, a comment should be made in the column to the right.

   [From this point on, the teachers will be recording the presence of certain factors through the use of checkmarks. The actual items (e.g., the comments made by teachers on report cards) do not need to be written on the matrix. When it is time to decide whom to screen further, the cumulative files can be referred to again, if necessary.]
3. *Compare IQ and achievement test stanines.* Teachers should put a check in the appropriate column if there is a discrepancy of more than one stanine between IQ and any achievement test stanine.
4. *Report card and cumulative record comments.* Ask teachers to look for comments that indicate at least one teacher felt a child was more capable than

Figure 5.1: Identification matrix.

								STUDENT NAME H.R.	SCHOOL GRADE DATE	
								IQ Group (G) or Individual (I)		
								>1 S.D. drop in Reading Achievement tests over 3 years		
								>1 S.D. drop in Math Achievement tests over 3 years		
								>1 S.D. drop in Total Battery Achievement tests over 3 years		
								Declining school grades		
								Discrepancy of at least 1 S.D. between IQ/Achievement test/grades		
								Self nomination		
								Peer nomination		
								Parent nomination		
								Teacher checklist		
								Report card comments		
								Outside activity/community nom.		
								Creativity test score		
								Interview using Richert protocol		
								Product evaluation		
								CST screening/recommendation		

grades showed or that the child appeared bored or was a behavior problem. Examples might include:

"bright, capable, slow worker"

"highly creative, poor work habits"

"hard on himself; 'uptight' about academics; self-pressure evident"

"absent a lot; talks well, but doesn't apply himself when working independently"

"doesn't always perform to ability"

"not achieving as he should"

"not working to potential; perfectionist; erratic work"

"strong academics, social problems, self-image problems"

"relies on gab rather than work"

If similar comments exist, the appropriate column on the matrix should be checked.

5. *Report card grades.* Teachers should look for grades that have consistently declined over the years in school, particularly in reading and math in the younger grades, but also in science and social studies in the upper grades. Check also for those children whose lowest grades are handwriting or spelling or who have difficulty spelling in daily work although they do well on tests.

6. *Checklist of characteristics.* When all the cumulative files have been reviewed, the final step is to ask teachers to review the Checklist of Behavioral Characteristics of Gifted Underachievers that you provide (see Appendix A). Ask them to decide if any children they teach now or have taught in the past fit a number of those characteristics, especially the starred attributes. If so, ask them to complete a checklist on that child. When checklists are completed, they should be given to the child's current homeroom teacher who can mark the matrix to indicate a behavioral checklist is available on that child.

At this point, the teachers have finished their part in the identification process. Matrices and behavioral checklists should now be given to the person in charge of the screening process. The teachers should be informed that additional indicators will be included in the search for candidates.

Make it clear to the teachers that some underachieving gifted students may only be found through their outside accomplishments and that the community will be solicited for these recommendations. Another way that children who only appear successful outside of school may be found is through a nomination form that includes both positive and negative signs of giftedness. If the district uses multiple criteria for identifying gifted children, a parent nomination or teacher nomination form that elicits negative qualities associated with giftedness as well as positive may already be used. It would be wise to search through those nominations for any child who had many negative attributes noted. (Districts not currently using such a nomination form might consider beginning to do so. A sample is included in Appendix A.) If a public-relations campaign was mounted, it is quite likely that some parents have called the school to say, "That sounds like my child. Is it possible he or she needs this program?" Notes or calls from a community member, for example a piano teacher who recommends that you consider a certain child, may have arrived already. When a child is referred by someone outside of the school family, the information should still be recorded on the child's homeroom teacher's matrix.

Now determine the final number of children the program in your district can accommodate. Six to eight students per class are recommended. This is small enough to allow for individualized instruction, yet large enough to allow group dynamics to be effective. The eventual number of classes will depend on the size of the district, but to start it would be wise to begin with just one class. (A small start means small mistakes that can be corrected more easily.) In the initial screening, consider about three times the final number of children who will be served.

From the matrices, highlight any students who have six or more checkmarks overall *and* any that have community or parent nominations regardless of the number of checks. This process may still leave a number that is unwieldy. If so, rank those nominated by school information in order, from greatest to least number of checks. Contact the parents or community nominators to obtain further information about the children they brought to the district's attention. Skim both piles until the number of students that can be handled for the final screening is reached.

At this point, contact the parents or guardians of each student being considered for the pilot program. Do so by phone so that any questions the parents have about their children or the program can be immediately answered. Explain that their children seem like possible candidates for a gifted program that is designed to help those who are not achieving all they might. Explain that students in this candidate pool will be screened further to learn more about them. Be sure parents understand that screening does not guarantee placement. Describe the way you will screen the pool and when your final decisions are likely. If the parents are even remotely interested in having their children considered for the class, tell them you will send home a release form so that they can authorize you to continue with the process. Tell them the date by which the form must be returned if their child is to be considered. Record to whom you send the forms and when they are returned to the school with a parent's signature. As the release forms return, set up individual files on each child for whom you have signed consent. Include the data from the matrix. Return to the cumulative records and copy for your file all IQ, achievement, report card and behavioral information relevant to the matrix data.

The next step is to arrange an interview with each child. The interviews take about 20 minutes each. Spend a few minutes warming up with each child. Then briefly describe the program. Explain that the school hopes to find out who among the students being talked to is most likely to benefit from such a program. Tell the child that only some of the people being talked to will be selected to participate. During the interview, use a protocol to be certain each child receives the same cues. This assures obtaining the same type of information from each, thus allowing fair comparisons. A useful protocol, found in Appendix A, was modified from one developed by E. Susanne Richert (1982). Record the child's answers next to the questions asked, and record your impressions from the interview on the chart below the questions. At the close of the interview, thank the child and give him or her a letter to take home explaining that the interview took place and what parents can expect in terms of a decision. Encourage parents to call with questions.

It is important to ask the child if he or she thinks the special program that is described might be helpful. Occasionally a child among the candidates will have no desire to take part. Although the parent might feel the UAG program would be beneficial, without the child's interest, success is doubtful. It seems foolish to begin by coercing a child to participate when there are many who are anxious for a fresh chance. By explaining this rationale to the parents and assuring them that the child will be reconsidered at a later time if he or she becomes interested, most will accept the recommendation graciously.

When all the interviews are complete, meet with the child-study team to learn whether any of the candidates have already been referred, but not classified. Determine the students about whom more information is needed and complete any referral process and forms that are needed.

Call together a representative subgroup of co-workers, for example the child-study team, to help you make the final selection. The decision at this point is a professional one, with no one criterion weighing more heavily than another. Attempt to choose students who evidence the greatest need at that point in time on the basis of the data available on each student. After the initial group is chosen, rank the remaining students so that if a parent refuses permission at this point or if attrition occurs for other reasons, those to be considered next are readily available.

When the UAG program was first established, everyone involved was surprised to learn that every child selected had an IQ over 120. Certainly this was not planned as a criterion, but the fact that it happened made the initial program more acceptable to people who view IQ as a strong indicator of giftedness. A strong caution is in order. No child whose IQ is lower than 120 should be eliminated from consideration if both giftedness, as evidenced by some other indicator than IQ, and need, supported by the screening process, are clearly evident. IQ measures such a small part of intellectual functioning and is often culturally biased. It is highly dependent on anxiety levels and socioeconomic status. Excluding any child who did not "measure up" due to these factors would be indefensible.

One last point. Keep all the original screening forms for at least five years. The information may be needed to answer questions that aren't anticipated at the start. The records of some, especially of those students who are included, may be useful for an even-longer period.

Notifying Parents and Students

Parents of students who were accepted for the UAG class should be sent a letter notifying them of the decision. The parents will be asked to share the news with their children. A permission form to be returned by a specified date should also be included. On the return date, additional letters to fill any spaces created by rejections, can be mailed. A second letter, explaining why a child was not to be included at this time, can be sent to the remaining parents. Again, ask that the parents share the information with the children. All form letters are in Appendix A.

A meeting for the parents of accepted students should be scheduled now. The purpose is to discuss the program goals, the ways in which the individual educational plan will be developed, the parent education classes, and the methods by which the students will be evaluated.

Notifying Teachers

All staff members can now be notified of the final groups of students. Do this in writing through faculty mail. Teachers should be encouraged to ask questions and to keep the teachers responsible for the UAG program informed of changes they see in any of the students who were considered. Make it clear that the door is always open, and encourage them to visit once the class is in operation.

START-UP TASKS

Children who have difficulty in learning benefit by having an instructional program designed to meet their individual needs. The first step in planning for those needs is diagnosis of both abilities and problem areas. Most of this assessment can occur before the students enter the adaptive class.

Developing Case Histories

Meet with the selected group to administer the Coopersmith Self-Esteem Inventory (1981) and a learning styles and interest inventory appropriate for the ages of the students. Analyze the results of these measures, and add the analysis to the data gained on each child as part of the screening process. Observe each child in class, and describe apparent personal and social adjustment, motor coordination, use of language, and any other noteworthy behaviors seen. Then meet with the child's classroom teachers. Record any suggestions the teachers have for instructional strategies that are successful with the child. A representative sample of current work in the subject areas for which the teacher in the UAG class will be responsible can be collected and diagnosed to find strengths and weaknesses in each child's work.

A thumbnail or outline sketch of each student can now be written, synthesizing information into the following categories:

1. Family background, including any known minority factors
2. General appearance
3. Health history
4. Aptitude and achievement discrepancies
5. Peer and social relationships
6. Preferred learning styles and strategies
7. Self-esteem information
8. Areas of interest and special abilities
9. Personality traits

These vignettes help the teacher have a well-rounded, clear picture of each child.

Meet with the child-study team to update the children's records based on the team's assessment of any students that were referred. A multidisciplinary evaluation by the child study team should be completed on each enrolled child, if at all possible. Assessment of a large group of children all at once may overtax the capabilities of the child-study team as the new program starts. At the very least, an individual assessment of achievement is recommended. Teachers can be trained to administer the Woodcock–Johnson Assessment Battery, Part II (Woodcock & Johnson, 1977). A child-study team member might complete the administration and interpretation of other sections of this battery, beginning with students who are suspected of having learning disabilities. Full-team workups can be scheduled on most students after the teacher has the opportunity to work with students in class. Some advocacy for underachieving gifted students and the support of the administration may be needed if the district's team is overworked, as many are.

With the available information, formulate specific goal statements and objectives for each individual child. What does this particular child need? Goals in both the cognitive and affective areas should be developed. Many thorough explanations of ways to write individual educational plans are available to help schools meet the requirements of PL 94–142 (Education for All Handicapped Children Act, 1975). Most guides, however, focus exclusively on students' weaknesses. Use what is available, but remember to capitalize on and build students' areas of strengths. The individual plans for gifted underachievers should include:

1. *A statement of the child's levels of performance.* Strengths should be emphasized. Synthesize data into two categories, strengths first followed by weaknesses.
2. *Annual goals and short-term objectives.* It helps to rank the annual goals. The most essential needs (areas of strength to encourage and areas of weakness to build) of the students should be listed first. Short-term objectives should be developed with input from the student, and should state how the student will reach the selected goals.
3. *Specific special education and related services to be provided.* If a gifted student has a learning disability discovered through screening for the UAG program, special education services may be used in addition to the adaptive program for gifted. Some students with serious gross motor problems may need adaptive physical education. These commitments for related services should be written in the student's plan.
4. *Dates for the initiation and duration of services.* These should be both of the adaptive class and any related services.
5. *Evaluation procedures.* These should include criteria for knowing that the objectives are achieved, and who will be responsible for performing them.

Preparing for the Change in Teacher Responsibilities

Talk at greater length with those teachers whose students who will be leaving them to come to the UAG class for instruction during part of the day. Clarify the fact that the curricula and the instructional strategies used with the UAG students will differ from those they use in the regular classroom. Share a copy of the student's individual plan. The classroom teacher, who will still be teaching the child for part of the day, should be knowledgeable about the individual goals and objectives set for the child. The classroom teacher should know what the student will be learning in the UAG class so she may help reinforce these learnings. Reaffirm for teachers that the teacher in the UAG class will be assuming total responsibility for the subjects students will now miss in their regular class. Give the teachers a memo stating the subject areas for which that responsibility is being assumed. Tell the teachers they are free to share this memo with the student's parents.

Explain how report card grades will be assigned for the subjects taught in UAG. It is suggested that the same policy as that used in the district by special education resource teachers be followed. The classroom teachers are accustomed to this practice and will have little difficulty understanding and accepting the change for UAG purposes. If the district does not have a standard policy, it may be helpful to do the following: The regular classroom teachers complete their report cards for the subjects they teach the students. Insert NG (no grade) in the subject area space for any students in the UAG class for that subject, then add a narrative report form. Grades can be reported on a narrative report card form, rather than on the regular report card. This difference emphasizes the difference in curriculum. The narrative can also detail the objectives reached and the areas still needing attention.

Ask to be included in, or informed of the results of, grade-level meetings when decisions are made that will affect the students in UAG (for example, field trip plans or special grade-level projects). Encourage the staff to discuss problems and conflicts as they arise rather than waiting for a problem to compound.

Orienting Students

Shortly before the first day of class, hold a meeting for each group of students, those who will be in UAG, and those who were screened but not included at this time. Enrolled students can be welcomed, told what they will need to bring to class and why, and given their starting date. Advise them that this is only their first meeting and that there will be many others. At class meetings, they will make and decide how to enforce agreements about classroom routines. Ask the students to think about how they would like the classroom run if they hope to do better in school. Their ideas, to be shared on the first day of class, will shape the rules they will live by in their new room. Tell them that meetings during the year will teach them how to govern themselves, just as they will have to do when they get out of school. Answer any questions, and dismiss the students.

In a second meeting, explain to the students who were screened, but who will not be in the adaptive program why choices needed to be made. While it would have been wonderful to include everyone in the adaptive class, explain that the class had to be kept small if it was going to work right. Try to have something special in mind for these students, too. An arranged time for them to set up and plan an independent or small group investigation (Renzulli, 1977) can be appropriate. This is optional, of course, but encourage the student to participate. Set aside one planning period per week to work with those who take on this activity.

CAN OTHER TEACHERS DO IT?

There are many exceptional professionals in the field of education. There are people who care deeply about gifted children in general and who worry about those who don't achieve. Many people can assume the administrative responsibilities necessary to orchestrate the start-up of a new program. The planning and the implementation take time, but, with patience and persistence, the end is achieved. Other teachers can implement the curriculum once the program is set up. Three very different teachers have assumed total responsibility for the UAG program over the course of five years. When affective and cognitive growth achieved by the students under the first two teachers were compared, it was apparent that the second teacher's students exceeded the first in affective growth and showed approximately equal cognitive growth. Given that the first teacher had twenty years of experience, ten of which were in the field of gifted education, and was earning a doctorate, while the second teacher had only two years of classroom teaching experience and a bachelor's degree in special education, it is obvious that people with various preparations can do the job. The teachers who replaced the first teacher in our program found help in the curriculum outlines we have included in Part III.

SUMMARY

In this chapter, the process of identifying students for a first class for gifted underachievers is thoroughly outlined. This initial screening process involves every teacher in the school and considers every student, even those who seem unlikely. The initial screening is followed by interviews with the student. Finally the selection procedures, involving the child-study team, and notification of all people involved are detailed.

The start-up tasks that are recommended once the students are screened and before they actually enter the class are also discussed. These procedures include preparing case histories, formulating specific goals and objectives for each student, and preparing for the changes in teacher responsibility. It is essential during this period to keep open the lines of communication with all school staff members. Finally, students are oriented to their new placement.

Remember, these are suggestions only. The identified students, the teachers' styles, and the school context will impact on what works. Be ready to modify almost everything as the UAG grows and develops. Add new materials and curricula that were not yet available when the first class began. Keep an open mind, be rigorous in insisting that what is adopted and adapted is based on research, and continue to learn.

PART THREE

CURRICULUM

CHAPTER 6

The Reading–Writing Connection

One of the most pervasive myths about gifted students is that they all excel in language arts and reading. Some of the gifted do. But not all gifted children read well, nor do they enjoy reading. In fact, some gifted underachievers would do anything to avoid reading. Nonetheless, reading is an important tool, and all children deserve appropriate reading instruction at their ability level so they become literate adults.

I begin this chapter by summarizing the research on teaching reading to the gifted. Second, I provide a practical approach to teaching reading that does not rely on basal textbooks and that does involve the students at their varying levels of readiness. Finally, I include sample lesson plans and students' reactions to the UAG reading program.

WHAT RESEARCH SAYS ABOUT READING FOR THE GIFTED

Very little has been written about differentiated reading instruction that is appropriate for the gifted. Primarily, there were position papers that recommended accommodations for the gifted (Cushenberry & Howell, 1974; Labuda, 1974), but little research to support those positions. If reading instruction, as it existed in most cases, kept the gifted interested in reading widely and with a critical mind, there might be no worry. However, a study by Martin (1984) shows that gifted students do not all display such attitudes toward reading. The population surveyed included 126 sixth, seventh, and eighth graders in a single school district. Martin found negative attitudes towards reading instruction among a large percentage of this gifted population. (These were not underachievers, but rather the more stereotypical, achieving gifted students.) Based on his findings, Martin made recommendations, but these also indicated that a good reading program for the gifted was little different from a good reading program for any other students. Pacing and content, perhaps largely because of the pacing, might differ. The same idea was supported by the work of Mangieri and Madigan (1984), who studied the status of reading instruction for the gifted, surveying 150 school districts across 50 states. The analysis of the data revealed five major findings. First, the key focus of gifted reading programs was enrichment, although wide variations existed among definitions of enrichment. Second, students were selected for such programs primarily by teacher recommendations. Third, the same basal series was usually used with these readers as with other students in a district, although sometimes the work was accelerated or enriched. Fourth, the regular classroom teacher was primarily responsible for reading instruction for the gifted and talented. Fifth, this person usually had little or no training in appropriate modifications for a reading program for the gifted, not a surprising finding given the dearth of relevant research on the topic.

Rupley (1984) discussed implications of the research on reading-teacher effectiveness for teachers of the gifted. From the literature on teacher-directed instruction in reading, he concluded that lesson pacing and presentation should differ to build on what students already know. Less teacher direction should occur in creative or inquiry situations. Rupley concluded that diagnosis of skills to identify instructional goals for gifted children should be based on questions such as: (1) Is this skill needed to improve students' reading comprehension capabilities? (2) Are there opportunities for learning this skill based on the students' existing capabilities? (3) Are weaknesses in these skills impairing the students' comprehension? Only if the answers were yes should the skill be taught. Isn't this, also, what should be done for those not identified as gifted?

From these studies, there appear to be no clearly different, research-supported recommendations for reading instruction for the gifted. People believe pacing and content should differ, but do not explain how to bring about such differentiation. Instruction for these children at present, even for the achieving gifted students, is often fragmented and ill-defined.

The inference to be made is that those who are interested in adapting reading instruction for the gifted, including the gifted underachiever, would be advised to learn what constitutes quality instruction in reading for all students. That instruction can then be modified by adjusting the content, the pacing, the process of instruction, the student products expected, and the environment where learning occurs to differentiate instruction appropriately for the gifted.

RESEARCH APPLICATIONS

Knowledge from both strands of research—reading instruction and gifted education—should be considered to find opportunities for reading encounters that will advance the reading abilities and interests of gifted students.

Developing Good Reading

Recommendations for effective reading instruction, reported in *Becoming a Nation of Readers* (National Institute of Education, 1984), included many ideas as important for gifted students as for other students. The report stated that

1. Teachers of beginning reading should present well-designed phonics instruction that should end by second grade. Although most children were taught phonics, most phonics instruction was "poorly conceived."
2. Teachers should devote more time to teaching reading comprehension. Such efforts clearly promote reading achievement, but were rare. One study cited by the panel showed that only 45 minutes of comprehension instruction occurred during 17,997 minutes of instruction.
3. Children should spend less time completing workbooks and skill sheets. These activities consume a large proportion of reading instruction in most classrooms, but little evidence exists that they help reading achievement.
4. Children should spend more time in independent reading and in writing. Independent reading is a major source of vocabulary growth and reading fluency; writing promotes ability in reading.
5. Schools should introduce more comprehensive assessments of reading and writing. Standardized tests should be supplemented with evaluations of reading fluency, critical reading ability, and amount and quality of independent reading and writing.

Two recent studies of reading instruction provide a look at the social setting in which we try to teach reading. Both are based on a social-process theory proposed by Vygotsky, a Russian cognitive psychologist. The first study (Palincsar & Brown, 1984) tested whether mediated learning experiences, with the teacher providing different types of assistance at different points in a child's understanding, can assist student learning. The second study by Duffy, Roehler, Meloth, Vavrus, Book, Putnam & Wesselman (1986) concluded that instructional talk—what teachers said to students—had a powerful influence on student learning.

Vygotsky's Theory

The crux of Vygotsky's theory is that all higher psychological processes are originally social processes. People learn by sharing. In schools, the sharing usually occurs between children and adults, and the best instruction is that which advances understanding at the highest level possible for each child. This instruction can be achieved by adult mediation that guides a child through what Vygotsky called the *zone of proximal development* (ZPD). The

ZPD, a map of the child's readiness, is bounded at the lower end by the existing level of competence and at the upper end by the level of competence that can be achieved under the most favorable circumstances (Brown & Ferrara, 1985).

Wertsch (1979) used the task of developing speech to help explain the different stages in the ZPD. Adults, he said, make accommodations for the different levels that exist in a child's use of speech. At first, the child's understanding of words is so limited that communication is very difficult. The adult must shift to speech and gestures appropriate for the child. At the second level, the child realizes that the adult's speech means something, but cannot infer meaning. The adult must help the child make inferences. At the third level, the child understands what is being said and can make inferences. The child assumes significant responsibility for trying to understand, while the adult provides support and feedback. In the fourth and final stage, the child completes the takeover. Language is then the child's, and adult accommodation is no longer needed. Wertsch explained that levels one through three are in the zone of proximal development. Based on this theory, he claimed the issue for instruction in school was not, "Is the adult providing strategic assistance?" but rather, "What type of strategic assistance is the adult providing at what point in the instruction?" Does the assistance match what a student needs at a given point in time?

Vygotsky insisted that education should be aimed at the upper rather than the lower boundary of the zone of proximal development (Brown & Ferrara, 1985), an idea that has profound implications for instruction of the gifted. Wozniak (1980) cited work by Luria, Egorova, and Tsymbaliuk who found wide, measurable differences in the ZPD in children of the same age with identical IQ results. Wozniak concluded that appropriate educational placement and instruction might require assessment sensitive to these differences in ZPD rather than to differences in IQ. Brown and Ferrara (1985) tried to develop an assessment of ZPD suitable for use in the United States. They worked with typical IQ-test tasks, but combined them with graduated degrees of training. By so doing, they learned that IQ did not predict learning speed and/or degree of transfer efficiently. Several clear profiles emerged from their work, two of which probably apply to gifted children. Specifically, they found fast learners (high IQ) who were wide transferrers and fast learners who were narrow transferrers (context-bound). These distinct patterns, even in children of the same age and IQ, mean differences in their readiness to tackle various reading tasks. Instruction has to account for such differences. It is not reasonable just to teach the same thing faster and expect students to be successful. We have to determine how close the students are to being able to perform the tasks required on their own. We then have to supply the appropriate assistance to that student to help the student move to autonomy.

Feuerstein (1979) believed children could be made aware of the rationale for their learning activities and would eventually come to acquire the knowledge they needed to monitor their success on their own. Building on Vygotsky's theory, Wertsch, McNamee, McLane, and Budwig (1980) studied the adult–child dyad to understand how the social processes led to the child's later functioning as an independent cognitive agent. They found that before the child was able to function as an independent, self-regulated learner and problem solver, the adult in the adult–child dyad functioned to plan, regulate, and reflect on the problem-solving task at hand. In other words, the teacher assumed the metacognitive responsibilities for the student in each new task until gradually the student was able to assume them for herself.

Without a way to measure ZPD in the UAG class, teachers tried to assess through practice at what stage the children operated. Adhering to Vygotsky's idea that teaching should take place at the optimal level, they most often began reading instruction at stage three. When a child was not successful at certain tasks, adjustments were made in teaching strategies to match the part of the zone that child appeared to be in. The level was raised as fast as possible. A remedial mode would suggest starting at the bottom and working up; instead, in UAG, instructional expectations are kept as high as possible. Instruction starts at the top and backs up when needed.

In order to provide appropriate instruction for gifted underachievers, we need to understand both the individual students and the tasks that good readers perform. Was any child unaware of a particular task, such as summarizing? Did any child not know that it helps comprehension to ask questions and set purposes for reading? If so, the teacher needed to model the process at the child's level. Was any child in the second stage, aware of the process, but not understanding its importance or the fact that he or she might perform the task? The teacher needed to "sell" the effectiveness of using the strategies of the task, break the task down, and have the child mimic. Or was a child in the third stage, trying to use the strategy, but not using it proficiently? Then the teacher needed to support the child, giving feedback on his or her successes and difficulties.

STRATEGIES FOR EFFECTIVE READING INSTRUCTION

The following is offered as one possible instructional design that accounts for a child's giftedness and for his or her need for appropriate reading instruction at varying stages of growth through the ZPD. It provides one field-tested design with evaluation data to support its effectiveness. Appendix C contains addresses for several of the resources mentioned as well as some that seemed promising but had not yet been tried in the UAG class as this book went to press. As stated before, no matter what strategies are used, it is important to begin at the highest stage of development possible, dropping back only if a child has difficulty with a reading process.

Group Discussion in an Independent Reading Program

Reading instruction in our schools too often means a series of skills to be mastered by completing workbook pages and skill sheets. There is little connection between these activities and the task people face of trying to make sense of the written word in real life. Reading is not seatwork; it is not filling in the blanks. Reading is communication. Authors combine words into sentences and paragraphs and chapters to share what is important to them with a reader. Obtaining meaning from those words demands responses from the reader. The reader first has to determine what the author is saying, then what the author means by what is stated. The final step is to decide how to accept what is meant. Reading instruction should teach students to do these things.

Students can be taught how to respond by using discussion groups. Thinking and talking with others about the books they read can enrich their understanding of what the author is saying. How they respond personally to the author's thoughts can be brought to a conscious level by a teacher's use of carefully crafted questions. When all children in a group read the same selection, discussion of an author's ideas is easy to facilitate. But this situation is not lifelike for most of us.

How can a teacher bring about deep thinking if the students are each reading a different book? Think about how you discuss your own personal reading. Some people have the time to join a book-discussion club. Others are too busy, only managing to squeeze reading into leisure minutes, not hours, and only managing to talk about their reading over lunch or in the car on the way to work. Yet people do read and do talk about what they've read. When others listen, they can gain insights into their own reading—or their own lives. Questions prompt those who are discussing a book to reconsider what they think the author is saying. And both the reader and the discussant are richer for their talk, however brief.

Since part of the teacher's job is to prepare children to be lifelong readers, children in the individualized reading program in the UAG class do as adults do. They share what they've read, gain insights from others, and broaden their understanding of life through what they and their peers read, even though they are all reading different works. The following strategies, based on lifelike experiences rather than the more traditional reading group concept, developed in our classroom, where each child chose a different personal reading selection. No two children read the same book at the same time. Each of the techniques described was used with the entire group at least once a year so the children could practice all the strategies. Favorites were then repeated at the request of the children as they finished a book they loved.

Bloom's Taxonomy and Creative Thinking

Bloom's taxonomy and several creative-thinking skills were taught to the students during the whole-group reading lessons as they were reading and discussing their first selection of the year. Students rapidly became aware that the higher-level assignments and discussions were far more enjoyable for them, but that they needed knowledge and comprehension of their text before they could extend their learning.

A helpful book for our teachers during this unit was *Reading: A Novel Approach* (Szabos, 1984). The students chose and read a work of fiction from the school library. Each day, they shared a summary of the part of the book they read. For independent work, they completed teacher-selected activities from *Reading: A Novel Approach*. Activities encouraged children either to think at various levels of the taxonomy or to use a creative-thinking skill. At the close of the first unit, students shared what had been their favorite independent activity. They gave reasons for their enjoyment and cited specific things of which they were proud. The rest of the group then offered positive comments about the thinking of their peers, asked questions about the activity or the story described, and suggested other activities or similar books that the student might also find enjoyable.

The Socratic Method

A second technique was the use of the Socratic method (Jacobs, 1986). This method is useful with any literary form students read. It is an excellent technique to suggest when a child responds to reading by saying, "I don't think a person would really act that way," or, "It was stupid of so-and-so to ————," or makes other value judgments. Students who use this strategy are asked to present a synopsis of the selection they've read and the issue they wish to explore with the rest of the group. The teacher or student then leads a discussion to explore others' ideas.

When the technique was first taught, a primary storybook, *How Yossi Beat the Evil Urge* (Chaikin, 1983), was used because of its conciseness and theme. The story was read aloud to the group, then summarized as follows: "Yossi was impulsive and easily distractible. He also became totally focused when he was involved in the creation of song and dance. The story made me wonder what adults should do if they have a child like Yossi in their family or in their class."

The children discussed what adults should expect of Yossi in various situations and what options Yossi had for responding to those expectations. Once they brainstormed several ideas, they placed the possible, realistic op-

Figure 6.1: Chalkboard diagram to accompany discussion of *How Yossi Beat the Evil Urge.*

MOST CONSERVATIVE			LEAST CONSERVATIVE
•	•	•	•
The adults should never permit Yossi to follow his impulses and should send him away to private school.	Yossi should be punished when he breaks the rules. When he starts to follow them, he should be praised. He should forget about creativity.	Yossi should be encouraged to find the best times for his songs. He should be reminded, but not punished if he forgets.	The adults should allow Yossi to always follow his impulses and not follow any of the rules the other children follow.

tions on a continuum on the chalkboard, as illustrated in Figure 6.1, with extreme positions at either end.

They analyzed what occurred in the story, discussing the probable short-term and long-term consequences of each option that might follow for both Yossi and the adults. The students decided for themselves, then shared with the others, what they thought the adults should do and gave reasons supporting their conclusions. They compared their decisions to what they thought Yossi would have liked and to what was best for him. Then they thought about their own lives and came to a final conclusion on their own about the story's themes. They realized that people differ for good reasons.

Interactive Questions

Interactive questions place responsibility for knowledge and comprehension of the selected books squarely on the students, while allowing group discussion that is automatically held at the level of analysis, synthesis, and evaluation. A question such as, "How did the author make you believe that the main character was a real-life person?" forces students to focus on character development while they read and to make decisions about what the author intended when the characters speak and act. A question such as, "How might your opinion of this story be changed if you grew up in very different circumstances, for example, as a victim of abuse?" insists that students think about their own life circumstances and decide how their personal experiences affect their understanding and appreciation of an author's words.

Interactive, group-reading lessons were held three times each week. For 20 minutes on each of those days, students (and the teacher) read silently. As they read, they thought about the one interactive question that the teacher chose for that day. About 18 minutes into the reading time, the teacher quietly asked the children to find a good place to stop their reading, then to wait silently, and to think about how they were going to answer the question. After two more minutes, each child shared a brief synopsis of the part of the book read. This gave the children practice in selecting key events and summarizing so that others in the group had a frame of reference for the student's answers to the interactive question.

Once the summaries were complete, the students participated in teacher-led discussion. The teacher, also, answered the question in terms of the book she was reading. Sometimes her response took place before the children contributed so she could model an appropriate response. At other times, with a question type that the children had practiced, the teacher asked the children to respond first, encouraging appropriate responses, and helping students clarify and improve less acceptable answers. As children became proficient, they selected and posed the question, then led the discussion themselves. In this way, the teacher was able to be sensitive to differences in children's abilities to perform certain tasks associated with reading comprehension and to help them take charge of their own learning.

The interactive questions (one is sufficient for any one day) were answered by each student in terms of his or her own book. But discussion didn't stop there. Each student was expected to analyze a book, then compare his book to the others being discussed in this interactive session. At the conclusion of the discussion, students synthesized their observations about the various approaches used by differing authors. They also evaluated, giving reasons why they did or did not like the approach used by their own author.

Some of the questions that were used in the interactive approach follow. The creative teacher will think of many more. Over the course of a year, the teacher can guide students through many differing questions. Questions are grouped into three broad categories: (1) feelings about the book; (2) understanding what the author said; and (3) understanding the author's language and what was meant.

FEELINGS ABOUT THE BOOK

1. What feelings did you experience while you read this book? What caused them? Count how many different kinds of feelings books can make people have (based on the books being read by your group).
2. Have you ever felt like the main character or another character in your story in your own life? When and why? If you were the character you described, what advice could you give in this situation? Have other students in the group each respond to the situation you describe. Explore why your answers may differ.

3. Did you like the feelings you experienced while reading this book? How did the feelings affect your enjoyment of the book in general?
4. How might your opinion of this story be changed if you grew up in very different circumstances (e.g., as a victim of abuse, in a foreign country, in a different kind of family)? What do you think you would not understand or would view differently?

UNDERSTANDING WHAT THE AUTHOR SAID
Literary Appreciation

1. Give an example of figurative language from your book that you especially liked. What did the author mean? What other ways could the same idea have been expressed? Why do you think the author chose this way?
2. Describe the characteristics of the genre you are reading. Share examples of how this work does or does not fit all the characteristics of the genre. Would the same theme be effective in a different genre? Discuss why you think the author selected this form.
3. What characteristics of this work make you know it is a poem? From the work of poetry, share examples of the rhyme pattern if one exists. Tap out the syllables of the lines of the poem. Is there a rhythm? Does it stay the same through the whole poem? Why do you think the author chose to use the rhythm and rhyme he or she did?
4. Choose a stylistic technique (e.g., local color, point of view, propaganda techniques, or connotative language). Find an example of the technique in your book, if it exists. What is the author actually saying in the part you read? Discuss how this technique affects your thinking and enjoyment of the work.

Comprehension

1. If you had to write a one-paragraph summary of this book for a catalog to try to sell the book to libraries, how would you state the main idea? What else would you include, and why?
2. If you were creating a storyboard, what would the eight most important events in this story be? How would you arrange them? Is this the way the author built the story? Where does the most exciting point occur? Could any of the steps be omitted? Why or why not?
3. How did the author make you believe the main character was a real-life person? How did this character change during the course of the story? Which characters could be left out of the story? How would leaving them out affect the story?

4. Describe in detail an especially enjoyable part of the story. You may be creative in the way you choose to present this. Describe in detail a part of the story that disturbed you. Discuss why you chose this.

Critical Thinking

1. What mood did the story have? Did all the characters share this mood? What story elements (setting, plot, characterization, etc.) helped to create this mood? How did the mood affect your enjoyment? Why do you think the author chose to tell the story in the mood he or she did? Could it have been told using the most opposite mood you can think of? What elements would have to change? How?
2. How did the author choose to tell the story—herself? Or did he have a character tell it? Or did it appear that someone who was not part of the book, but knew everything, told it? How did this choice affect the writing? What can and can't an author do who chooses this point of view? Would another choice have made a more interesting story? Discuss why you think so.
3. Choose one event in the story. What caused it? Use your own ideas and change what happened in some way. How would the rest of the story be affected by this one change? Are some changes your group suggests more significant than others? If so, why do you think so? Identify a situation in your own life where you had more than one choice. What would have happened if you had selected a different course of action? Would you have been more or less pleased with the possible outcomes? You may want to read Robert Frost's poem, "The Road Not Taken," when you discuss this.
4. In a work of nonfiction or fiction, select one item you are sure is fact and one you believe is opinion. Be able to tell why you selected the items you did. See if your classmates agree with your evaluation. Discuss what it is that makes some people believe one thing while others disagree. Then discuss whether or not the present discussion (thinking about beliefs) will make you think any differently in the future when you read or have a discussion.
5. Select a part of a book that you think shows an obvious cause-effect relationship. (For example, in *Bridge to Terabithia* [Peterson, 1977], one child thought the other died because of an error the first made.) Analyze what appears to be the immediate cause and decide if you think that is the only cause. Look for other incidents that led to the effect. Remember to consider characters and setting as well as plot. List these as clues and decide in what order they occurred. Offer these clues one at a time to your classmates. See when they are able to guess the outcome of the book. Discuss

whether any of the other ideas your classmates give are as logical as the one the author chose.

UNDERSTANDING THE AUTHOR'S LANGUAGE AND WHAT WAS MEANT

1. The connotation of a word is its emotional importance. Often, especially in drama, it is important for the reader to be sensitive to connotative language. Pick a section of your book with a lot of dialogue or conversation. Ask to have two photocopies of the page made. Then, sentence by sentence, practice emphasizing different words in different ways. (You can underline the part you decide to emphasize, so you remember.) Read the two different versions to your classmates. Ask them to tell you what emotions each of your versions created in them. Decide which is more in keeping with the tone and theme of your book. Then discuss with your group how your silent reading can be affected if you misunderstand the connotations of words.
2. Shakespeare, T. S. Eliot, Mark Twain are famous authors whose language is not familiar to us because they lived in a different time or place. But what they wrote is still funny, dramatic, exciting, thought-provoking, and important for us to think about. Learning to read an archaic style is a challenge. Try it!

   Choose a work like *A Midsummer Night's Dream* by Shakespeare, or *A Connecticut Yankee in King Arthur's Court* by Mark Twain. Pick a few pages and "translate" them into the slang of today. Give your classmates both the original version and your translation. You take theirs. Then discuss what differences the change in language makes. Talk about the ideas you would have missed if you had never read this work.

The Writing Project

We would be totally remiss if we did not mention the Writing Project in connection with our reading program. It is impossible to write without reading, so we made writing an integral part of our day. Writer's Workshop is a process approach, developed by Lucy Calkins at Teachers College, Columbia University. The experience grips youngsters, rapidly making them into authors. They are greatly encouraged by sharing what is really important to them, seeing those ideas in print, watching others read and enjoy what they created, and hearing the responses of readers to their writing.

Some examples. It was this approach that provided the key to learning for Jamal. Jamal's oral language was phenomenal, but when he entered the class, he refused to pick up a pencil or to read anything. He was expected to be part of writer's workshop, but at the start, his part was mostly listening to others or telling on audiotape what he wanted to share.

Jamal was familiar with the computer through games he liked to play. He was introduced to the use of the computer as a word processor. At first, the teacher typed while he spoke. As he learned to manage the keyboard and the software, he was encouraged to write a personal narrative on his own on the computer. He wrote several and used another piece of software to illustrate his work. The narratives were all very short, but well-constructed vignettes about himself—some funny, some poignant. When several were completed to his satisfaction and edited for fundamentals like capitals at the beginning of sentences and punctuation at the end, we helped him publish them for "the real world." Jamal was so pleased with the product that he made duplicate copies of his writing for each member of his homeroom class. His excitement was incredible! He could barely contain himself as he pulled his work in print from the copy machine. When he returned to the UAG room, Jamal—for the first time—pulled out his journal, and in pencil (a major breakthrough) wrote, "I feel proud, sensashunal, outrages, wonderful, great, crazy, wild, like I have a new life. thank you."

Jamal wrote from that time on. It was marvelous to see him come to school with many pages of loose-leaf paper filled with parts of a story he was writing or a new poem. Near the end of the year, he said, "I used to only like drawing. Now I really like writing, too." And he meant it. After several lengthier short stories and many poems, his last work of the year was a seventeen-page, typewritten story about a robot gone wild in a shopping mall. Published and left on the classroom library shelf, it had high school students, who dropped by to visit, engrossed. Quite an accomplishment for a student who never wrote and refused to read!

Writer's workshop involves students in independent writing and writing instruction by having them imitate what real writers do. As Lucy Calkins puts it, "We write because we want to understand our lives" (1986, p. 3). The writing process moves children's school experience with writing away from the stilted "What I Did on My Summer Vacation," or "How I Would Feel as a Piece of Bubble Gum," and toward recognition of and appreciation for the many experiences, memories, and stories they have to share. It is the flip side of reading as communication.

Starting the workshop. To initiate writer's workshop, the teacher began a mini-lesson on topic finding by asking what each child cared deeply about. Mike cared about giving up his room to his grandfather and moving in with his teenage brother. Juliet cared about horses and the freedom their movement suggested. Jamal cared about the day he was adopted for good after moving through seven foster-care placements. Ned cared about the closeness of his large family and the zany fun they had on family trips. Selecting a topic and deciding what they choose to share with others about that topic is the first step.

Writer's workshop continued, then, by giving children permission to write about their ideas without concern for spelling and grammar and punctuation. The children were expected to write, but not all their writing needed to be shared. They were afforded the dignity of choosing whether to have an audience other than the teacher respond to a particular piece. Especially in the beginning, children often struggled to put things into print, and it was risky for them to ask others to respond to their innermost selves. In a mini-lesson, the children were taught, by modeling what was expected, how to give positive feedback, and only positive feedback. When the students felt ready to be heard, they deserved and got encouraging responses to their ideas.

It was only after a while, after the level of trust developed in the class, that the students had the courage to ask other class members to give them critical feedback on ways to improve specific parts of their writing. The children learned to ask questions about their own writing that were similar to the interactive questions they asked about the writing of published authors. "I'd like you to listen and tell me if you think this character would really act like this?" "Do the short choppy sentences make you feel nervous like I felt when this happened?" "Have I spent too much time creating the setting?" "I'm not sure whether to tell this story in the first person or third. I'd like your opinion about the way it sounds now." In dyads and small groups, they learned to risk themselves. They learned how their writing touched other people and learned how they might improve it.

Once students worked on a piece, got response to it, polished it to their satisfaction, and were ready to publish, they had the honor of sitting in the author's chair. At this point, feedback was only positive: No one was permitted to make a critical comment because sitting in that chair meant the author was pleased with it exactly as it was and wanted to share. The students were well aware that people's tastes differed and that what one person liked a great deal, another might not care for. That was to be expected. When someone shared themselves, what they received in return was how they touched others in a positive sense.

Then the mechanical editing began. Each student had specific grammar and usage skills that she or he was learning. These lessons took place through individual conferences with the teacher during the writing time. The student's personal editing checklists were kept in the writing folder. When editing, the student was expected to apply those skills on the editing checklist correctly. (Be assured that there were many skills not yet on each student's editing checklist. Children rarely run out of things they need to learn. New skills were added as the children mastered a few at a time.) Once the editing was done by the student, another writer helped check for the correctness of the skills on the checklist. A final draft would then be carefully copied onto white paper. Illustrations could be added if the child wished. The final product was then bound and placed in the classroom library.

Occasionally, a child chose to share his writing beyond the classroom. If the writing would be published "in the real world" (hung on the wall outside of the room, or if the school library was to receive a copy), additional editing took place. The teacher acted like a book editor to help the child prepare the manuscript for the public. Final editing corrected any mechanical errors that remained before going "public," but the writing remained totally in the child's voice.

Teacher Involvement. The teacher in writer's workshop is responsible for both instruction and orchestration. The writer's-workshop format creates a classroom environment in which writing, not the teacher's directed lessons, is the valued activity. On any day, an observer in the UAG classroom would see a five-minute mini-lesson on some aspect of writing. The purpose of mini-lessons was to help children gain more power over what they wrote. Mini-lessons focused on things like topic finding, choosing descriptive words, matching the form of writing to its content, and varying sentence structure. They also taught children how to respond to one another and to the teacher. Always, at the close of the mini-lesson, the teacher suggested that students might use the idea when they wrote that day, but never were students required to use a new strategy on the same day it was presented.

Once the mini-lesson was over, the children worked on their own, doing any of a number of purposeful writing tasks: brainstorming a new topic, collecting ideas to use in a piece, beginning a rough draft, revising a piece on which they were working, sharing with a partner to get feedback, or preparing a published copy. While the children worked, the teacher followed a conference schedule, meeting with each child for ten minutes on a rotating basis. In the UAG class, by meeting with two children daily, each child was personally monitored at least once, and usually twice, a week. Conferences were used to provide feedback to a child's writing, to model a writing technique or grammatical principle pertinent only to that child, to help a child make inferences about the writing process, or to track a child's progress and provide encouragement. These are the same types of activities used in reading to meet a child at the correct point in the ZPD.

Press Club

Students' involvement with this project sparked wide reading of nonfiction, reading in content areas, and extensive library work on the part of formerly reluctant learners. Children dealt with weighty social and moral concerns of deep interest to them. Issues such as the death penalty, treatment of the aged, pollution of the groundwater supplies, and nuclear disarmament were raised as the students brainstormed ideas about which they wanted to express their opinions. Students scoured the local newspapers and weekly news magazines for additional topics of interest.

From the master list, each student chose one topic. For one week, students read everything they could find on their subject, using many library sources for the search. On the first day of the next week, they framed 20 interview questions to help them learn what other students thought about the topic. From the twenty, the students selected their five best questions to begin their roundtable.

For a roundtable discussion, students sat with the desks formed into a table. Each student's place was marked with a name tag in "Meet the Press" style. The student discussion leader acted as facilitator and did not express his or her opinion at this point. Other students spoke freely. These comments gave the discussion leader more information about what children had to say about the topic they were exploring. The roundtable discussions were audiotaped. (A *good*-quality tape recorder is needed for this.) Students identified themselves by name before speaking and spoke loudly so the tapes could be transcribed more easily. (Not an easy task!)

When the student leader received the transcript, she wrote the correspondent's report. These reports expressed the children's views about their world. We sent one copy of the final report to "Children's Express," a syndicated column written entirely by children under thirteen years of age. We stored the second on a news-data disk, which we kept in the classroom to use with "The Newsroom," software by Springboard (1985). When several stories were completed, we published our own class newspaper.

Borland–Jacobs Interdisciplinary Model
(Borland & Jacobs, 1986)

Although not conducive to group discussion, another effective means of individualizing reading instruction was an adaptation of an interdisciplinary model of instruction (Borland & Jacobs, 1986). This strategy was particularly successful with children who had a strong special-interest area, and it helped us teach children the skills they needed for their achievement tests. The interdisciplinary model guided teacher instruction and student independent activities during the two days each week when individualized lessons were planned. We drew a wheel and placed the student's area of interest in the center of the wheel (see Figure 6.2). In the spaces between the spokes of the wheel, we wrote activities that focused on the student's interest for each sub-

Figure 6.2: Borland–Jacobs wheel.

ject we taught. The activities were planned with the student's instructional objectives in mind.

Telecommunications

By taking advantage of telecommunications, students were able to share their ideas in a new way, through the world of computer bulletin boards. Telecommunications takes some practice to master, but its possibilities seem limitless. Very quickly, students began to read via computer. The computer screen, itself, seemed to motivate many students. With a local bulletin board, the children linked up with students in other schools. Pen pals are nothing new, but reading and writing messages via computer is! Through networking, they quickly learned about and became participants in several toll-free bulletin boards. The Young Astronauts Program provided students with information, updated monthly, from NASA. The County Agricultural Extension Center linked the elementary school to Rutgers University for information and bulletin-board privileges. The students became involved in a *National Geographic* project, collecting scientific data and depositing it in a data bank with students from across the nation via telecommunications. If a computer is accessible, consider adding a modem, software to run the modem, and a telephone line to your classroom equipment.

EVERYDAY INSTRUCTION

Annotated Bibliography

When a new class is organized, it is helpful to have a well-established file cataloging high-quality children's literature that deals with the issues and problems facing the students. Building such a file is time-consuming, but worth the effort. It allows the teacher to use some of the techniques of bibliotherapy (Frasier & McCannon, 1981) and to offer worthwhile suggestions when children hit a reading rut. Students can add to an annotated bibliography using a computer database.

Perfect references are impossible to give. The problems and strengths of students in one district will be different from those of the initial group of students. Nonetheless, some of the books our students found and that our teachers sought out are worth knowing. They are listed in Appendix C. The students used the Bank Street Filer to create the database. It was not the easiest to use because of the limited space for comments on books, but it served the purpose and forced them to summarize succinctly. Each time a book was completed, the student added a record of that book to the file. Other students then referred to the file to help them select a book they might enjoy. When a student was the second person to read a book, he or she added a comment to the one already written. The format for recording this information in Figure 6.3 was useful.

Skills Scope and Sequence (Compacted)

When the UAG program first began, the school district was committed to a skills approach to reading instruction. While we of the UAG program did

Figure 6.3:   Library format used by students to record reading choices.

Title: Encyclopedia Brown Solves Them All	
Type of Lit: mystery	#pp.:
Author: Sobol, D. J.	Reading Level: 6.5
Publisher: Scholastic, Inc.	Copyright: 1968
Reviewer: Gretchen	Location: UAG library

Comment: This is a short book containing ten mystery stories about Encyclopedia Brown and his friends. Etc. . . .

- -

Title: Octopus Pie	
Type of Lit: realistic fiction	#pp.:
Author: Terris, S.	Reading Level: 7
Publisher: Farrar Straus Giroux	Copyright: 1983
Reviewer: Pat	Location: Middle Sch. Lib.

Comment: This book describes the adventure of a family that adopts, etc . . .

not philosophically subscribe to reading instruction that was divorced from the true reading process, we considered it politically wise to be aware of students' areas of weakness. To be sure that the students were not penalized, we completed an analysis of the district's curriculum guide and the scope and sequence chart in the basal reading series used by the district. The skills were listed in each of the following areas tested on the district's standardized achievement tests:

1. Phonics
2. Structural analysis
3. Vocabulary
4. Comprehension
5. Literary analysis
6. Language and mechanics
7. Study skills

The students were pre-tested on the skills they would need to know for their grade-level achievement tests. Mini-lessons were prepared for students deficient in any of the skills. The most frequent weaknesses were study skills or language and mechanics items, which were addressed through lessons in writing workshop. Some students had difficulty drawing inferences from their reading. Since it was felt that this ability could be developed better through a holistic approach to reading, the students did not drill the skill with isolated workbook pages. Instead, questions that required the students to read between the lines and to draw conclusions were emphasized during the reading sessions.

Ned was an exception to this process. He had serious difficulty reading anything. When further testing was completed, it was discovered that he was perceptually impaired. We addressed his difficulties in two ways. Arrangements were made for Ned to work in the resource room. While the special education teachers worked with him on fundamental word-attack skills and methods he could use to circumvent his weaknesses, Ned continued to be included in the interactive lessons. When Ned found a book about an adolescent boy who finds his first love, it was evident that he was finally a reader. No one could get Ned to put the book down to begin any other work.

Individual Record-Keeping

A student–teacher planning conference was held at the start of each marking period. The conference allowed the student and teacher to discuss what literary types the students would read that marking period and what he or she would try to take control of in his or her own reading during that marking period. Students understood that their final grade would depend on two things, first, how much they improved in what they chose to work on and, second, what tasks they did and books they read (both quantity and quality counted here) to improve their ability. The following procedure was helpful to keep track of student growth.

In the back of a marbleized notebook for each student, based on the administered skills pre-test, were listed the achievement-test reading skills the student had not yet mastered. Also listed were other things observed during reading lessons that the student could improve. Examples of these were the following:

1. Needs to summarize a reading selection briefly, telling only key points
2. Needs to think of better questions about the reading selection
3. Needs to learn to interpret the author's meaning when it is not directly stated
4. Needs to think more about cause and effect
5. Needs to make more realistic predictions based on what she or he has read
6. Needs to relate his or her own life to that of story characters

During the planning conference, the mutually selected objectives were highlighted. Literary genres, chosen from a list of genres to which students in our regular classes were introduced at varying grade levels, were also selected and highlighted.

Instruction and Assignments

The teacher then planned individualized instruction for that student on the chosen skills. When a skill was introduced, it was marked with an **I**. When the student felt the skill was mastered, he or she marked it with an **M**. **M**'s were reviewed on a weekly basis through short assignments created by the teacher and written in the reading notebook. A final review of the **M**'s took place during an individualized lesson just before the marking period closed. At the close of the marking period, the student and teacher sat with their original agreement and discussed the student's progress. Notebook assignments were reviewed for prompt completion and overall correctness (assignments were always corrected immediately). A practical exam to assess the student's current ability to perform the reading tasks he committed to rounded out this conference. The grade was assigned, and new plans were drafted for the next quarter.

A standing assignment for the students was to read a minimum of twenty minutes per day. Students were also expected to complete one reading competency assignment daily. Directions to each student were written in the student's notebook. The students were to check their notebooks before beginning to read to see if there was something special for them to do when they were done. Most assignments aimed to build the achievement test skills and real-life reading abilities that were chosen cooperatively by the student and teacher at the conferences. Direct instruction by the teacher always preceded a reading assignment based on a newly introduced skill. Supervised practice always occurred before students were put on their own to reinforce a new skill. All independent assignments were long enough to practice a skill, but short enough for the teacher to check understanding before any serious mislearning occurred. First assignments usually had from three to five examples. In this way, an occasional misunderstanding could be clarified before it was embedded through practice.

After the initial learning, practice was scheduled intermittently to reinforce learning. Students were encouraged to try on their own first and to turn to their peers only if they still needed help. If their peers were unable to help, they were to wait until the teacher could meet with them to provide further assistance. The students knew that it was important for them to overlearn new skills. They knew about the rate of forgetting. They knew about the need to move new concepts from short-term to long-term memory and that practice was the way to do this. Because students knew the research on learning, and thus the rationale for the way things were done, there was little resistance to the practices we used. They assumed command; they chose what they needed to learn. They were in control; when they realized they did not know something perfectly, they knew the appropriate action was to get help and relearn it. It was okay to forget things at times because everyone does; it was not okay to ignore the problem and hope it would go away.

Scheduling the Week's Instruction

There are many ways of handling individual needs in a program like this. One that worked well involved splitting the week. On Monday, Wednesday, and Friday, reading lessons were group lessons. All students, regardless of reading level or ability, participated in an activity planned by the teacher to increase reading comprehension. On Tuesdays and Fridays, ten-minute time blocks were used for direct instruction on skills needed by only one or two children.

Student Reading Choices

The choice of reading matter was left to the student within certain parameters. Students knew from their reading conference with the teacher that they would need to read at least one selection of each literary type listed in the district's reading curriculum to complete what was called a reading level. The students could read more of whatever new literary type they particularly enjoyed or of a type they enjoyed from earlier levels. But they had to manage at least one of each of the types for their current reading level before moving on to the next higher level. Students began reading literary types at level one to be sure they were exposed to all types of literature. Since they were not using a basal text and since their instruction was not keyed to a publishing company's conception of student skill, there was no stigma. Everyone started at level one when they first entered the UAG program with books of appropriate difficulty for them.

Each reading choice was recorded (author, title, publisher, date of publication, starting and ending dates, and literary type) in the student's notebook. It was important to substantiate that the students were reading regularly and broadly as part of their instruction. The list of works completed was also supplied to the receiving teacher when students left the UAG program. Some students tracked their independent reading in this manner as well. In these cases, an asterisk marked the books that were read independently and not used for instruction.

Students were strongly encouraged to do independent reading, which we knew increased their fluency and vocabulary development. Many motivating techniques were employed. We encouraged and fostered *noncompetitive* reading and the achievement of reading goals. We avoided contests and competitions, which destroy the real purpose of reading—communication—and emphasized winning. One activity used by a teacher in the UAG program had the students chart on quarter-inch graph paper the number of minutes each student spent reading independently in class as a free-choice activity. For each minute a child read, one square of the graph paper was colored with marker. The minutes added up rapidly; additional sheets were filled in quick succession. The vivid charts remained up as bright, graphic reminders of what can be accomplished by a group working minute by minute.

Readability Level

Controversy surrounds the use of reading-level designations for textbooks. Too often, books have been rewritten, destroying their literary merit, to meet the reading level requirements of schools. However, students in UAG were not using "adjusted" books. It was important to have a way to judge whether a book that a student chose, either because another student recommended it or because the student liked the cover, was appropriately challenging. With some students who were reluctant readers, the concern, especially when the child hoped to use it as the foundation for instruction, was that she or he might feel frustrated because a book was too hard. Therefore, we used both an informal and a formal method of assessing reading level.

The students learned the "rule of thumb" (D. Strickland, personal communication, February 1987). After selecting a book they thought they would like to read, they were to turn to three places in the book and begin reading one page. Each time they came to a word they didn't know, they were to put up one finger, beginning with the pinkie and working toward the thumb. For a recreational book, if they got to the thumb on one page, it was probably too hard. For an instructional book, if they reached the thumb on two of the three pages, the book was very difficult, and they were encouraged to select another. A second method of determining difficulty used a piece of software that figured readability levels using seven different formulas. The results were, if anything, morale boosters. Because the books were not "dumbed down" to fit a grade-level requirement, many students read books well beyond their grade placement. After they completed a book, the software was used to check the grade equivalent. The information was used to reinforce the students' self-concept. A learning disabilities specialist, reading teacher, or other professional on your staff may have such a program in your district already. If not, explore what is currently available.

One final word of caution is in order for those using readability formulas. When children are reading in areas of interest to them, the teacher should remember that conceptual level and reading level are not the same. Children with a specialized interest may be able to read texts of far greater difficulty than their measured reading level might predict. Conversely, if the subject area is brand-new to the child, readability level may predict that the child will be able to pronounce the words and "read" the sentences while she or he, in fact, may not make any sense out of the text.

SAMPLE LESSON PLANS

All lessons taught in the class follow the same planning model as the lessons included here. A few things should be noted before reading the first lesson. Each objective states a thought process (for example, explore or decide) expected of the student and a way the student will demonstrate this thinking. Following the objective, in the section titled "skills level," I list the levels of critical-thinking skills the teacher should encourage from the students. As is appropriate for gifted students, each lesson should move as quickly as possible to the analysis, synthesis, and evaluation levels rather than concentrating on the knowledge and comprehension levels typical of regular classrooms. In addition, I list the creative-thinking skills that can be addressed through a lesson. I hope that teachers will consciously choose to encourage divergent thinking. After the skills are enumerated, I include the necessary materials, the procedures that can be used by the teacher, and at least one way of evaluating whether the objectives were achieved.

Lessons like this were planned for every ten-minute block, although not all were written out so extensively as the plans included here. The teachers became accustomed to teaching at the higher levels of Bloom's taxonomy and were adept at encouraging creative thinking, so these goals did not need to be stated routinely. Objectives, materials, activities, and evaluation were written in abbreviated form.

What follows are samples of some whole-group lessons that show how UAG reading lessons differed from standard reading group lessons. Since the children were not nonreaders for the most part, most lessons were directed at the third level of the ZPD. Most of our students were polishing their reading strategies and needed feedback on their success or failure in those strategies. Following the stage-three lessons, are lessons at level one and two. These were used when it was discovered that most of the students did not realize their first comprehension task when reading was to figure out and be able to restate what the author said. Convincing them of this was an important task. Then, backing up further, the students needed to be taught how to summarize.

Stage Three: Polishing the Task
Giving Feedback on Reading Tasks Being Learned

LESSON ONE
Reading the Newspaper

Objective: Students will explore alternate positions on an issue in the news and decide on their own position by preparing a list of open-ended questions to be discussed with the group on a newsworthy topic. (Conditions: The questions need to elicit other students' opinions on the topic. The topic needs to have been treated both in news reports and in editorials. Students may work in dyads if they wish.)

Skills Level: Comprehension, analysis, synthesis, evaluation
Originality, fluency, flexibility, elaboration

Materials: two weeks of newspapers at the child's reading level; reading notebooks

Procedures:
1. Have students read and summarize the topic and major points made in editorials during the last week.
2. Students choose the editorial topic of greatest interest to them.
3. Students then skim newspapers to find at least two news reports on the same topic. They read and summarize the "who, what, when, where, why, and how" stated in each article.
4. Students analyze the facts presented in the news and the positions taken by reporters and editor.
5. Students decide on an alternate position that could be taken by another person.
6. Students brainstorm a list of at least ten questions they could ask other people to determine the positions of those people on the issue.
7. Students select their three best questions and direct the discussion.

Evaluation (written in notebook):
1. Accurate summaries of editorial and news articles
2. Statement of alternate position a person could take
3. Brainstormed list of ten open-ended questions on topic, with three best starred
4. Class discussion of questions

LESSON TWO
Being Aware of Main Events in a Story

Objective: Students will evaluate which events are the most critical to the plot of a fairy tale by selecting eight that they will sketch on a storyboard (to be translated at a later time into an 8 mm animated film or video, if your camera has single-frame capabilities).

Skills Level: Comprehension, evaluation
Originality, flexibility

Materials: Children's fairy-tale books, storyboard paper, sketch pencils, reading notebook

Procedures:
1. From a selection of children's fairy tales in the library, each child chooses one to reread for this activity.
2. The children reread the fairy tale to refresh their memories of events; they list key events in their notebooks.
3. From their lists, the children choose eight that will allow them to tell the story in pictures to other children.
4. Children sketch, using stick figures, those eight events, one per frame, on the storyboard paper.
5. Children share their storyboards, justifying their choices of events used and eliminated.

Evaluation:
1. Listing of all major story events in notebook
2. Selection of eight events sketched on storyboard
3. Oral justification for eliminating certain events and not others

LESSON THREE
Interactive Questions

Objective: Students will compare examples of author's techniques of character development
Skills Level: Comprehension, analysis, flexibility
Materials: Individual reading selections; copy of interactive questions to be used

Procedures:
1. The teacher introduces the questions to be discussed before the silent reading time. For this lesson, the questions are:
   a. What did the author do to make the main character in your story seem alive and real?
   b. Did the author make this character change at all during the part you read today? Did she or he change at all since the beginning of the story?
   c. Do people you know act like the main character in your story? In what ways? How are the people you know different from your main character? Could the main character act exactly the way your friend or acquaintance does? Why or why not?
2. Students are given a minimum of 20 minutes to read silently. The teacher reads, too, and prepares to answer the questions in terms of her own book.

3. Discussion of the questions posed prior to reading with each person responding to at least one of the questions, preferably all.

Evaluation: Responses to oral questions

Stage One: Modeling a Strategy
Demonstrating What a Good Reader Does

LESSON ONE
Summarizing What the Author Said

Objective: The student will learn that readers can summarize what an author said in a paragraph without imposing interpretations on what is written.
Skills Level: Knowledge, comprehension
Materials: A work of fiction or nonfiction of interest to the children

Procedures:
1. Tell the children that one thing good readers do is to try to understand exactly what the author is saying. You will show them how you do this by voicing your thoughts while you read.
2. Read aloud a paragraph that you selected. If you are aware of thoughts you have while you read, share them with the children at the point they occur.
3. Restate in your own words, without imposing your own opinions, what the author said in the paragraph.
4. Ask the children to signal if they agree that your words say the same thing that the author said.

Evaluation:
1. Children will signal agreement showing they detect the similarity between the author's words and the teacher's restatement.
2. Children will be able to restate one thing you thought about while you were reading.

Stage Two: Taking Over Tasks
Convincing Students to Try for Themselves

LESSON ONE
Deciding How to Use What They've Read

Objective: Students will know a reason for summarizing what an author has said.

Skills Level: Knowledge
Materials: A book of interest to the students

Procedure:
1. Tell the students that once they can summarize what an author says, they can do more exciting things with what they read.
2. Read aloud a paragraph from a book of interest to the children.
3. Summarize in your own words what the author said.
4. Ask the children to respond if your summary was correct.
5. Have them tell you what they were thinking about while you read.
6. Ask them to tell you something else they can think about after they know what the author really said. Suggest that one thing you do is to decide if you think the author is right, but that you can't do that well if you don't have a clear idea of what the author actually stated.

Evaluation:
1. Students state one thought they had while you were reading.
2. Students state one thing they can do with what they learned.

STUDENT RESPONSES TO THE READING CURRICULUM

In *Listen to the Children* (Supplee, 1987/1988), students reported instructional strategies they felt were helpful in reversing their underachievement. All of the successful students cited individualized learning, peer teaching, the use of notebooks rather than workbooks, and choice and control over their goals and objectives as critical. These were all part of reading instruction in the adaptive class. Most students also cited ten-minute mini-lessons, small-group instruction, reading instruction based on library books rather than basals, and active involvement in learning as important. The teacher behaviors found helpful included challenging students to think hard, making students responsible for finding and correcting their own errors, and helping students see problems in their work when they couldn't find the problem themselves. The students in class also felt that having a teacher know students' abilities in each subject, "going just fast enough" for the student, using student interest to help them learn, and making them responsible for setting their own goals were important.

Achievement gains were also impressive. The Woodcock–Johnson Achievement Battery, Part II was used as a pre- and post-measure of growth in reading. Five months separated the two testing sessions. The data are included in Table 6.1. Mean gain in reading achievement was 27 months in five

Table 6.1   Changes in Academic Achievement in Reading as Measured by the
Woodcock–Johnson Achievement Battery, Part II

| | READING ACHIEVEMENT* | | |
SUBJECT	pre	post	change
Cal	7.2	11.4	+4.2
Portia	12.9	12.9	+6.0**
David	11.4	10.5	−0.9
Mike	7.0	10.1	+3.1
Ricardo	10.9	12.9	+2.0
Doug	6.0	7.6	+1.6
Karen	8.2	11.9	+3.7
Marcia	3.9	4.5	+0.6
Ned	3.0	3.4	+0.4

*Grade level scores.
**Age scores used to estimate growth due to student surpassing 12.9 grade level.

months of instruction. This far exceeded our expectations at the outset of the program (Supplee, 1989).

With results like these in five months, we can confidently state that a change of approach with gifted students who are not achieving is worth the effort.

SUMMARY

In the first part of this chapter, research on teaching reading to the gifted was discussed. The conclusion drawn, based on position papers and the minimal amount of empirical research in the literature, was that good reading instruction for the gifted does not differ from good reading instruction for anyone except that pace may be accelerated and content enriched. Vygotsky's theory of the zone of proximal development was elaborated on. The teacher must be conscious of the stage within the zone in which each learner is currently operating. It is the teacher's responsibility to meet the child at that point and help him or her develop.

The second part of the chapter elaborated on practical approaches to daily teaching responsibilities. The use of Bloom's taxonomy, the development of creative-thinking skills, and the use of interactive-reading questions, the Socratic method, the Writing Project, the Press Club, the Borland–Jacobs Interdisciplinary Model, and telecommunications were described as strategies to engage the students in reading for real purposes. To deal with the routines of reading instruction, use of an annotated bibliography was suggested. Ways to cope with meeting a district's requirement that the students progress through a skills scope and sequence were discussed. Methods of record keeping that worked efficiently, details of the types of assignments, student reading selections, readability levels, and lesson scheduling rounded out this section.

The last part of the chapter provided readers with some sample lessons used in the UAG class. Several lessons in the third stage of the zone of proximal development and one each at the first and second stage were presented. Student responses to the reading instruction and their achievement gains were included to substantiate the effectiveness of the nontraditional approach to instruction used in the UAG class.

CHAPTER 7

Mathematics

Mathematics education in the United States comes under frequent fire. Newspapers report that we are well behind our economic competitors in the world market, while popular magazines run articles on how far ahead of American youngsters foreign students are in mathematics. Even our gifted students do not measure up to their gifted peers from other nations. The barrage of criticism has led researchers to look carefully at mathematics education in our nation. Their work, particularly in the fields of cognitive science and effective teaching, has led to recommendations that should improve math curriculum and instruction.

MATHEMATICS FOR THE GIFTED: A REVIEW OF RESEARCH

When trying to decide how to raise the mathematics achievement in gifted children who underachieve, I first turned to the current literature on mathematics instruction in general. I then narrowed my focus to studies advocating specific, differentiated instruction for the gifted. With three bodies of research in mind, mathematics education for the gifted, cognitive science, and effective teaching, I formulated a curriculum and devised instructional strategies that served our gifted underachievers successfully. While preparing this manuscript, I updated my search of the literature. This search of the most recent publications confirmed that the curriculum choices made and instructional strategies designed for UAG at its inception were appropriately differentiated for gifted learners and foreshadowed what would be recommended for all learners.

National Council of Teachers of Mathematics (NCTM)

The position paper, *Curriculum and Evaluation Standards for School Mathematics* (Commission on Standards for School Mathematics of the National Council of Teachers of Mathematics, 1989), offers a framework for curriculum development. It specifies key elements of a high-quality school program but does not offer a scope and sequence or grade-level listing of skills. The paper does state five broad goals that cross age and grade lines for students in mathematics. The council believes that students should

1. Learn to value mathematics
2. Learn to reason mathematically
3. Learn to communicate mathematically
4. Become confident of their mathematical ability
5. Become mathematical problem solvers

While the goals cross age lines, the standards themselves are clustered into three grade-level groups: kindergarten through grade 4, grades 5 through 8, and grades 9 through 12, with developmentally appropriate differences in each cluster.

Certain values guided content decisions. First, the council believes that "knowing" math is "doing" math. Math is not memorizing and using formulas. Rather, it is thinking and making decisions about what math to use when, why to use that math, and then deciding whether to estimate or to find an exact answer. Only after this decision point is reached is knowing how to find that estimate or exact answer important. Until now, only the last step received attention in schools. Second, the council recognizes that certain aspects of "doing" math have changed rapidly in recent years. Because of the applicability of math in many disciplines, the ability to create mathematical models, structures, and simulations is important for all students. No longer is the algebra-geometry-precalculus-calculus sequence, with its primary applications being in engineering and the physical sciences, the ideal sequence. Third, the council believes that technology has dramatically changed the discipline. Because of these changes, NCTM proposes that

1. Appropriate calculators be available to all students all of the time
2. A computer be available in every classroom for demonstration purposes
3. Every student have access to the computer for individual and group work
4. Students learn to use the computer as a tool for processing information and performing calculations to investigate and solve problems (p. 8).

NCTM also has specific recommendations for expected student activities, both those that should be deleted from common practice and new activities that should be incorporated in every math classroom. Students should not be developing isolated skill competencies. There is no data to support the contention that teaching a skill in isolation allows students to transfer the skill to a real-life context. Isolated paper-and-pencil computations, rote practice, and memorizing equivalencies, rules, procedures, and the names of geometric figures should significantly decrease. Using clue words to determine the operation to use in a problem, using one-answer and one-method problems, and working word problems all of a certain type should be eliminated. Less attention should be given to teaching by telling, worksheets and texts, extended periods of seatwork, and testing for grading purposes only.

In contrast, the council believes instruction should emerge from problem solving with the need for certain knowledge to solve a problem providing the rationale for learning. The problems students encounter need to be real, complex problems that may have more than one appropriate solution. Since cognitive science suggests that mathematics knowledge is constructed by students through varied experiences, NCTM believes that instruction should utilize several strategies. Opportunities for students should include appropriate project work, group and individual assignments, discussion about mathematics between teacher and student as well as among students, practice on mathematical methods, and exposition by the teacher (p. 10). Mathematics should involve collaborative as well as individual work. Students should be actively involved in a caring environment that encourages them to explore, test, develop, discuss, and apply ideas. The importance of the development of thinking and reasoning ability cannot be overstressed, and students should have access to a wide variety of manipulative materials to help them make the abstract more understandable. Finally, learners should know that mathematics is purposeful and has real applications in their immediate world. Mathematics includes a broad range of content, far broader than the traditional emphasis on computation would imply.

The final section of the NCTM recommendations concerns evaluation. Evaluation is not the simple, narrow task of assessing an individual student's skills; it is a long-term, ongoing process, assessing the conceptual development of students. The evaluation section also recommends assessment strategies related to curriculum, to instruction, and to the math program in all areas: problem solving, reasoning, communicating mathematically, concept building, and procedure learning.

The Missouri Math Model

Good and Grouws (1988) build on the direct instruction model to suggest strategies that increase mathematics learning. Their broad findings on effective teacher behaviors imply that the classroom presentation of superior teachers in mathematics is meaningful, i.e., clear, practical, and related to other concepts. The teachers are active decision makers; they sense when they are not successful from student feedback and pace their lesson accordingly. Expectations are appropriately positive; effective teachers believe the students can learn what they are teaching. Good classroom management is in place, allowing the teachers to progress at a brisk pace through the curriculum. Time is used effectively for instruction, not discipline. Appropriate review and reinforcement assignments are scheduled.

Good and Grouws (1988) recommend 60 minutes of math instruction daily, with quality time being critical. A three-to-five minute review of homework should begin the period. (They contend that if more time is needed to clarify misunderstandings, the assignment was probably too difficult.) Following review, five to ten minutes should be spent on mental computation and estimation. At least one problem that requires mathematical thinking (as opposed to mere computation) should be discussed with the class every day; as Good and Grouws (1988) state, "Asking students to *think* about mathematics is going to require some pretty serious adjustments on the part of children, but it should be our goal." The development portion of the lesson should occupy the greatest portion of time. At least twenty minutes, preferably 50 percent of class time, should focus on developing understanding and the meaning of the mathematics concept in question. Guided practice should follow the development portion. Homework should be brief, success-oriented, and contain at least one review problem. Calculators should always be available for student use.

Good and Grouws (1988) also recommend variety in class lessons. While whole-class instruction is favored for general use, small groups should be formed occasionally for remedial or enrichment work. For talented students, Good and Grouws suggest horizontal enrichment, especially data gathering on real problems and research applications of mathematics. Whole-class instruction should also be supplemented with time for all students to do some problem-solving work in groups, for discussion of mathematical ideas, and for cooperative learning.

Class climate is important to produce high mathematics achievement. The affective climate in effective teachers' classes supports responding, risk taking, and question asking. The students need to understand that they are not expected to know everything, but that they can learn what they need to know. They also participate in problem solving *with* the teacher. The teacher does not need to know the answer to these problems but should model good problem-solving strategies.

Grouws (1988), in speaking about mathematics curriculum and instruction reform, lists several things that need to change before improvement will be noticed in our students. First, he says, math shouldn't be subdivided into isolated subtopics and skills to be drilled independently in a step-by-step manner. Second, skills in isolation do not need to be mastered before the student moves on to applications. An integrated approach through problem solving is more effective and fosters flexible thinking and creativity in mathematics. Problem solving points out the need to develop multiple approaches to solutions and different schemes for organizing data. Third, mathematics instruction that is isolated from real-world problems should be eliminated. Only by doing so will any reform movement in mathematics have its intended impact.

Research-Based Adaptations of Recommended Math Instruction for Gifted Students

The research and successful experimental projects of Julian Stanley (George, Cohn & Stanley, 1979) confirm that acceleration is an appropriate alternative for gifted students, particularly in the field of mathematics. Stanley used the SAT test at the seventh-grade level to identify talented youth (those who scored 700 or above in seventh grade). He then taught such students advanced-level mathematics in a compressed, accelerated manner. The striking advancement of the exceptionally bright students with whom he worked demonstrated that such acceleration was possible and that the students thrived on it. They were not damaged socially or emotionally by the acceleration (Daurio, 1979). Fifteen years of research with mathematically precocious students supports Stanley's conclusion that acceleration is the most appropriate option for mathematically gifted students.

NCTM argues for appropriate gifted education in its publication *Providing Opportunities for the Mathematically Gifted* (National Council of Teachers of Mathematics, 1987). Their position is that superior students should move at a faster pace and should be allowed to explore wider options. In other words, NCTM suggests that acceleration and enrichment in tandem are appropriate modifications for gifted students in mathematics. The position paper adds that gifted students should be held accountable for knowing more when they are in a special program and that the content of any gifted course should be of substance, not piecemeal curiosity topics. NCTM continues its recommendations by insisting that a solid program for such students requires continuity and should not be a one-year-only effort because of one teacher's concern or interest. One of the biggest drawbacks, they found, to appropriate modifications of the curriculum for the gifted was precisely the lack of continuity. The other was inadequate preparation of mathematics teachers.

More recently, Daniels and Cox (1988), in *Flexible Pacing for Able Learners,* collected descriptions of accelerated programs, particularly in mathematics, that are in place across our nation and are working effectively. Daniels and Cox emphasize that, whatever the pace of learning, mastery of content is still the point and that artificial barriers to progress should be eliminated. Selected features of the flexible-pacing systems that appear to work include:

1. Capitalizing on whatever is already available in a district
2. Providing supplementary materials for students in alternative media
3. Capitalizing on what the professional literature offers in the ways of special ideas for varying student learning, projects, team teaching, etc.
4. Starting a little at a time
5. Winning support and cooperation through collaboration.

THEORY INTO PRACTICE

When the UAG program began, its mathematics model varied from the traditional mathematics program in the school. The traditional goals of elementary school mathematics had been reassessed. Since a computer and calculators were readily accessible in the UAG classroom and in the student's everyday world, and since computers and calculators perform operations more quickly and accurately for adults in today's culture, the emphasis on computation-related objectives for UAG students was reduced. A broadened view of mathematics was adopted. Mathematics became problem solving, with computation, drawing, chart and graph making, and the use of manipulatives serving as helpful aids in solving problems. Mathematics became a way of organizing information and using numbers and ideas about numbers to solve problems that occur in both the students' lives and the lives of others. (Mathematics as problem solving should not be equated with the word problems often found in math textbooks. Such problems are no more than an application of the computation skill just covered in the text. They require no real thinking in an alternate language, no real solution finding.)

Mastery of mathematical ideas became the students' goal. When they needed to know a fundamental process to solve a problem, they had built-in motivation to learn. Math was something real, not just something in a book. Students became responsible for their achievement. Cooperative learning increased. The teacher's role changed to that of a concept builder and guide through creative problem solving rather than that of lecturer and homework grader and tester.

Development of the Scope and Sequence in Mathematics

Despite the change in focus for math instruction, the content in the scope and sequence that was developed for the UAG class evolved from the school district's curriculum. As with the reading curriculum, it was recognized that the responsibilities of a school district to the students included a responsibility to help students pass high-stakes tests. This curriculum was already aligned to the High School Proficiency Test, an achievement test administered by the New Jersey State Department of Education that students must pass before graduating from high school. To this curriculum were added the recommendations from the National Council of Teachers of Mathematics (Conference Board of The Impact of Computing Technology on School Mathematics, 1985) that were not included in the district curriculum. The recommendations were incorporated at appropriate points in the sequence of objectives. Finally, the entire package was reviewed by a mathematician who resided in the district. All suggestions made were incorporated into the final product, which appears in Appendix D.

Instructional Decisions

Based on the research, students were permitted to accelerate. A vertical curricula approach similar to the Johns Hopkins math program was used. The students were pleased that they no longer had to work every problem on a page in order to prove their competence. Of course, using an accelerated, differentiated curriculum involved a risk. Coordinated change was not likely to take place simultaneously throughout the district and the receiving high school. The intent in this model was to return students to the mainstream as soon as they were able. Despite the risks of an uncoordinated program, the belief that teaching students meaningful mathematics in a meaningful manner at a pace that matched their ability was more likely to affect their long-term achievement than would mere enrichment of the standard curriculum. Therefore, a transition back to the "real world" was planned. Children would be placed across grade levels, if needed, in a mathematics class that best matched their progress when they returned to the mainstream. They were also reacquainted with more traditional materials and approaches as they became ready to return to the real-world classrooms. By our capitalizing on their improved metacognitive skills and teaching them how they could monitor their own learning, they could continue to use the techniques and strategies they learned in the UAG class to enrich and extend their mathematical learning and thinking. When a student was ready to return, a conference was held with the receiving teacher. The conference explained what the students had mastered and some of the most successful adaptations in the program for each of the students who "graduated" from it.

Assessment

Another potential problem is that existing standardized achievement tests do not measure the depth of students' mathematical comprehension, nor their improved real-life problem solving skills, nor their ability to deal with computer logic, probability, statistics, randomness, negative numbers, alternative base systems or the other advanced concepts that the students were learning. On standardized tests, it may very well appear that the students are only learning at an average rate—only equal to their peers in mainstream classes. While an average rate of growth on a standardized achievement test is not bad, it is deceptive. In this case, "average" means average in terms of the average curriculum with its strong emphasis on computation—deemphasized in UAG class instruction.

Martin (1988) states that "education today suffers under the tyranny of standardized testing . . . and [these tests] are so powerful and pervasive that they are likely to determine the curriculum" (p. 94). Standardized achievement tests skew the focus of mathematics. Martin cites the National Council of Supervisors of Mathematics to illustrate the seriousness of the situation.

> Nationally-normed standardized tests that are currently in use do not match the objectives of a mathematics curriculum designed to prepare students for the 21st century. . . . At this time the use of standardized tests to monitor student progress and evaluate the effectiveness of instruction is harmful. Existing standardized tests perpetuate the domination of the mathematics curriculum by lower-order skills, and their results give a false sense of accomplishment. (National Council of Supervisors of Mathematics, 1988, p. 4)

It is important to develop criterion-referenced tests and other assessment measures that are aligned with the additional parts of the math curriculum and the changed purposes of effective math instruction. Without evidence that the children are learning different mathematics as well as basic-skills mathematics, it will appear as if their progress is not accelerated.

Teacher Competencies

The staff must be encouraged to overcome dependence on textbooks and to use concrete manipulatives and alternative materials to help students master mathematics. It is important for the teachers to be well-grounded in mathematics, not just competent in the operations used in math. The teachers' knowledge should be sufficient so that, when they are teaching a concept, they know how that knowledge will help the students make mathematical connections in later grades. For example, teachers should know that a clear, thorough understanding of place value in the primary grades helps students learn decimals in the later middle grades and other base systems in the junior high years. Without that knowledge, teachers are tempted to skip or only mention briefly those things for which they themselves don't see meaning.

When teachers know connections, they can answer the question, "What do we need to know this for?" with certainty and confidence. The UAG students in the model progressed to the point where some were learning first-year algebra and first-year geometry. That meant the teachers needed to be confident of their ability to teach at that level. To teach problem solving well, teachers had to have confidence in their ability to teach higher math, to develop abstract thinking, to sharpen higher cognitive processes, to practice creative problem posing and solving, and to enlarge on their individual methods and styles of inquiry. In UAG, this meant "refresher courses" for the teachers through self-study and through enrollment in university courses. Another approach that could have been used is computer tutorial programs.

In addition to having content knowledge, teachers must also be solidly grounded in how students learn mathematics and the types of environments that support individual differences and mathematical thinking. Because of the philosophical position taken, teachers need to be sensitive to the kinds of difficulties students might experience and errors they may make as they progress through the curriculum. A diagnostic-prescriptive approach is effective, so teachers should know how to implement this. Teachers also need to know how to ask questions about the underlying concepts and to listen to and watch student responses, so as to be able to diagnose their difficulties.

An example. When Ricardo was first learning how to solve algebraic word problems, he had great difficulty with the logic needed to solve the problem because he made error after error, never arriving at a correct solution. We used the "talk aloud" technique to diagnose while he worked through the problem. (The student said aloud exactly what he was thinking while he was solving the problem.) The difficulty became clear. Ricardo's trouble had nothing to do with logical thinking or his approach to problem solving. Rather, his problem was with subtraction involving exchange, the computation process he was trying to use to solve the problem.

When the teacher discussed the problem with him, Ricardo revealed what had happened when he was younger. He was bright enough to devise his own algorithm for this process. No one was aware of his lack of understanding because, while he obviously must have made some errors, he didn't get enough problems wrong on his homework or his tests for a teacher to realize the malfunction in his thinking. His algorithm worked well most of the time, breaking down only in specific cases. By focusing on only one example with him and diagnosing the thought processes in that example, we recognized the flaw in his thinking that pages upon pages of subtraction problems in the earlier grades had failed to point out. Once Ricardo's problem was diagnosed, he turned to concrete materials, building and demonstrating the concepts he lacked. When the teacher felt fairly sure that he had corrected his thinking, Ricardo worked a few problems similar to those that had given him trouble. His success made him confident that he understood the correct algorithm. A practice set of problems was selected for work during the next few days, two or three to be done and checked each day. His accuracy on those confirmed that he did, indeed, know what he was doing and that he could move on, using the process confidently in the future.

Success Breeds Success

The changes in math instruction that are recommended are many and often appear difficult to implement. This should not discourage districts or teachers from trying a UAG class. Our suggestion is to manage the change carefully—one thing at a time. Even one small change in procedure or teacher knowledge can affect these students powerfully. As always, success breeds success. The second change will be easier, and the third. If needs were rank-ordered, the most immediate need is developing teacher competence, something that may require time outside of the classroom. Within the classroom, the first change to be made is the introduction of concrete materials and manipulatives at all grade levels taught in the UAG program. These can help both teachers and students understand math concepts better. (A section is devoted to the use of manipulatives later in this chapter.) The second most important recommendation would be the inclusion of computers and calculators. These are techniques the children can learn and apply to their learning when they leave UAG, whether or not their regular classroom instruction includes them.

Student Placement in the Curriculum

We used the Woodcock–Johnson Assessment Battery, Part II (Woodcock and Johnson, 1977) to establish instructional levels and made a philosophical decision to capitalize on students' strengths. Again, in contrast to the approach used in remedial programs and in line with Vygotsky's learning theory, as discussed in Chapter 6, the upper reaches of the instructional level provided by this test were used to guide placement of students in the curriculum. This decision improved the students' sense of self-esteem immediately.

There were no difficulties presented by this decision that were not easily handled. During instruction, if an obvious gap in skill development was evident, the students very willingly backtracked to learn the skill because they saw the purpose for it. Such an approach was far more motivating than a purely remedial approach could ever be. The approach said, better than any words could have, "You are intelligent and capable. If you can do _____(the advanced skills), it will be a cinch for you to learn _____(the missing skills)."

ACCELERATION AND ENRICHMENT TOPICS: FITTING IT ALL IN

How did everything recommended by the research fit into 100 minutes a day, when there were also other things to teach? Is an individualized, accelerated math program that also focuses on problem solving an ideal, but unreachable goal? Certainly not; it proved workable in a small, individualized classroom like UAG.

Instructional Strategies

With the schedule segmented into modules of ten minutes each, it was possible to schedule one whole-group problem-solving session daily. Two individualized math meetings were also held daily, and two approaches were used in the daily time block for problem solving. On Tuesday, Wednesday, and Thursday, a single problem was presented and solved during the period. Early in the year, the teacher modeled a strategy to solve the problem, explaining her thinking aloud and encouraging the children to join her when they could. The problem was not one the teacher necessarily knew the answer to, but the answer was immaterial. It was the process the teacher was teaching. As the group solved the daily problems, they labeled them, creating a mental library of problem-solving strategies. Later in the year, the teacher could refer to one of the methods that had been modeled earlier by saying, "This is like the book problem," or, "This is like the pizza problem." By the end of the year, the students were classifying problems by type.

The second problem-solving instructional strategy encouraged cooperative learning in small groups. A "Problem of the Week" was presented on Monday and discussed on Friday. Once introduced, the problems were placed in a learning center. Students were expected to work on the solution by themselves or cooperatively with other students in the class. As students arrived at what they thought was an answer, they signed and dated a sheet attached to the center. When succeeding students arrived at an answer, they were expected to compare their solution and the process of arriving at the solution with those who already signed the sheet. It was understood that there were several ways to solve most of the problems and that often there was more than one correct answer. What they were to do by checking with one another was to view the problem in another way and decide if that solution, too, was a possible one. On Friday, each of the individuals and groups that solved the problem presented their solutions and the problem-solving process to the teacher. Mathematical ideas underlying the problem were brought out by the teacher and discussed at this time.

The problem-solving times gave every student whole-group math instruction every day. The individual needs of students could be addressed during the other ten-minute blocks. Students met with the teacher at least twice a week for direct instruction on a concept at their math achievement level. When several students happened to be working on the same concept or skill (and they frequently asked to do so), the students had more than two meetings a week with the teacher. With the revised approach to elementary mathematics, significant portions of time normally devoted to algorithms and practice on multiple-digit calculations were reduced and other mathematical goals could be reached more easily.

To build concepts during the individualized instruction time, the teacher either used commercially available manipulative materials, created his or her own materials, or selected specific activities from a wide variety of standard materials, including computer-assisted instructional software, math texts or workbooks, problem-solving kits, estimation activities kits, and thinking skills books. Direct instruction was the primary mode employed during these mini-lessons, but several nontraditional strategies were utilized. The talk-aloud was one. This method, asking the students to say aloud everything they are thinking as they perform an operation or think through a problem, is one of the most effective means devised to assess students' conceptual awareness during instruction. It allows the teacher to plan appropriately for continued growth. Experience with manipulatives and other concrete representations at all age and grade levels was another.

Using Manipulatives With Children of All Ages

What is a manipulative? It is an object that appeals to several senses. It can be touched, moved about, rearranged and otherwise handled. It can be from the environment (like money and measuring instruments) or specifically designed to teach math concepts (like number cubes and Cuisenaire rods).

Why use manipulatives, especially with older children? Because concrete materials are as helpful to students learning three-dimensional geometry and probability as they are to younger children learning to add or subtract. Students' mental ideas and abstract images are based on experiences. The more that students involve themselves in manipulation, the clearer the images they form that support an abstract concept. Everyone, even an adult, who is introduced to a totally new idea, benefits from "seeing" the idea.

An example. It is far easier to understand and recall a concrete representation of an idea than to create a mental image of the same from just hearing it. For example, think back to a time when you asked a stranger for directions to reach a destination that was new to you. "Go to the next light, turn right, then go about three-and-a-half miles. Look for a large garage on the left. When you see it, go three more blocks, turn right, then left at the next street. It's in the middle of the block." Sound familiar? Are you mentally there, or will you need to stop again later because you got lost after the first turn? Isn't even the sketchiest map easier to use and to remember? Imagine how much easier yet it would be to remember once the route was traveled. Even a simulation, such as a physical representation of a map, similar to a Monopoly board, with simulated landmarks, makes it easier to remember the way. It is that type of concrete representation we are giving students when we use manipulatives.

From a meta-analysis by Parham (cited in Suydam, 1986) of 64 research studies using elementary school students, it is clear that lessons using manipulative materials have a higher probability of producing greater mathematics achievement than do lessons in which such materials are not used. The effects are seen in problem solving, as well as in topics such as place value, measurement, and geometry. Research also supports the idea that manipulatives are not only appropriate for use with very young children. According to Driscoll (cited in Kennedy, 1986) manipulatives also help children in the intermediate grades develop new concepts. Thornton and Wilmot (1986) discussed using manipulatives effectively with mathematically gifted students, stating that manipulatives can serve at least six functions with these children. They can help gifted students

1. Build concepts and related vocabulary
2. Improve spatial visualization
3. Allow discovery of patterns and relationships
4. Provide problem-solving experiences
5. Teach the essence of verification or proof
6. Promote creativity.

Manipulative materials do not have to be expensive, as can be seen from the examples given in the lessons. However, if a little money is available, you may wish to purchase some of the materials listed in Table 7.1. Their colorful appearance and the attractive feel of such manipulatives can "sell" an otherwise dull idea to students. In addition to the manipulative materials, some of the uses for each material and the types of questions that can be asked of the students to improve their mathematical thinking are listed in Table 7.1.

One favorite tool of the UAG students for concrete representations in numbers and numeration, basic operations, and problem solving were scored natural wooden blocks. These include centimeter cubes, tens rods, hundreds

Table 7.1 Useful, Commercially Available, Manipulative Materials

MANIPULATIVE MATERIAL	USES	SAMPLE QUESTIONS
Attribute blocks	Set notation Logic Classification	Can you make a circle of ten blocks, each with two different value differences from the adjacent blocks?
Cuisenaire rod sets and *Roddles*	Prime numbers Composite numbers Multiples Factors Fractions Ratios Proportion Sets Bases Problem solving	Can you show me that the sum of two squares of the two legs of a right triangle is the same as the square of the hypotenuse?
Pattern blocks	Pattern finding Geometry Fractions Symmetry Functions Logic Area	Can you make a design with exactly three lines of symmetry?
Mira	Symmetry Congruence Perpendicular lines Parallel lines Angle bisectors Transformations Properties of figures	Can you show that this angle has been bisected?
Geometric solids	Faces Edges Vertices Surface area Volume	Can you demonstrate that the volume of a cone is one-third the volume of the corresponding cylinder?
Measurement equipment	Standard and metric measure Problem solving	If we turn the couch sideways and place it next to the counter, will we have enough room to walk past it, or will it be too tight a squeeze?

Table 7.1 (*continued*)

MANIPULATIVE MATERIAL	USES	SAMPLE QUESTIONS
Tangrams	Geometry Problem solving Seeing spatial relationships Perimeter Area Congruency Similarity Kinds of angles	Make a design. If a square has a value of one, what is the value of your design? Can you make a parallelogram using four pieces? five? six?
Geoboards	Plane geometry Transformations Measurement Number patterns Coordinates Perimeter Area Fractions	Can you show me that the area of a triangle is one-half the area of a rectangle with the same height and base?
Game pieces ("men," dice, and tokens)	Basic facts Negative numbers Problem solving Probability Equality Fractions Percent	Here are 48 men. Show me how many groups of 8 there are in 48.

flats, and thousands blocks. They were stored and "served" on a dime-store silver platter. Again and again they proved their worth in the UAG classroom, and word soon spread. Soon other teachers in the building were borrowing the "silver tray" on a regular basis. If only enough money to purchase one item is available, this is the one to buy.

Direct, one-to-one contact with students using concrete materials was not the only way we taught math. Students were expected to complete one math competency assignment daily. All assignments were short, ten minutes a day being the expected norm. This strategy provided the independent practice that students needed to reinforce previously learned concepts and skills. Selected practice exercises were handwritten or photocopied from prepared materials and pasted in students' math notebooks. Others were written as if the notebook were an assignment pad, with software or book title, page, and problem numbers noted. Still others were original examples, including directions to "find a manipulative material that will help you do this work." All assignments were clearly dated. Though some very routine materials were used, a student never had a "math book" through which he plodded his way page by page. The personalization of assignments was well received; in the UAG evaluation (Krantz, 1986), one student noted that a positive feature of this class was that "we don't do the same math problems over and over."

Basic Facts, Estimation, and Calculators

In the UAG class, the importance of students' knowledge of basic facts was emphasized. This competency is required for efficient mental calculations and accurate estimation, both of which remain important in a calculator/computer technology. Unlimited calculator use was permitted once a student demonstrated mastery of basic facts. Until that time, calculators were only available at the learning center for advanced calculations that might be needed to solve the problem of the week. Once a student mastered the facts and calculators became available to her all the time, it was necessary to teach discrimination between situations in which calculators were more and less efficient. This was fun. Humans versus calculators! Calculators were put to the test against the teacher's mental operations, such as multiplying a number by 1000, and paper-and-pencil tasks, such as reducing a fraction to its lowest terms. When it was evident to the students that the teacher could do some things faster than the calculator, they wanted to learn the "tricks" that were used. Once learned, students more adeptly chose when to use the calculator and did not rely on it indiscriminately.

Students were also encouraged to use calculators to confirm estimated answers and vice versa. Estimation skills were considered an integral part of every mathematics lesson. Three styles of estimation were used: front end, rounding, and adjustment. After these types were understood and used well, the children learned about special circumstances that affect correct estimation (such as having a limited amount of money to spend, requiring students to estimate up to avoid being short of money). From the beginning, children were encouraged to decide which method was most appropriate for the task at hand and to routinely use estimation to confirm the correctness of an answer reached through mental operations, paper-and-pencil tasks, and calculator/computer tasks.

Students need to develop a number sense, that is, to recognize the relative sizes of numbers, to estimate well. One activity the students enjoyed that helped develop this sense was estimating the number of corn kernels, jelly beans, or other small objects in a jar. They counted a small portion and estimated the number of times that portion would fit into the jar. They then estimated the number that would fill the entire jar. Finally, they estimated how much space (in terms of classrooms, desks, cars, etc.) one thousand or one million or one billion of these items would occupy. The concept was extended by calculating the number of minutes until their next birthday or since the year zero. A third activity that was especially enjoyable was estimating how much space a million unpopped popcorn kernels would occupy once they were popped. Problem-solving skills, estimation skills, and number sense were developed—and the tasty leftovers weren't bad, either!

Data Gathering, Organization, and Presentation

Problem solving is based on a student's ability to handle data effectively. From the youngest students, right up through the oldest, data management was practiced extensively. As often as possible, real-life situations were used. We encouraged students to organize lists, sort, make geometrical sketches, web ideas, graph, and draw to handle number information they collected as they solved actual school problems, such as how much good food is thrown in the cafeteria garbage cans or how many students preferred an early opening time versus a later opening time for a school day. Data gathering, organization, and presentation were also facilitated by computers with appropriate software for spreadsheets and graphing.

DAILY LIFE WITH DIFFERENT MATH

Record Keeping

The record-keeping process was very similar to the one used to systematize the reading instructional program. Each student had a mathematics notebook. Marbleized notebooks were the most effective; as the pages did not tear out easily, the students were forced to be accountable for work assigned on a particular day. It was hard to "lose" a page. These books were also convenient because they were bound with a hard cover that allowed the students to work at places other than a student desk.

At a quarterly conference, the teacher and student discussed what mathematical topics from the curriculum the student hoped to work on individually for that marking period. The number of choices remained open; frequently adjustments were made as students learned something more quickly than they thought possible. But the planning conference choices served as goals. Students understood that their final grades depended on the quality of their efforts to achieve their personal, individualized goals and on the quality of their problem-solving work. In the model, the following procedure was helpful to keep track of student growth.

Students were pretested on the concepts in their chosen topic at the level of mathematics achievement indicated on the Woodcock–Johnson Achievement Test. Concepts the student had already mastered at that level of the curriculum were highlighted on the printout. During the planning conference, the student and teacher decided which of the unhighlighted concepts in the topic were to be goals for the quarter. Since math is more sequential than many subjects, the order was sometimes pre-established within topical areas, but the students could see the reason for a more limited choice.

The concepts selected for study were recorded in the back of the marbleized notebook. The students' outlines of curriculum concepts were filed until the next conference. In this way, the number of things to learn did not become overwhelming and the agreed-upon goals were handy for planning.

As the concepts were introduced by the teacher, they were dated and marked with an **I** in the mathematics notebook. As students demonstrated understanding, brief practice and review assignments were given. These were checked immediately by the teacher. Then intermittent reinforcement was planned on a daily, weekly, and monthly basis. Once the students felt they had mastered the skills that had been agreed upon, they marked them with an **M**. M's were reviewed by both teacher and students just prior to report-card time and a test was administered to give the students feedback on whether their perceptions of mastery were correct.

SAMPLE LESSON PLANS

Several model lessons are included here to give an idea of both the problem-solving lessons and the individual progress lessons that occurred in the UAG class. Only plans for the developmental portion of the lessons are included. Guided practice followed each of the individualized developmental lessons and independent practice after the students knew the concept. Independent practice reviewed and reinforced a previously learned skill.

LESSON ONE: MEASUREMENT
(Level 4)

Objective: Student will be able to record time to the nearest second using the proper notation.
Skills Level: Knowledge, application
Materials: Computer, stopwatch, notebook, and pencil

Procedures:

1. Have the student suggest some occasions when it is important to note time to the nearest second. (Most students will mention sporting events; suggest they think of academic competitions, medical uses, recording fire drills, computer time, etc.)

2. Turn on the computer and access the clock (in some you need only to type TIME; check your user's manual). Have the student observe how the computer registers time to the tenth of a second.

3. Demonstrate the use of the stopwatch. Show the student how to read, then write the time to the nearest second using the notation 00:00:00.0 for hours, minutes, seconds, tenths of a second, just as the computer does.

4. Have the student time several things going on in the classroom using the stopwatch. After each event, read, then write the time elapsed.

5. For review and reinforcement, have the student set up an outside play activity. The student can then measure and record the length of time it takes to complete the activity.

6. Have the student suggest other times when the new skill might be used.

Evaluation: Accurate reading of the stopwatch, recording of the time using the correct notation, and application to real-life activities.

LESSON TWO: GEOMETRY
(Level 7/8)

Objective: The students will be able to find the area of a right triangle, first using a geoboard, then without using the geoboard.

Skills Level: Knowledge, comprehension, application

Materials: Desk-size geoboard and elastic bands (one per student and teacher)

Procedures:

1. Have the student create a rectangle 5 nails wide by 9 nails long. The student should find the square area of the rectangle.

2. Have the student take a second elastic band and place it on the diagonal from one corner to the opposite corner.

3. Student should observe, with the teacher's help if necessary, that the two sections into which the rectangle is divided are equal.

4. Have the student prove the equality of the two sections by counting nails along each outside edge and recognizing that the diagonal is common to each section, and so must be the same. A second method of proof can

be considered. The student can count squares and half-squares in each section, proving to the teacher and himself that the two are equivalent.

5. Have the student deduce that if both are equal, then each section is half of the rectangle.

6. Lead the student to the conclusion that if each section is half, in this case the area of the triangle formed with the second elastic band is one-half the area of the rectangle that had the base of 4 (made with 5 nails) and height of 8 (made with 9 nails).

7. Have the student begin a chart:

Base of rectangle	4	2	3
Height of rectangle	8	3	4
Area of rectangle	32	6	12
Area of right triangle	16	3	?

8. Make several more rectangles and follow the same procedure. When the student appears to see the generalization that the area of a right triangle is one-half the area of the corresponding rectangle, have the student estimate the area of a triangle without the use of the geoboard. Once the estimate is given, have the student check by using the geoboard.

Evaluation: On succeeding days, give the student two or three problems with the base and height of a right triangle given. Have the student compute the area of the triangle without using the geoboard.

LESSON THREE: NUMBERS AND NUMERATION
(Level 3)

Objective: Develop the concept that the place furthest to the left in a number has the largest value.

Skills Level: Knowledge, comprehension, analysis, evaluation

Materials: One deck of cards, numbered 0–9

Procedures:

1. Have the student draw a series of lines, representing the place value positions of numbers, for a numeral in the millions. The lines should look like this:

—,———,———.

The student's objective is to make the largest possible number. If the student understands that the places to the left are those of greatest value, e.g., millions, and those to the right are of the least value, e.g., ones, by writing in the numbers that are drawn on the cards, placing the largest number in the places to the left and the smallest numbers in the places to the right, the student has a good chance of winning. (There will still be an element of luck because not all the digits are drawn in any one round.)

2. Mix the cards and draw one. The player writes the number in one of the blanks. There is no erasing, and the numbers must be written as soon as they are drawn. Continue until seven cards are drawn. Compare to see if that is the largest number by reorganizing the individual cards to make the largest number.

3. Variation:
   Try with more or fewer blanks.
   Try with addition to make the largest sum.

$$\begin{array}{r} \underline{\,\underline{}\,\underline{}} \\ +\underline{}\,\underline{}\,\underline{} \end{array}$$

   Try with multiplication to make the largest product.

$$\begin{array}{r} \underline{\,\underline{}\,\underline{}} \\ \times\,\underline{} \end{array} \quad \text{or} \quad \begin{array}{r} \underline{\,\underline{}} \\ \times\,\underline{}\,\underline{} \end{array}$$

Evaluation: Students will be able to explain why the number is the largest.

LESSON FOUR: BASIC OPERATIONS
(Level 3)

Objective: Develop an understanding of the division algorithm through concrete materials.

Skills Level: Comprehension

Materials: Base-ten blocks (the pieces from the set that will be needed are the hundreds "flats," tens "rods," and ones "cubes") or cardboard substitutes.

Procedures:

1. Have the student work as a "banker." Give the banker 8 hundreds "flats," 5 tens "rods," and 2 ones "units." The banker has to divide the amount equally among 4 imaginary (or real) people in a group.

2. Write the division problem on the board and record each step as it is transacted with the blocks.
   $$4\overline{)852}$$

3. Lead the students through the process:
   Can each person get 1 hundred "flat"?

Can each person get 2 hundred "flats"?
Are there any "flats" left?
Record the number of hundreds "flats" that you gave each
person on the blackboard in the correct answer place.
Can each person get 1 tens "rod"?
Can each person get another tens "rod"?
How many tens "rods" were given out?
How many tens "rods" were left over?
Record that information on the board.
What are we going to do with the one tens "rod" left over?
(exchange it for 10 ones "cubes")
Now how many ones "cubes" does the banker have?
Distribute the ones "cubes" to each person.
How many ones "cubes" did each person get?
Record that on the blackboard.
Count what you have left in your hand.

Evaluation: Student will be able to perform a similar division and record the
work correctly on the chalkboard without teacher assistance.

LESSON FIVE: PROBLEM SOLVING
(Level 6)

Objective: Use logic, working backwards, and a table to help solve a problem
Skills Level: Knowledge, comprehension, analysis
Materials: Sample logic problems (*Mind Benders,* by Anita Harnadek [1984]
available from Midwest Publications are excellent)

Procedures:
1. Explain to students that sometimes we use logic to help us solve prob-
    lems. Logic can eliminate things we know are not true to find out what
    is true. This is a form of working backwards to find the answer to the
    problem.
2. Present students with a sample problem.
        The grocer, teacher, and cook of the town of Amityville are named
        Ben Grocer, Keith Teacher, and Laura Cook, although not neces-
        sarily in that order. Match each person to his or her job. You have
        the following clues.
        No person holds a job that is the same as his or her last name.
        Keith is not the grocer.
3. Tell students that they can use a chart to help them organize what they
    know about the problem. Draw the following on the board, explaining

why you are setting up the parts you need to match up by placing the names in a column and the jobs in the top row.

	grocer	teacher	cook
Ben			
Keith			
Laura			

Clue 1 tells you that no person holds a job the same as his or her name. Therefore, you know that Ben is *not* the grocer, Keith is *not* the teacher, and Laura is *not* the cook. You put **X**'s in the places where those names meet.

	grocer	teacher	cook
Ben	**X**		
Keith		**X**	
Laura			**X**

Clue 2 tells you that Keith isn't the grocer. So you place an **X** where Keith and the grocer cross. That leaves only one thing that Keith can be, so you place an **O** to show he's the cook.

	grocer	teacher	cook
Ben	**X**		
Keith	**X**	**X**	**O**
Laura			**X**

Now you know two more things. If Ben and Keith are not the grocer, that means Laura must be the grocer because she's the only person left. You can put an **O** to show Laura is the grocer. Also, if Keith is the cook, that means Ben can't be the cook. You can put an **X** to show Ben isn't the cook.

	grocer	teacher	cook
Ben	**X**		**X**
Keith	**X**	**X**	**O**
Laura	**O**		**X**

You know now that if Laura is the grocer, she can't be the teacher, and if Ben is neither the grocer nor the cook, he must be the teacher. You can complete the chart.

	grocer	teacher	cook
Ben	**X**	**O**	**X**
Keith	**X**	**X**	**O**
Laura	**O**	**X**	**X**

Evaluation: Have the students try another, similar problem and help them through the solution. The students should assume as much responsibility as possible for the logic, but you should guide them when they need help, pointing out any faulty logic they try to employ. When students seem to have mastered the process, a more challenging problem of the same type can become a problem of the week.

LESSON SIX: PROBLEM OF THE WEEK
(All levels)

One "Problem of the Week" should be introduced to the class on the first day of each week. The students then have the rest of the week, except for the last day, to try to solve the problem. The students may work cooperatively, and more than one solution should be possible for each problem. If the students solve the problem rapidly, they should be encouraged to find other solutions to the same problem that are equally correct. On the last day of the week, the students should share the solutions they discovered and evaluate the process they used to solve the problem.

Objective: Apply any of several problem-solving strategies to a complex problem and compare, with other students, alternate solutions and alternate processes of arriving at those solutions to the same problem.
Skills Level: Comprehension, analysis, flexibility, fluency, evaluation
Materials: Complex problems that have more than one solution prepared and placed in the learning center area, calculators, computer, computer software that may be appropriate

Procedures:
1. On Monday, present the problem of the week to the class. (Sample problems can be found in Figure 7.1, Figure 7.2, and Figure 7.3. Place each problem in a separate, colorful, appropriately decorated file folder with any helpful manipulatives enclosed in an envelope glued inside the cover.) Make sure all vocabulary is understood, that students understand there may be several processes that lead to correct solutions, and that there may be several solutions that are equally correct. Be sure, also, that they know they may work with others to solve the problem, and then when they believe they have a solution, they are to sign the sheet attached to the center. If they are not the first to sign, they are to present their solution to the students who have already signed to see if the first group(s) arrived at the same solution in the same way they did.
2. On Friday, each student or group who reached a solution, explains the process they used and the solution they found to the teacher. There

Figure 7.1:   Problem of the week. Bull's-Eye problem.

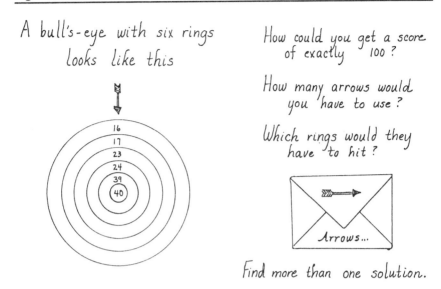

A bull's-eye with six rings looks like this

How could you get a score of exactly 100?

How many arrows would you have to use?

Which rings would they have to hit?

Arrows...

Find more than one solution.

should then be discussion of the strategies employed and the mathematical principles underlying any solutions achieved.

Evaluation: All students have reached solution by Friday and are prepared for discussion.

STUDENT RESPONSES TO THE MATH CURRICULUM

In Chapter 3, we discussed the factors that, in the eyes of students who became successful as a result of the UAG class, were significant in changing their achievement. Four students were selected as representative of all the successful students in the program, that is, the students who had been enrolled in the UAG program and returned to the mainstream. Case studies were developed independently on each of the four students. When all four agreed, the assumption was made that other students who were also successful would respond similarly.

All four successful students selected math as it was taught in the adaptive class as one of the three subjects most helpful in making them a better student (Supplee, 1987/1988, p. 111). Wording on the interview schedule that elicited the students' perceptions about math frequently evoked the response that it

130

Curriculum

Figure 7.2: Problem of the week: Toothpick trick.

You can make a triangle that has three sides the same length with three toothpicks.

If you had six toothpicks, you could make two triangles.

Actually, you could make two triangles with equal sides with only 5 toothpicks.

Here's the problem:

Use six toothpicks and make four triangles that have all the same length sides.

TOOTHPICKS

Figure 7.3: Problem of the week: The sum of two squares.

I'll bet that sum of them can't!

The number 20 can be written as the sum of two squares:

2^2 (which means 2×2) = 4
+ 4^2 (which means 4×4) = +16
_____
20

Find all the numbers less than 50 which can be written as

the sum of 2 squares.

was how the subject was taught that made the difference in their success, not the different content, goals, and objectives. There appeared to be real differences in the use of math manipulatives, student choice, and control-of-learning pace; the use of notebooks rather than page-by-page textbooks also had an impact on how the students saw themselves and how they learned mathematics. The instructional strategies chosen by every successful student as being helpful in learning math were

1. Individualized learning
2. Peer teaching
3. Using notebooks instead of commercial workbooks
4. Having choice and control over goals and objectives
5. Using the talk-aloud method.

Chosen by three of the four (75 percent) students involved were

1. Ten-minute lessons
2. Small-group instruction
3. Use of the computer as a tool
4. Math manipulative materials
5. Learning how their learning occurs
6. Taking an active part in the learning of math.

In another section of the study, students' attributions for their success on the math tasks were explored. The researcher tried to learn whether students believed it was within their power to become successful math students or whether they felt it was a matter of luck or something else over which they had no control. Results showed a fairly distinct pattern. Table 3.1, in Chapter 3, shows a regular decrease in responses indicating helplessness and a corresponding increase in mastery orientation. Students in the "not included" group showed the greatest sense of helplessness. The sense of mastery increased in the "not yet" group and increased again in the "successful" group. While cause and effect cannot be absolutely determined, it appears that the instruction that occurred in the UAG class affected the students' perceptions of their ability to master mathematics.

SUMMARY

A review of research began this chapter. The most recent recommendations of The National Council of Teachers of Mathematics (NCTM) and Drs.

Tom Good and Doug Grouws, researchers who developed the Missouri Math Model, were presented. Following this, research on appropriate differentiation of the mathematics curriculum for the gifted was discussed. Radical acceleration, as proposed by Julian Stanley; a combination of acceleration and enrichment, as proposed by the National Council of Teachers of Mathematics; and the flexible pacing system laid out by Daniels and Cox were treated.

The research was applied to the scope and sequence already present in the district to guide mathematics education. Acceleration through the enriched curriculum was permitted. Student placement in the individualized program, and modifications that allowed the students to return to the mainstream with little trouble, were discussed. Two difficulties were discussed: assessment using only standardized achievement tests, which tended to mask achievement in the enriched portion of the curriculum; and the need for a broad range of teacher competencies in order to teach the mathematics curriculum.

The last part of the chapter dealt with the practical day-to-day activities involved in teaching mathematics. Methods of scheduling, setting up daily routines and assignments, the use of manipulatives to teach mathematical concepts, and record-keeping ideas were presented. Issues facing classroom teachers, such as how much emphasis to place on basic facts, the use of calculators, and how to incorporate the gathering, organization, and presentation of mathematical data were addressed. Several sample lessons were outlined at differing levels of the curriculum. Finally, the students' responses to the curriculum were defined.

CHAPTER 8

Affective Studies

Gifted students who underachieve are disaffected students. Whitmore (1980), an educator, believed students' problems generally began once they reached school age. She concluded that disaffected behavior was one result of inappropriate school situations. Rimm (1983), a psychologist, believed the inappropriate behaviors stemmed from the home situation and were first seen when children were confronted with a social environment (school) that pointed up their maladjustment. Neither view is totally correct. Many factors affect each child. Personality variables, school settings, disabilities, family problems, and more have an impact on a child's way of dealing with his or her daily life. Cause and effect are nearly impossible to determine and, more important, are immaterial. Home and school factors become part of an interactive web that is impossible to untangle. What *is* important is the way the children and the significant adults in their lives learn to react to and manage these variables. If neither home nor school support the gifted child, there is little hope that giftedness will emerge. If either environment is supportive, there is some hope. Of course, if both work together, the child has the best chance possible to achieve great things.

It is also nearly impossible for giftedness to emerge when non-intellective skills are missing, or when children's original learning has led to inappropriate or self-destructive behavior. It is possible, fortunately, to help children learn new ways of behaving and reacting. In most cases, such change does not happen spontaneously. The easiest course, though not always the least painful or the most healthy, is to continue behaving in pre-established patterns. Most people, children and adults alike, can exert more control over their own actions and reactions than they do. However, it takes conscious effort to become aware of the behavior patterns being used and to use alternate behaviors instead. It takes decision-making skills to choose those behaviors they want to have, and it takes task commitment to practice the new behaviors until they become habitual. It is hard work for students and their parents to look at themselves objectively and to choose to make changes in themselves. The teacher's role, when implementing the affective curriculum, is to present choices and to teach decision making and task commitment. The teacher becomes a clarifier and facilitator, not an enforcer or reinforcer. Considered choice is essential. Choice protects the dignity and the importance of each participant.

CHANGING STUDENT BEHAVIOR

The affective curriculum does not rely on behavior modification or management strategies. While these strategies were recommended as effective ways to change our students' inappropriate behaviors, we chose not to use them.

Behavior Management: Why Not?

Only extrinsic motivational techniques are operating if behavior modification or management includes

1. The adult selecting a behavior to extinguish
2. The adult selecting a positive behavior to replace the undesirable behavior
3. The identification of a reward system (whether concrete, such as the use of M&M candies, or more abstract, such as the use of tokens to be exchanged for desired rewards)
4. The recognition by the adult of the desired behavior with regular reinforcement, eventually replaced by intermittent reinforcement
5. The ignoring of undesirable behaviors.

Even if the children are involved in certain parts of the decision making and in their own record keeping, behavior management is not philosophically in line with the approach taken in UAG. Behavior management places far too much emphasis on external controls, rewards, and adult decision making. The adult, not the child, is in charge of the child. When adults choose what behaviors the children should have, the implicit assumption is that the children aren't capable of such choices and/or do not already have an internal locus of control. It is assumed that they need adults to provide external controls until the students do what the adults believe they should.

If Not Behavior Management, Then What?

In contrast, the UAG program operated under the assumption that children are capable of thinking, of making choices, and of taking charge of themselves. Adults can aid children most by helping them recognize self-defeating behaviors and by pointing out the direct consequences of those behaviors. Adults can also help by providing the students with several alternatives to a self-defeating behavior, discussing with them the pros and cons of each, and then allowing them to choose which alternative they are ready to try. In so doing, an entirely different climate is created. The students are recognized for their own ability to control their lives and are dignified by being expected to take that control. Natural and logical consequences provide the rewards and punishments for the choices students make. The adult continues to support and encourage the child's developing internal locus of control until, finally, the child is on his own.

The belief that the development of internal locus of control is crucial to helping students overcome their handicapping conditions is supported by a four-year study sponsored by the Spencer Foundation. The study sought to determine which personality traits and actions helped propel disadvantaged youths out of poverty and into extraordinary success in the fields of business, academia, and government. Harrington reported that internal locus of control was critical ("Beating the Odds," 1985–86). According to Harrington, the personality traits that make a student appear to resist external controls, which are inherent in behavior management strategies, could be evidence of a strong sense of internal locus of control that should not be destroyed if students are to have any hope of breaking out of the past.

Besides being a facilitator, the teacher's role is also one of a model of behaviors that are productive and supportive of giftedness, rather than counterproductive or destructive. By bringing to the conscious awareness of children the fact that everything they, as adults, do has a "price" to pay or a consequence, the teachers help children see the lifelong value of thoughtful decision making. As adults, they would choose to do things certain ways because they can live with the "price" of their choice more easily than another choice. The children have the chance to consider new ways to approach life if they get to think about, and then select among, several alternatives, each of which has certain consequences.

For example, to teach students about productive work-study skills, the teachers modeled several appropriate ways to manage time. One thing they did was to list the schedule of mini-lessons on the chalkboard as a reminder to themselves and the students to keep the pace of instruction moving. The teachers then used direct instruction to point out that they were consciously choosing to use their time in the way the schedule defined it rather than another. They reminded the students that there were consequences of this choice. In the case of the daily schedule, a good consequence was that time was fairly apportioned to every student for every planned lesson. A negative consequence was that it didn't allow for the extra time if a student had difficulty with a lesson. If the teacher and student chose to stay in one lesson longer, another student would miss a lesson. The teachers asked students what other choices were available to the teachers regarding the use of time and what the "price" of each choice would be. Children then talked about whether the teachers' strategy or another that had been discussed had the best "price" if they were to choose. The group discussed how scheduling time might help them solve a problem in their own lives. Students were encouraged to try to apply the processes.

Gradually students assumed responsibility for using some of the new behaviors learned in the adaptive classroom. They planned when and how they would introduce the new behaviors in other contexts as well. As was discussed in the more cognitive subjects, the teachers helped the students through the zone of proximal development (Wertsch, 1979), this time in the affective areas and in developing the non-intellective skills important to success. New social, work-study, stress-reduction, communication, and other skills permitted their giftedness to emerge.

An example. One of the stress-reduction strategies the UAG students learned was to consciously, physically relax their bodies when they recognized that stress was beginning to incapacitate them. The strategy was learned in stages. Students learned first to recognize the feelings that tension produced in their bodies by deliberately creating tension. They tightened up every muscle in their bodies by contracting them all simultaneously. Then, one muscle group at a time, they deliberately relaxed that tension. A deep sense of relaxation results, particularly when the tension is released from the top of the head down to the toes. It feels as if tension is flowing from the body right out through the toes.

Marcia was particularly pleased with the effect this exercise had on her. She practiced enthusiastically in the UAG classroom while the group was learning the technique. Before long, it was possible to see her using the technique on her own in the UAG classroom. She employed it most often when she had a disagreement with another student and when she was facing a test on her return to the regular classroom.

In the spring, when standardized testing took place, Marcia's regular classroom teacher came to the UAG teacher with a story that made both laugh. Marcia found achievement tests to be particularly stressful, and now she knew she had a strategy that could counteract the stress. She used the technique in the regular class; she tensed, then relaxed her body totally unconcerned about what the other children's reactions might be while the teacher was passing out the materials for the testing session. One of the non-UAG students observed her tensing her body, and not knowing what Marcia was doing, called the teacher's attention to the fact that Marcia needed to use the lavatory before the test began. The teacher asked what Marcia was doing, and Marcia explained in a straightforward manner. At that, the other students asked to learn how to relax. The teacher later reported better results for the entire class on that subtest than on any other subtest. The entire class apparently benefitted from the strategy Marcia used.

CONTENT FOR THE STUDENTS

The goals of the affective curriculum are to help the students improve their attitudes towards school, their school behaviors, and their self-esteem. There are several subcurricula within the affective curriculum. These include group self-direction skills, pro-social skills, cooperative sports and games, work-study skills, and stress-reduction skills. Since each part had separate objectives, each is discussed separately.

One mini-lesson, lasting about twenty minutes, was taught each day in one of the subcurricula. After much experimenting, we found the best arrangement for us to be a class meeting first thing Monday morning to teach group self-direction skills and to help students organize their week. A meeting in the middle of our class periods on Tuesday was used to teach pro-social skills and communication skills. On Wednesday, the same time period was used to teach cooperative games, and on Thursday to teach work-study skills. On Friday, the group again met first thing in the day to learn a new stress-reduction skill. Since creative production was one way students learned to manage their stress, this lesson often introduced a new center in the creative arts. Having the lesson early in the day allowed students to plan their time well to finish the week's work and begin an arts activity.

Group Self-Direction Skills

The objective of group skills was to help the students learn how to participate positively in a group. They needed to learn how to determine what "agreements" (Clark, 1986) rather than "classroom rules" were needed to make their mini-society work efficiently, to learn how to manage themselves successfully in that "mini-society," and to learn how to manage the agreements when problems arose. Class meetings were the vehicle for instruction.

Initially, the class meetings were used to establish the agreements the children needed in their mini-society. The teacher brought to the class a set of possible agreements that would protect the rights of each person in the room and that would imply certain responsibilities for each person if the agreements were to work. The agreements were few (four at first, but finally three) and were stated simply with reasons for their being. The students discussed the proposals, adding to, deleting from, and changing to simpler language, those they didn't like. When the agreements were worked out so that every hypothetical situation the students could think of that might disrupt classroom life was covered, the agreements were charted and posted in a place easily visible from every part of the room.

The final results from our first class were

1. I have the right to learn what I need to know. Therefore, I have a responsibility to listen in class, to be ready for my lessons, and to do my work. I also have the responsibility to allow others to do their work without being disturbed.
2. I have the right to be safe physically and emotionally. Therefore, I have the responsibility to take care of myself and to treat others the way I would like to be treated. I have the responsibility not to hurt another person's body or feelings.
3. I have the right to work in a pleasant place. Therefore, I have the responsibility to take care of the class environment and to be a pleasant person. If a problem arises, I will handle the problem with the person who can do something about it.

(Other samples of a different type of agreement are mentioned in *Optimizing Learning* [Clark, 1986], p. 136.)

Our students decided that if a person found it impossible to follow the last sentence in agreement number 2, he or she would need to leave the room until able to follow it again. For the other agreements, the students decided they wanted to be reminded of the agreement if they broke it. They wanted to be asked what made it hard for them to follow that agreement at the time they broke it. If it seemed that the natural consequences didn't help students remember the agreements or if agreements seemed impossible to keep, the students decided they would bring up the problem at a class meeting. They would revise the agreements until they were modified to the satisfaction of all the students and a logical consequence for not living by the agreement would be determined by the group.

This happened more than once, but the first time taught a lesson that years of sermonizing and adult control would never have done as effectively. Our room had an area set aside for socializing with food available for snacks. A table and two chairs in the areas were often used by the children who needed breakfast or as a self-selected reward to celebrate reaching a goal. Some of the children were careless about cleaning up after themselves, making the area an unpleasant place for the next person. Others overextended their time in the area, limiting access to others. Marcia brought up the problem at an early class meeting as a violation of agreement number 3. Although other students also believed the problem existed, they felt the agreement shouldn't be changed. What made it hard to follow, they decided, was that there was no one to remind them to be courteous in the area. To solve the problem for themselves, the students decided to make a list to post near the area. This would remind them of the things they needed to do when cleaning up after themselves. They also agreed to limit their time in the area to once a day for ten minutes, and they posted a sign-in, sign-out sheet. They decided that a logical consequence if someone forgot the agreement was not to be allowed into the area for three days. As was classroom practice, modifications were to be tried out for one week only to see if they worked.

As luck would have it, Marcia was the first to forget the kitchen clean-up agreement. Yet she lived with the consequences and admitted that they helped her remember to clean up when she was next allowed to use the area! Had an adult suggested or imposed what the children finally agreed to and had Marcia then broken the "rule," she might never have assumed her own responsibility for the problem. Far more likely, she would have blamed the external controller (teacher) for being unfair, for not giving her another chance, for giving her a punishment for some little thing that she really didn't deserve because "the other kids did it, too." Probably her anger would have interfered with the business of learning and working in the class. Instead, Marcia had no one but herself to look to: She brought up the problem, she agreed to the solution, she forgot the agreement, and she lived with the consequence. She was angry with herself, but she knew the limits of the consequences and could pay the "price." For her, it was a real-life lesson in personal responsibility and accountability in the workings of a democracy. Class meetings, after all, had a greater purpose than scheduling kitchen time and clean-up problems. They were a forum for the beginnings of the determination of personal values, self-government, conflict resolution, consensus seeking, yielding to a majority, long-range goal setting, criteria development, and planning skills.

Before any of these loftier goals could be reached, the children had to learn how to use basic democratic processes. They learned how to run a political meeting and how to conduct a group discussion so everyone was heard. The students agreed to be responsible for presenting an issue as they saw it. They were expected to have their thoughts clearly organized and to speak briefly about the problem, not about individual people, when their turn came up on the agenda. They knew to listen to the points of view of others and learned to recognize that not everyone saw things the same way—or needed to. They learned the value of an agenda to help organize their plans for action and devised a system of writing the issues they wished to discuss at the class meeting in a specially designated notebook. They also learned the need for recording minutes to recall exactly what was decided and what might need refinement as the decision was carried out.

During the early weeks, the teacher modeled how to conduct the meetings and a student recorded group decisions, which the teacher initialed to signify a "certified copy." Later, the children practiced the role of leader and were capable of running their own meetings and recording and verifying their own decisions. They shared the chairperson and the recorder responsibilities on a rotating basis.

In a typical meeting, the first five minutes were devoted to a mini-lesson on a group discussion skill. Sample objectives for these lessons included

1. Stating an idea briefly and clearly
2. Stating a problem, not criticizing people who may be creating the problem
3. Staying on the subject
4. Asking for clarification of an idea
5. Proposing an alternative idea
6. Coming to consensus.

The second portion of the meeting, also kept very short, was devoted to announcements (usually about expected observers, guest speakers, class trips, special recognition for a student, or teacher absences due to professional responsibilities), and correspondence. The third portion, and one that was not always necessary, was old business. Any unworkable solution to a previous issue could be reintroduced for revisions. When an issue was presented in old business, it superseded any new business and occupied the last five to ten minutes. If no old business needed work, the last section was for new business and devoted to a problem a student placed on the agenda. Problems were considered in the order in which they were written into the book unless something new was truly pressing. If the majority agreed, the agenda was amended and the new item was considered ahead of the others.

For any new or old business, the person who wrote the item in the agenda book or who introduced it under old business presented the classroom problem that needed solving. Different ideas on the same issue were expressed by the others in the group, both students and teacher. At the end of five to seven minutes, tentative solutions to the problem were brainstormed by all group members. The consequences that could be anticipated for each solution were considered, and the one appearing to be best was adopted for a trial period of one week. The "one-week trial period" concept kept class meetings from bogging down. Almost any decision can be tolerated for a week if there is hope of change the next week.

As time passed, instruction in group processes became less necessary. By the end of the first semester, many minor problems were ironed out and students found they had few problems to solve. They learned then that governing bodies don't only solve problems from the past, that they also consider their involvement in a wider community, in this case the school. Governing bodies also look to the future and make plans for a better life for the communities of which they are a part. Our students did likewise, planning and managing changes in their classroom routines and environment, helping out in schoolwide projects, organizing field trips, arranging for speakers to come to class, and designing celebrations for students who reached a particular goal or who "graduated" from UAG.

The class-meeting procedures we followed are adapted from the family meetings suggested in *Children: The Challenge* (Dreikurs & Soltz, 1964). Based on Adlerian psychology, Dreikurs and Soltz devised family councils as a way of encouraging children to take responsibility for themselves and to recognize the rights of others within a family. The procedures worked as well in the UAG classroom "family" as they do in a typical family.

Did this curriculum matter to the children? In *Listen to the Children* (Supplee, 1987/1988), the responses from a group of students who were not involved in the adaptive class were compared to those students who were in the class for at least a short period of time. Both groups were asked: "Do you feel you have a say in the rules that run the class? Do you run it well? Do you find it easy to live by your rules?" A second set of questions included, "Do you find that our management routines give you a comfortable feeling in this classroom? Do you feel you have some control over the way this classroom operates? Please explain." A third set asked, "How would you describe the way the people in this room were disciplined if they did not live up to the expectations?"

The students "not in" the adaptive class recognized some aspects of the self-governance in their regular classes. When the enrolled students were asked if there were differences between self-governance processes as they were used in the regular classroom and in the adaptive classroom, they noted the sense of equality that existed in the adaptive room (Supplee, 1987/1988, p. 140). They commented on the fact that in the adaptive room, the students' ideas were as important as the teachers' and consensus was used to reach agreement on class issues. This equality gave them a feeling of their own importance, building their self-esteem, one of the original goals. When the program was evaluated by the Center for the Study of the Gifted (Krantz, 1986), the evaluator commented on the evident sense of purpose in the classroom among children who had been difficult to involve in school prior to their enrollment in the adaptive class.

The following sample lesson plans have been included to help others design lessons of their own that will help students develop their ability to manage their own society. All references to cognitive skill levels refer to Bloom's Taxonomy of Cognitive Objectives (Bloom, 1956) while the affective skills refer to Kratwohl's *Taxonomy of Educational Objectives, Handbook II: Affective Domain* (Kratwohl, D., Bloom, B., & Masia, B., 1964).

LESSON ONE
Stating the Problem, Not Criticizing a Person

Objective: (a) Students will be able to distinguish the problem behavior from the person demonstrating that behavior. (b) Students will be able to state a problem without naming a person causing that problem.

Skills Level: Cognitive: analysis, evaluation, synthesis

  Affective: receiving/attending, responding

Materials: No special materials required

Procedures:

1. Begin the mini-lesson by stating the objectives.
2. Explain that sometimes people say things about others that make them feel really threatened and angry. Personalize the lesson by stating that if someone accuses the teacher of doing something wrong, the teacher doesn't want to hear about it because she thinks she'll get into trouble. For example, if a teacher is accused by a parent of being late for playground duty and a child gets hurt, the teacher might be afraid she'll be sued.
3. Ask the students what they think the teacher probably feels like doing when she feels angry or threatened by someone.
4. Ask whether the students have ever felt the same way when someone accused them of doing something wrong.
5. After a brief sharing, again personalize the lesson. Explain that the teacher knows that some of the things she does cause another person a problem. For example, if she leaves her books in the middle of the couch, another person can't sit there. That causes a problem. It doesn't make the teacher the problem, nor does it make her a bad person, because the teacher can fix the problem once she knows it is a problem. But if she feels angry or threatened, she is not going to want to fix the problem, she's going to feel as the students already discussed—angry, resentful, etc.
6. Explain that if the person who has the problem can say what the problem is without accusing, a person will probably fix the problem, especially if that person doesn't feel angry or scared and most especially if

the person doing the asking is important to the person causing the problem.
7. State that today the students will practice stating some problems without naming the person. A person could state the problem the teacher made with the books by saying, "When there are book spread all over the couch, I can't sit down. I'd like to be able to sit there." The person could then offer a solution. "Would you mind moving them to the bookshelf, or mind if I do?"
8. Have students discuss the feelings a statement of this kind will probably generate in the person causing the problem. Have them predict what kind of response they probably will get.
9. Ask students to share one problem at home that each person would like to solve. Have them practice restating the problem without naming the perpetrator. Have them practice saying the same problem several different ways (and be prepared for a sense of humor in some students!).
10. Ask students to think carefully about the problem on the agenda today. Have them mentally think how they would state the problem without naming the person. Then begin the new business portion of the class meeting.

Evaluation: Observe whether the student is successful in stating the problem correctly. Ask other students if they might have stated it differently.

LESSON TWO
Coming to Consensus

Objective: (a) The student will learn that consensus seeking is an alternative to voting as a way to reach a group decision. (b) The student will know that consensus requires compromise. (c) The student will practice arriving at consensus.
Skills Level: Cognitive: knowledge, comprehension, application
Affective: receiving/attending, responding
Materials: No special materials needed.

Procedures:
1. The teacher asks how students make decisions in their regular classes when the teacher allows them to decide something (most often, the response is voting).
2. Discuss how people feel after a vote is taken if they voted on the winning side/on the losing side.
3. Tell the students there is another way of making a decision, called con-

sensus seeking. In this method, there is no voting, so no one clearly wins or clearly loses. Instead, people try to compromise until they find a spot somewhere in the middle between two points of view that they can all live with. At the end, no one is totally unhappy with the decision, although no one may be completely happy with it either.

4. Ask students to think of a time when it might be important to come to consensus rather than vote. If no one can think of anything, remind them of their original agreements. What would have happened if voting was the way the agreements were reached. Would everyone follow them willingly? What might happen?

5. Give students practice arriving at consensus. Suggest they plan to buy one new snack for the kitchen area. They must buy something that has not been in the kitchen before; everyone must like it; and everyone must be able to eat it (no food that allergy-prone students can't eat).

6. Ask the students if this process would be helpful sometimes during class meetings. Have them suggest a time, and apply it as soon as possible.

Evaluation: Students will arrive at consensus on a new snack. Students will apply consensus during a class meeting.

Work-Study Skills

The students renamed our work-study skills curriculum, "school-survival skills." School survival included instruction in the non-intellective skills that are very necessary for success in school but normally are not taught there. Some students, adept at picking up cues or learning how to play the game of school from parents or peers, have no difficulty excelling in school. Other children just never figure out on their own how to do what the teachers expect of them. For some, their exceptional academic abilities permit them to breeze through the first few years of school, but trouble develops in the middle grades as the demands to be independent, organized learners increase. Still other children must learn to cross cultures, acting in a way that would be unacceptable at home (because of cultural mores) yet is expected of them in the school.

Our school-survival lessons were generally taught through role playing. In a small group, students were introduced through a brief discussion to one skill that might make it easier for them to be successful in school. Together the students and the teacher brainstormed a list of guidelines that might be evident if someone was particularly good at that skill. A short discussion about why the skill might be valuable—"What are the good things that might happen to someone who does these things?"—helped the children clarify whether they would find the skill under discussion useful.

Then the teacher and a student who had rehearsed with the teacher enacted a situation that demonstrated the desired skill. It was especially effective if a student who very much needed to develop a particular skill was selected to "teach" the others through this role-playing. The rest of the class watched to see which of their guidelines—the things they thought they should see—were actually observable. The student assistant then chose two other students to demonstrate the same skill using their own role-play, this time unrehearsed. This second time, a brief critique was held again.

Students were encouraged to "try on" each skill for at least a week before deciding whether or not they would "buy it." We posted the list of guidelines and benefits which the students developed for "try-on week." To provide appropriate, consistent practice, students were "flagged" on one particular day during the week. Flagging meant that the student's name appeared on the chalkboard in the morning in a flag. This was a signal that it was that child's day to be particularly aware of practicing the school-survival skill of the week. The teacher and the other students were responsible to find a time to compliment the flagged students when they noticed the skill being practiced. This procedure kept everyone aware of the desired skill every day of the week following the lesson. Either they were "flagged" and practicing for others to see, or they were watching to see whether the "flagged" person used the desired skill.

The following week, the guidelines remained up. During this second week, the students were encouraged to write "graffiti"; that is, to jot down a brief note on the bottom of the chart describing each time that week that they successfully used the skill either at home or in the regular class. The graffiti served as our "bridging" activity. The students could let one another know how a new skill helped and when it was useful. At the beginning of the next week's lesson, compliments were paid and the children decided if the skill needed additional reinforcement or if the chart could come down.

In essence, a new skill was introduced in one 20-minute lesson. It was reinforced daily for the following two weeks. After the first week, two skills per week were the center of attention, one being "flagged" and one being "graffitied." When the cycle of lessons did not last the school year, those skills that needed reinforcement were repeated. Any new skills that the teacher or students noticed they needed could easily be added to the list below.

The following objectives were included in our school survival skills:

1. Listening, and looking as if they were listening
2. Asking a teacher or a friend for help
3. Bringing needed materials to class
4. Following written and oral instructions (this may need at least two separate lessons)

5. Memorizing efficiently
6. Learning to use an assignment pad well, with a correlate of planning a study area and study schedule at home
7. Studying for tests
8. Completing short-term assignments
9. Completing long-term assignments
10. Contributing to a class discussion
11. Ignoring distractions
12. Asking a question in class
13. Deciding what to do when assigned work is finished
14. Setting medium- and long-range goals
15. Dealing with an accusation
16. Accepting consequences for mistakes in work or behavior
17. Negotiating with the teacher
18. Making good decisions
19. Dealing with time pressures and schedules
20. Learning to set priorities
21. Rewarding themselves for tasks well done
22. Learning to say no when work must come first
23. Overlearning something to be sure it's mastered

What follows is a sample lesson from this curriculum.

LESSON ONE
Looking as if You Are Listening

Objective: (a) The student will know that teachers read body language to help them decide if students are doing what they should be doing. (b) The student will know that when a person is speaking to them, in most American schools, the students are expected to look at the teacher. (c) The student will understand that in some other cultures, to show respect, students do not look at their teachers, but look down.
Skills Level: Cognitive: knowledge, comprehension
   Affective: receiving, responding, valuing
Materials: Chart paper and markers

Procedures:
1.   Begin by stating that in America, students are expected to look at the teacher when the teacher is speaking to them. This is not true in all cultures. For example, in Mexico, students are taught by their parents to cast their eyes downward as a sign of respect when adults are speaking to them, especially if they are being chastised.

2. Ask the students to brainstorm what a person in an American school would do to show the teacher that he or she is really listening. These are listed on the chart (e.g., the student will be quiet, the student will be looking directly at the teacher, the student will not be writing or doing anything with his or her hands or mind).

3. Select a student to role-play a situation with the teacher. The teacher begins to talk to the student. The student practices sitting quietly, looking directly at the teacher, and not doing anything with his or her hands. Have the others give the student who is role-playing some feedback on whether the elements were all there.

4. Have the students explain what good things might happen if they are able to use this skill well in our school. Add these ideas to the chart.

5. Have the student assistant choose two other people to role-play a similar situation. Give these students feedback as well on their ability to meet the guidelines.

6. Place the chart with the skill, the guidelines to good practice, and the good consequences of using this skill in an easily visible spot in the room. Remind the students that they will be "flagged" during the week on their use of the skill. That means they will be expected to use the skill very well on one day and that the others in class will be looking for times to compliment them on their use of the skill. On the days they are not flagged, they should be looking for the skill to be used by the person whose name is in the flag.

Evaluation: Students will demonstrate effective use of the skill on the day they are flagged; they will also recognize effective use of the skill by their peers on the days they are not flagged.

Interview data in the program evaluation by Krantz (1986) indicated that there were changes in students' abilities to live successfully within the school culture. Teachers said, "Children seem to like it; they're less antsy when they return to my room," and "takes part in discussions; couldn't get participation before." The students' comments included, "get work done better and faster now," while parents noted, "improved her ability to start homework and finish it without my nagging," and "has the ability now to sit through tests without messing it up. It's incredible. He's a different person."

Cooperative Sports and Games

Most of our students were accustomed to thinking of school in terms of work and pain. These activities were so much fun it was hard to believe they were important for school! We entered the UAG program with the belief that we would have to develop trust and a sense of family quickly if we were going to be successful with a multi-age group. We had to trust the students and they had to trust us and one another. Cooperative activities seemed to be the answer to that problem. We had no idea at the time of the extraordinary impact this subcurricula would have on the students with whom we worked.

As we were designing the curriculum, we looked to formerly tested programs such as Project Adventure and Outward Bound for ideas. Two books proved particularly helpful, *Cow's Tails and Cobras* (Rohnke, 1977) and *The Cooperative Sports and Games Book: Challenge Without Competition* (Orlick, 1978). Later, we found *More New Games! . . . and Playful Ideas From the New Games Foundation* (Fluegelman, 1981), which offered additional good ideas and was very clearly organized. From these resources, we developed a mini-curriculum nicknamed "coop" games by the students.

Project Adventure activities led to a challenging outdoor ropes course, available to us locally at our county vo-tech high school and at several environmental education centers nearby. To prepare for these programs, each week a 20-minute class was devoted to indoor and outdoor games designed to build trust and confidence and eliminate competition among the students. Most of the school-based games took minimal supplies and equipment. When the students were ready, that is, when they could allow other students to touch their hands or arms and could allow others to stand behind them without fear, a very rewarding field trip, in terms of the group cohesiveness that developed, followed. On this trip, the children accomplished feats that they were sure were going to be impossible for them, such as scaling an eight-foot wall with only each other as tools. What an ego boost!

After the trip, coop games continued. They provided a weekly break in activities. They allowed the students to interact with one another for pure fun, but also to support one another. None of the games had winners or losers. The object was for everyone to win through the efforts of all. While no one was forced to participate and occasionally students asked to pass when the activities began, for most of the students this was an activity where success was evident and laughter was key.

Indeed, cooperative sports and games were perceived by the students as the most valuable and different portion of the affective curricula in the adaptive class (Supplee, 1987/1988). One anecdote is worth repeating to demonstrate dramatically the differences students saw between these activities and their typical physical education classes and classroom games. After several months in the adaptive program, Marty decided he wanted to play a "real" game—basketball—instead of the "coop" games. The teacher was reluctant and commented on the differences in the ages and sizes of class members. The group called a class meeting, and since the entire group reached consensus, the teacher conceded. They gave the real game a try. It was disastrous!

Children who had been supportive, encouraging friends for months with seldom a cross word were screaming at one another. When Helen, one of the younger children, burst into tears, the teacher reconvened the class meeting.

A powerful discussion followed. Children were able to name what they felt on the court and discuss what the "game" made them think of their friends. They analyzed the differences between this and the cooperative games. They were able to state that, although they could play competitive games in their regular classes quite well, in this group, competition was a violation of trust. It meant trying to be better than another at any expense, as long as it was "within the rules." It was a game of power and control of the big over the little and in this social setting, that was not acceptable. They felt it was still fine to play competitive games, but not in the adaptive classroom where people could get hurt emotionally.

Competition is a fact of life in our nation. America's economic and political systems are based on competition whether between varying products and industries or between party lines. As such, people need to learn to deal with competition. The schools, as an instrument of that social system and a reflection of it, have incorporated competition into their structure. Because competition is such a pervasive element in American society, its appropriateness in the schools has rarely been questioned. Based on the responses of our students, we question whether it is good for students to be so competitive in the regular classroom. The students' selection of cooperative games as important to them and the clear evidence from the anecdote cited of the changes in their attitudes towards one another when they engaged in the competitive play typical of their regular classrooms indicate that competition among these children may be a destructive element of their school lives.

By its nature, competition ordains that someone wins and someone loses. People who win all the time, or who win more often than they lose, develop a liking for competition. But what about the frequent loser—who may lose because she is shorter, or because of a mental disability, or because her mind was on family problems? Does losing, whether it be in a game, on an assignment done incorrectly, or on not meeting the social expectations of others, powerfully influence a student's future ability to win? A fundamental philosophical question arises about the nature and purpose of school in our society, particularly for these children. Should schools begin and encourage the stratification that will eventually face people in our nation? Or should they deliberately and methodically plan for a noncompetitive atmosphere in order to allow every student the opportunity to be all she or he can be? It seems evident that these underachieving gifted students needed a cooperative atmosphere, at least for a while.

The results of this study also lend support to the day-to-day decisions teachers in any class, including the adaptive class, need to make about time use. It was precisely this subcurricula that drew questioning looks from fellow staff members when the adaptive program was first implemented. The teachers felt unspoken, yet subtle pressures from those looks, which implied, "These children are gifted, and failing, and you're playing games with them?" The "Why?" in their looks can now be answered with greater assurance: The games make a substantial difference in student perceptions of themselves and others (Supplee, 1987/1988).

In the following section are two lesson plans. The first is a trust-building exercise and can be repeated several times. It is a good idea to have mats available for this if you are working inside. The second is a sample of an energizing activity, the kind that makes people feel good about themselves.

LESSON ONE
Trust Building

Objective: Students will be able to allow another student to touch their shoulders, walk behind them, and eventually do a "trust fall" into the arms of another.
Skills Level: Affective: responding, valuing, organizing
Materials: Mats, if indoors and students are ready for "trust fall"

Procedure:
1. Explain that different students have different levels of trust. The activity of the day is going to be students' helping one another in order to build trust among the people in the room. Tell students they will only need to do what they are comfortable with. At any time, anyone can say, "That's my limit for today," and all the rest of the students will respect that decision.
2. The teacher begins by working with a student who is quite trusting. The teacher faces the student and asks, "May I stand about a foot away from you?" If the response is yes, the teacher moves to that position.
3. A series of questions follows, each demanding greater trust on the part of the participants:
    "May I put my left hand on your shoulder?"
    "May I leave my hand there and step out of your line of sight?"
    "May I step behind you?"
    "I am behind you. May I put my two hands on your shoulders?"
    "I am stepping one step backwards. My hands are still on your shoulders. I am going to move them a few inches away. Can you rock backward until you touch my hands? I will catch you."
    "I am several steps behind you. I will catch you if you lean back. Can you lean back?"

4. After modeling, the teacher asks the students to pair up with a classmate and go through the steps with which they are comfortable.
5. After several coop days when this has been tried, students discuss whether they feel any difference from the first time they did the activity. Have them talk about why they feel as they do.

Evaluation: Students will exhibit a gradual increase in trust among class members until they are able to complete the trust fall either on a mat or outdoors.

LESSON TWO
Giraffes, Elephants, and Kangaroos*

Objective: (a) Students will feel energized. (b) Students will be able to enjoy a game where there are no winners.
Skills Level: Affective: responding, valuing
Materials: No special materials required

Procedure:
1. Students and teacher stand in a circle. One person is appointed the ring-master. As the ringmaster points at a person standing in the circle, that person and the two people on either side must make that person into the animal the ringmaster calls out: giraffe, elephant, or kangaroo.
2. To make the kangaroo, the person pointed to must create a pocket around the belly area with both arms. The two people on either side must make the kangaroo's tiny ears with their fingers placed in a circle beside the head of the person who was pointed to.
3. To make a giraffe, the person pointed to must create a long neck by raising both arms above the head, while the people on either side create spots with their hands.
4. To make an elephant, the person pointed to must create a long trunk by hanging both arms in front of the face while the people on either side create large ears by making circles with their arms.
5. The ringmaster is replaced by anyone who is pointed to that cannot immediately create the animal called out by the ringmaster.

Evaluation: Lots of laughter and no complaints as the children rotate through the ringmaster's position because of their mistakes.

Source: Train the Trainer Workshop, *Here's Looking at You, 2000,* Sept. 26–30, 1989, Princeton, New Jersey

Pro-Social Skills

Many children learn appropriate social skills through plentiful interaction with other children and adults in their formative years. But not all children do. Some have not had the benefit of preschool experiences; others have attended but were not well accepted by their peers even at very young ages. What most children pick up from their environment, some of our students needed help learning. Our pro-social skills curriculum was designed to teach children the non-intellective skills they were missing in the social area. They included:

1. Friendship-making skills
2. Skills for dealing with the feelings of others and the feelings that others engender in them
3. Alternatives to aggression with peers
4. Creative problem solving skills for handling unique social and other difficulties
5. Effective communication skills for use with both peers and adults.

To teach skills in the first three categories, we often used the book *Skill-streaming the Elementary School Child: A Guide for Teaching Pro-Social Skills* (McGinnis & Goldstein, 1984). This is a well-thought-out teacher's manual that task analyzes the social skills children need to develop. The book also offers useful guidelines that define successful practice of each skill. Role-playing ideas, to be used in class, and black-line masters, to be used as "homework," are an integral part of the McGinnis and Goldstein program. The workbook quality of the assignments and the role-playing format suggested were not so effective in teaching social skills as "rap sessions," which were used nearly exclusively in the UAG class.

Twenty-minute group rap sessions were held in the living-room area of the class. For each rap session, students focused on one pro-social skill suggested in McGinnis and Goldstein or on a social need that grew out of a real-life situation. Instead of a formula-like lesson, the students and teacher talked and listened to one another as they explored whether the students believed a skill was needed, and how the skill looked and sounded when it was practiced effectively. Once the students decided a skill was useful, they practiced it with one another in situations they described from their own experiences. Other group members offered feedback on the effectiveness of their performance.

A typical pro-social session was started by the teacher who focused the group, reminding them that even into adulthood, social skills need continuous practice and updating. Each student was invited to listen during the discussion for one new technique that he or she might try that day or the next to improve his or her own social skills.

When the teacher's abilities to use the pro-social skill under discussion were challenged, she provided an example from her own experience and explained how she dealt with it. Students were invited to describe to the group their own experiences that demonstrated a similar problem. If they handled their problem successfully, they were encouraged to explain what they did. If they had a problem or were only partially satisfied with their efforts, they asked other group members to suggest what might have worked better. Suggestions were usually plentiful. Because the children were not in the heat of an emotional situation, they were able to draw from their previous experiences and build on the observations of others, reflecting clearly on what worked and what had not.

During the last five minutes, each student was asked to state what new technique he or she would try to put into practice that week. The teacher noted these and followed up with each student through journal comments and private discussions. Occasionally, a student said, "But I never know what to say," or "I don't know how to do that," when a suggestion was made. Role-playing, with their classmates acting as tutors, allowed on-the-spot practice. When the teacher or students were aware that a child was trying a new behavior, an encouraging comment let that child know someone was aware and proud of her for trying to grow socially.

What follows is a sample of one lesson used in the pro-social skills lessons.

LESSON ONE

Joining In

Objective: (a) The student will know it is natural to feel shy when trying to join a new group. (b) The student will know an opening line to use when trying to join a group already in play. (c) The student will role-play the skill of joining in. (d) The student will apply the skill during the week in which it is taught and reflect on the experience.

Skills Level: Cognitive: knowledge, application

Affective: receiving, responding

Materials: Chart paper and markers

Procedures:
1. Teacher example: "You know, recently I was at a convention as a speaker. I didn't know anyone else there and I was feeling pretty lonely, and I was also feeling shy. Has anything like that ever happened to you?" (student responses)

2. Teacher example: "Do you know what I did? I started to think I probably wasn't the only one there who was alone. If other people were alone, they were probably feeling shy, too. I started to think what the others might do. I figured some would go to their rooms and be lonely for the whole convention. Others would get up the courage to introduce themselves to people directly. Probably still others would look for an appropriate time to ask if they could join a group. I thought about which one I would feel most comfortable doing. I decided to look for a group to join. I waited at lunch until I saw there was one seat left at a table that looked as if it wasn't being saved. I then asked the people at that table if they were saving the seat or if I could join them. They welcomed me and when I sat down, I started to get to know those people. I really met some interesting folks! What would you do?" (student responses)

3. "Sometimes students [have trouble joining a group already playing on the playground]. What are some of the steps you might take to join that group? [List on chart paper]. Which one is most like your style? How could you do something different from your normal style? Let's practice saying some of the 'opening lines' with the tone of voice and body language you might use that would make people want to let you join their group." (student suggestions, then practice with one another; feedback on the words and the tone of voice, specifying how the person on the receiving end felt)

4. "Think back to what I did to join the group at the table. The best thing happened to me because the group invited me to sit with them. What would have been the worst thing that might have happened if I asked to join the group?" (student responses) [list on chart]. "What could I have done if the first worst thing happened?" [students generate alternate solutions, which are listed next to the worse-case scenarios].

5. "Think about the problems you told me you had in joining in. Consider what could happen if you tried each suggestion you made before (both good and bad). What could you do if the worst thing happens?" Discuss whether the risk is worth the price in each case.

6. Role-play, using the student-generated scenarios, a positive and a negative response to a "joining-in" effort. Ask the student making the effort to join in, how he or she feels at the response, and whether the feeling can be handled. What would he or she do next?

7. Going around the group, in round-robin fashion, ask each student, "Tell me one new thing you learned today that you might try when you want to join a group." Record these and look for instances when the student tries to use them.

Evaluation: Students will be able to state opening lines and role-play a situation in which they are accepted into a group/not accepted into a group.

Another aspect of the pro-social skills curriculum, creative problem solving (CPS) skills, were taught using Parnes's (1972) model. When an unusual social problem arose (what is called "the mess" in creative problem solving terms), application of this method became the focus of the week's pro-social lesson. By using the model, students saw that they were able to maintain control in difficult situations. In UAG class, social problems included both situations at school with peers and teachers and at home with parents and siblings.

The first step in creative problem solving, once "the mess" has been identified, is to make some sense out of it. Students learn to list what they already know about "the mess," then ask themselves what they still need to know. They brainstorm a list of questions, then go back and brainstorm all the possibilities for finding the answers to those questions. They search for all the related, helpful facts by viewing the problem from as many different perspectives as possible. This is the fact-finding stage of creative problem solving.

The next step is problem finding or idea finding. This is the point at which students learn to use brainstorming, indulge in fantasy, try synectics, and use SCAMPER (substitute, combine, adapt, magnify–minify, put to other uses, eliminate, reverse–rearrange) techniques (Eberle, 1977) to increase their innovative thinking. In this step, students list their responses to stems such as "How might I . . . ?" "In what ways might I . . . ?" or "What ideas might I produce to . . . ?" while looking at the problem from different vantage points. When done, they stop and ask themselves, "Now that I've looked at this mess from as many different points of view as I can, what seems to be the *real* problem? What do I really want to accomplish and why?" The essential next step is to define the problem carefully, to broaden, reword, or subdivide it so that the problem can be better understood and more easily solved.

In the solution-finding stage, students establish criteria against which the alternatives that appear to be good ideas are tested and the consequences of each alternative considered. Ideas are modified until the students reach the acceptance-finding stage.

Although somewhat cumbersome at first, the process improved over time. It is a good idea to practice with some relatively minor problems so that the process is familiar before a major crisis arises. By doing so, the tool is available when large troubles surface, as happened with Juliet.

Juliet lived in an especially difficult family situation: Her parents were chemically dependent. A deeply religious person, she turned to prayer for the answers to her problem. This helped her to the extent that she felt better for a while, believing that God would not desert her. But the underlying problem did not resolve itself, and Juliet became more and more depressed. We suggested to Juliet that she not abandon prayer, because it was helpful to her, but try applying CPS as well to see if she might find another way to help manage her problem.

Her trust in the group was such that she agreed and asked for time to discuss the problem during a pro-social lesson. With the emotional support of the other students clearly evident, through her tears Juliet explained "the mess." Gently the students asked questions until they felt they knew the facts as Juliet saw them. Together they brainstormed what else they needed to know to help her solve her problem. The discussion brought out what students had learned in health about alcohol dependency. They tried to help Juliet by reminding her that she didn't cause her parents to start drinking or to keep drinking. Alcohol dependency was their problem, and because it was theirs, she couldn't fix it. She could only fix things that were her problem. They looked at the portion of the problem that Juliet had made hers. Her problem was too much work. She was trying to do her own work as a student and also trying to do the work of her parents because she felt responsible for her brothers and sisters. The students' fact-finding also brought out some community resources that were available to help Juliet, whose biggest fear was that her family would need to split up in order to get her help.

In the problem-finding stage, Juliet tried to restate the real problem. The statement began as: "I have to make my parents stop drinking. They drink until they're drunk, and then I have to take care of the other kids." The statement became: "I am not old enough to be a parent for my younger brothers and sisters; I need someone to care for me, too. I don't know what choices to make so we stay together and I don't go crazy." Phrased this way, part of the problem was hers and there were places to go for help.

With the group, Juliet determined four alternatives in addition to prayer that might help her deal with her problem. One was moving out of her house and finding a friend's family to live with. This had the "price" of splitting up her family and neglecting her brothers and sisters, something she definitely did not want to do. Another was to keep doing what she was doing but also talking to the school psychologist when things were especially hard to bear. This had the "price" that other people would think she was "crazy." Another idea was getting someone to take her to Alateen meetings, with the "price" that she would have to let others know about her parents' alcohol problem, and she would be imposing herself on a friend's family. The last was getting counseling at our county mental health center with the "price" of needing to find a ride with someone she could trust and still being called "crazy" if anyone found out.

Juliet and the other students in class talked through the possible good and bad consequences of each alternative. Then Juliet decided which alternative best matched her criteria of keeping the family together and having a consequence that she felt was worth the risk. She chose two, making an appointment with the school counselor and finding someone to take her to Alateen. She initiated both steps. In class she practiced what she would say on the phone to find out about Alateen. She practiced how to ask for an appointment with the psychologist. She was able to take it from there.

Juliet's home situation was unchanged, but her response to it changed. She learned she wasn't helpless. She could do something in addition to praying to make her own life better. Had her first steps not worked well, she still had another alternative to try. When Juliet first shared her problem with the teachers, they could have told her what to do, could have initiated the contacts with outside agencies for her, but would have robbed her of a chance to feel the power of making decisions for herself and to develop conscious control over her own existence.

CPS is not a cure-all. CPS doesn't work all the time because there are some things that simply have to be endured. The price for changing is higher than the price for enduring. But a student who *decides* to bear a problem after considering the alternatives is far more empowered than one who never considers that there might be another way. Likewise, there are ethical dilemmas that present themselves to the teachers when children in an adaptive class begin to trust the teacher and the students enough to share what they see as their problems. Suppose Juliet had shared an instance of clear-cut child abuse. By law, the teacher would have had to report the instance to the Division of Youth and Family Services at once. Doing so might violate the trust Juliet felt, but child abuse is serious. It is not ethical for a teacher to ignore abuse in the name of practicing the CPS process with the children.

The last segment of the pro-social skills curriculum was a unit on communications skills. One resource for teaching effective communications was *Games Children Should Play* (Cihak & Heron, 1980). Another good source was *The Second Centering Book* (Hendricks & Roberts, 1977). The goal was to teach children to say what they needed to in an assertive, but nonthreatening manner. They also needed to learn how to listen and really hear, nonjudgmentally and with accuracy, what others had to say. The following lesson gives an example of a rap session on reflective listening.

LESSON ONE
Reflective Listening

Objective: (a) The students will know that reflective listening means hearing what another person says, then restating it for that person in different words so that both are sure they understand the same idea. (b) The students will apply reflective listening in a hypothetical situation.

Skills Level: Cognitive: knowledge, application

Affective: receiving, responding

Materials: No special materials needed

Procedures:

1. Focus the students by reminding them that people sometimes have dis-
    agreements because they have real trouble understanding each other's
    meaning even though they understand the words. One way to avoid mis-
    understanding is to use a technique called "reflective listening," when
    you think communication is not as clear as it needs to be to avoid a
    misunderstanding.
2. Give the definition of reflective listening.
3. Try a few examples. The teacher makes a statement such as, "When
    you're done, I want you to put your work away and find something to
    keep you busy until the next lesson." Talk about some of the things that
    might happen when a teacher makes this statement. Then ask, "Do you
    think the teacher really means you can do whatever you want?" If not,
    you can clarify what the teacher means by beginning a sentence with,
    "When you said . . ." or "Do I understand correctly that . . . ?" or "Do
    you mean . . . ?" and then saying in different words what you think the
    teacher meant. For example, in the statement made by the teacher
    above, you might say, "When you said, 'find something to keep
    you busy,' did you mean we could make our own choice of anything
    quiet we wanted to do, or are there only certain things we are allowed
    to do?"
4. Have a student role-play the student and another role-play the teacher
    to see what responses are given.
5. Discuss for a minute how this might solve a problem before it started.
    Can the students think of other benefits? Any drawbacks? If there are
    drawbacks, are they worth the benefits?
6. Have several other statements available so students can practice rephras-
    ing them to be sure both the student and teacher understand the same
    thing. Here are several for starters:
    > While we are on the bus for our field trip, I want quiet.
    > You may talk softly in the cafeteria.
    > Jason, please help Mary with her homework.
    > I want this entire room as clean as a whistle.
    > I want you to watch your baby sister until I get home from the
    > store.
    > Do your chores or there will be no dessert.
7. Ask the students to generate some examples of statements they have
    heard that have caused them trouble because they didn't understand
    what the other meant. Have them role-play listening reflectively.

Evaluation: The student will correctly rephrase the words of another to the
satisfaction of both students.

Stress-Reduction Skills

Stress is an inescapable fact of life. It is not always a result of negative experiences. Very happy events, such as weddings and the birth of a child, can be as stressful as losing a parent, a friend, or a pet. Isolated events may temporarily cause us problems. What is most debilitating is constant stress. Children are as subject to stress as adults. Many of the children we taught lived with incredible daily stress either at home, at school, or both. Some of their stress was externally caused. Some they generated themselves. Stress burdened them both physically and psychologically. What they needed to learn were ways to identify the stressors in their lives and to manage themselves in such a way that stress was not incapacitating.

Most children do not have effective stress-reduction skills. Seldom are such skills taught deliberately. Those who do not have built-in sensors to pick up the cues from society about ways to deal with childhood stress or those who are so stressed that they become blind to cues need deliberate, direct instruction. What the stress-reduction curriculum tried to do was to help children identify stressors that affect many people, pinpoint those they found especially difficult for themselves, and establish ways to deal with these stressors effectively.

One of the materials that is recommended highly is called *Coping for Kids: A Complete Stress Control Program for Students Ages 8–18* (Herzfeld & Powell, 1986). This is a series of tapes and organized lessons that cover many of the objectives in our curriculum. It was supplemented with teacher-designed activities to reach the following objectives:

1. Recognizing feelings
2. Naming feelings
3. Stating the feelings being experienced
4. Learning what stress can do to physical and mental well-being
5. Learning various mental relaxation techniques
6. Identifying the three ways most people deal with anger:
   Internalizing
   Reacting to the person or thing causing the anger
   Reacting to another unrelated person or thing
7. Identifying the way they usually deal with anger
8. Identifying the healthiest way to deal with anger
9. Dealing with fear, boredom, jealousy, embarrassment, failure, and other "negative" feelings
10. Using creative imagery as a stress-reduction technique
11. Determining physical outlets for stress that can be used almost anywhere

12. Identifying and then participating in creative outlets for stress (including the visual, performing, and practical arts)
13. Identifying the role professional counselors play
14. Knowing when and how to ask for the help of a professional counselor

Instruction began in stress-reduction skills by helping the students learn to identify, and then name, what they were feeling at any particular time. They got a clear, consistent message that all people have feelings all the time. The feelings themselves were uncontrollable. They just existed. Some of the feelings were pleasant, some were neutral, and some were unpleasant, but people were not good or bad people because of the feelings they had. What mattered was what people did about their feelings, because constant stress, whether from pleasant or unpleasant events had a bad effect on our bodies and minds.

Most of the children had little difficulty with positive feelings. What gave them trouble, both in identifying and in naming, were the unpleasant feelings. Anger was particularly troublesome. Many students denied that they ever felt angry. What follows is one lesson of several that was used to help students learn what anger is and what might be happening to their denied anger (see Figures 8.1, 8.2, and 8.3).

LESSON ONE
Recognizing What People Do With Anger

Objective: (a) The students will know three basic ways people deal with the anger they feel. (b) The students will be able to apply the theory to their own lives and recognize how they normally deal with anger.
Skills Level: Cognitive: knowledge, application
     Affective: receiving, attending
Materials: Chart paper and markers

Procedures:
1. Teacher example: "We have learned that all people have feelings, both positive ones and negative ones. We also learned that our feelings are *our* feelings. They are not 'good' or 'bad,' but what we do about them may be 'good' or 'bad.' Today, let's talk some more about anger. In our class, we have an agreement to solve angry feelings with the person who can do something about it, usually the person with whom we feel angry. In other words, we deal directly with the person. In this room that is a safe thing to do. But it isn't always safe in the real world, especially when someone more powerful than we are makes us angry. Recently, for example, I felt very angry when [give specific example]."

Figure 8.1: Direct Anger.

The healthiest way to deal with anger is to work out the problem with the person causing the anger.

Figure 8.2: Power figure building a wall to deflect anger.

In some cases, the price to pay for dealing with the person who causes our anger is too great. In effect, a wall is built that keeps us from dealing directly with the problem.

Figure 8.3: Indirect anger.

When a wall is built, our anger doesn't disappear. Instead, we do one of three things. We may direct the anger at ourselves, we may misplace our anger by directing it at another less powerful person, or we may get back at the person causing our anger indirectly. People using this technique usually find a sensitive spot to exploit in the person causing their anger. Some examples of this type of indirect attack by children on their parents include failing in school, becoming pregnant, or turning to drugs or alcohol.

2. "Are there things that have made you feel angry lately with a person more powerful than you?" (student response)
3. "When I felt angry, I [give example of way in which anger was demonstrated, e.g., scolding my own children for something minor that would not normally upset me.] It reminded me of a lesson I learned a long time ago about things people do with their anger, a lesson I forgot when I [scolded my children]. I will share the lesson with you so you can help me remember better ways to handle anger, and I can help you when you feel angry."
4. "When a powerful person makes us angry, we usually feel in our minds that there is a one-way wall between that person and us. The other person can make us mad, but our anger bounces off the wall and we can't get back at him directly because the 'price' we pay is too big. That doesn't make our anger go away. Our mind still has to do something with the anger. Usually, our mind does one of three things:

—It can find a way to go around the wall and get back indirectly at the person who made us angry

—It can find another target for anger (as I did with my children)

—It can turn the anger back on ourselves and make us say things to ourselves like, 'How could I be so stupid!' lowering our self-esteem, or it can give us ulcers or high blood pressure.

Let's see if we can think of some examples of times we have seen people use each of these methods." (student responses)

5. "Think about your own life, now, for a minute. Try to remember what you did with your anger the last time a more powerful person made you angry. Keep it to yourself. Now think about whether this is what you always do with your anger."

6. Ask the students who feel comfortable sharing to tell what they normally do with their anger.

7. Say, "At the next meeting, we will talk about some of the healthier ways of dealing with anger when the price of dealing directly is too high."

Evaluation: Students will be able to state how they normally deal with anger at a more powerful person.

Once the students learned to identify and name the things in their lives that caused them stress, several instructional activities were implemented. The school psychologist taught several progressive relaxation techniques to the children. These were followed up in class on a regular basis using the relaxation and practice exercises from *200 Ways of Using Creative Imagery in the Classroom* (Bagley & Hess, 1982). Several imaging and relaxation strategies that were used are also described in *Optimizing Learning: The Integrative Education Model in the Classroom* (Clark, 1986) and *Growing Up Gifted* (Clark, 1983a).

Guest speakers and field trips were a wonderful way to help children understand the physical consequences of prolonged stress. A local hospital may have an educational director or public relations head who can suggest an appropriate speaker or set up a field trip. With some tact and luck, it may be possible to arrange for the children to meet with a physical therapist. The same resource person may be able to help children understand how physical activity can be useful to relieve stress and tension. Ask whether a special exercise plan can be developed for each child through your guest speaker or while visiting the hospital.

If a hospital visit is arranged, it may be possible to also meet the hospital's nutritionist at the same time. This is a person who can discuss the proper diet to better prepare the body to deal with stress. The clear links that exist between a healthy body and mind make it essential that the children learn the connections between their diet and exercise choices, and long-term physical and mental health.

A third instructional strategy used to help students manage stress was teaching them how creative outlets could help manage tension. This was an ideal occasion to establish a permanent creative-expression learning center with changing activities the children could try. There are literally hundreds of resource materials that are available concerning art, music, drama, crafts, creative (no heat) cooking, building, dance, mime and so on. The difficulty is more likely to be choosing from the abundance. A few guidelines may help.

For starters, the children deserved to be introduced to the masters of any art or craft. The UAG class began with a series of center activities that allowed the students to explore the world of sculpture. Several activities allowed the children to try to create sculpture similar to that of Alexander Calder, Louise Nevelson, and other contemporary sculptors. A sample lesson follows:

LESSON ONE
Sculpture Center

Objective: (a) Students will recognize the stylistic characteristics of the work of a contemporary sculptor (in this case, Louise Nevelson). (b) Students will create a piece of sculpture similar in style to that created by the sculptor.

Skills Level: Cognitive: comprehension, application, analysis
Affective: receiving, responding

Materials: Styrofoam or cardboard meat trays; found objects; black and gold spray paints; art books containing large photographs of Nevelson's work

Procedures:
1. Have students examine photographs of several works of the sculptor under study. Ask students what they see that looks similar in each of the pieces in the photographs. Then have them analyze the differences between the pieces. Finally, have them decide what characteristics would make them suspect a work was by that artist. How would they know that the piece was an imitation and not an original?
2. Introduce the materials in the center. Explain that students may use these to try to create similar pieces to those they have seen.
3. Ask them to develop a list of criteria by which they might (not must) judge their own piece.

Evaluation: Students will complete a piece similar to the artist and be able to explain how it does and does not meet the criteria the class established.

This series of center activities on sculpture culminated with a trip to the Guggenheim and Whitney museums in New York City. There the children were guided by a young woman who knew the interests of the children through exhibits of the actual work of the artists the students had tried to emulate. The guide also, based on conversations during the planning of the trip, selected several other less-familiar artists to share with the children. What a joy it was to see a museum through children's eyes and to see the interaction between the students and the guide! How exciting it was when, as they were walking through a museum, they pointed ahead to say, "There's a Nevelson!" or "Look, isn't that a Rauschenberg?" and to hear them giggle at pop art, seriously critique a special exhibit, give reasons for their selection of a favorite piece, and decide ways they could try to imitate new works they saw. At the Whitney Museum, the children were introduced to twentieth-century painters as well as sculptors. The interest generated led to centers that explored color and the art of painting. Later, students were encouraged to try music as a way of expressing the same idea or feeling that had been expressed through a painting. Finally, the expression of the same and other messages through mime and dance and theater were explored.

A second guideline is to vary the activities in the center so they do not always focus on the visual and performing arts. The practical arts should be included as well, with quilting, cooking, and woodworking projects small enough to be completed in a short time frame. Weaving, using various media, is another good choice for a center and proved to be a favorite in the UAG room. There is something very calming about the repetitive nature of the over-and-under pattern-making. Rug making and stitchery provided the same feeling. Our students often chose to do work at the creative center on a practical project if they needed "time out" because of angry or upset feelings. A secondary benefit was the wonderful practice it provided for those who had difficulty with small motor control! The beauty of a finished work of art is far more motivating than a nicely written, but meaningless, handwriting practice sheet.

EVALUATION DATA

In order to measure growth in students' affect, we used the Coopersmith Self-Esteem Inventory (Coopersmith, 1981). This was administered on a pre- and post-basis for group results. The results suggest strongly that what we did worked. Table 8.1 compares students' self-esteem using raw scores. The mean gain in the overall scores was $+6.77$, a mean increase of 5.9 percent. Seven of the nine students showed gains ranging from $+2$ to $+28$ points out of a possible 100 points.

Table 8.1 Increase in General Self-Esteem as Measured by the Coopersmith
Self-Esteem Inventory

	PRE-TEST		POST-TEST		CHANGE	
SUBJECT 1	general	lie	general	lie	general	lie
Doug	32	(1)	38	(1)	+6	0
Cal	76	(0)	92	(1)	+16	+1
Juliet	68	(3)	52	(2)	−9	−1
Helen	40	(6)	24	(2)	−16	−4
David	42	(0)	70	(2)	+28	+2
Marty	90	(3)	92	(3)	+2	0
Ricardo	60	(3)	78	(2)	+18	−1
Karen	34	(0)	42	(2)	+8	0
Marcia	60	(2)	68	(2)	+8	0

The test also includes a defensiveness (lie) score. The purpose of having
this score is to determine whether the students were being honest in their
answers to the questions about their self-esteem. A student with a high defensiveness score is probably giving the answers he or she thinks the examiner
wants to hear rather than what is true. If the lie score is low, the answers given
are probably valid. In a pre- and post-test situation, if the scores remain unchanged, it is likely that the answers are reliable. In our class, these scores,
for all students except Juliet and Helen, remained unchanged or in the acceptable range of +/− 1 out of a possible eight. An overall decrease in defensiveness of 2.7 percent was shown. The students who had decreasing self-
esteem scores also showed a decrease in defensiveness scores, indicating that
the pre-test scores were probably less valid than the post-test. The student
whose scores appear to show the greatest drop in total self-esteem also showed
the greatest drop in defensiveness. It may be that her self-esteem didn't
change but that her honesty increased.

The academic/school subscale of the Coopersmith inventory measured
improvement in satisfaction in school. A mean gain for the nine students was
+ 1.33 out of eight items used, or an increase of 13.3 percent in school-related
self-esteem. These data suggest that students' attitudes towards school substantially improved from January (pre-test) to June (post-test).

We recommend that you not omit any of the subcurricula before trying
them. Modify them later to suit your group.

FINAL THOUGHTS

In carrying out the affective curriculum, we must outwardly acknowledge to the children that there are times in most lives when people find it very

difficult to deal with their problems. Despite their best efforts to be positive and to be in control of what they choose to do, everyone falls victim to chance factors. When life gets too overwhelming, there are places to find help.

Most UAG children eventually entered counseling while in this program. By openly discussing what may signal the need for counseling, what to expect when in counseling, and how to deal with any teasing that they may experience and that can be so hurtful, the way was smoothed for these children to benefit more quickly from the help they needed.

Parents were not left out of this process. The next chapter is devoted to a curriculum that was used with them to help them develop more effective parenting skills. They learned what their children would be learning, and they learned to distinguish between "passing phases" and behaviors that signaled the need for professional help. The more involved they became in supporting their children's affective growth and development, the more quickly the children achieved success and returned to the mainstream.

SUMMARY

The chapter opened by considering the points of view of Whitmore (1980), who believed inappropriate schools contribute to underachievement among the gifted, and Rimm (1983), who believed underachievement is a family problem. My position is that the cause doesn't matter. The problem is an interactive one that compounds itself unless behaviors are changed. Behavior modification is not used to bring about change because such change relies totally on extrinsic motivation. In the UAG class, we expended effort to develop students' sense of intrinsic motivation, which has been shown to be a key for disadvantaged youth trying to become successful. The roles of the teacher as facilitator and model in the process were explained, with the discussion being grounded in Vygotsky's theory of the zone of proximal development.

The content of the affective subcurricula was presented with objectives, sample lesson plans, and instructional strategies offered. The subcurricula included group self-direction skills, pro-social skills, cooperative sports and games to develop trust and group cohesiveness, work-study skills, communication skills, creative problem solving, and stress-reduction skills.

Evaluation data suggests that students' general sense of self-esteem as well as their school self-esteem grew dramatically. The UAG class was the only identifiable change in their lives, so it is reasonable to assume that the experiences there played a part in their improved outlook.

CHAPTER 9

For the Parents

In the past, attempts at reversing underachievement among the gifted have had mixed results. Counseling has been tried most often, with some evidence pointing to the success and some to the failure of this technique. McCowan (1968) worked with groups of male high school students: In one group, counseling involved students and their parents; in another, only parents were involved; in a third, only students were involved; and in a fourth, neither parents nor students received counseling. Post-testing showed that parent counseling was effective in improving academic achievement. The combination of student and parent counseling was also effective. Perkins and Wicas (1971), again working with male high school students, found even more encouraging results when counseling only mothers of the underachievers.

Experiments with elementary school students (Mink, 1964; Ohlsen & Gazda, 1965; Winkler, Teigland, Munger & Kranzler, 1965) found no significant improvement in elementary-age underachievers. The Mink study, however, involved only five hours of work with the parents of four students in seventh and four in eighth grade. Sessions were devoted to discussion of topics such as college attendance, children's aptitudes, and vocational opportunities. Ohlsen and Gazda (1965) were critical of their own design, and Winkler et al. (1965) did not include parents in counseling at all.

The findings of research on counseling the parents of elementary-aged children does not suggest that counseling the parents of young underachievers is ineffective. Both the design and the number of cases studied have been too limited to draw such a conclusion. Work with high school students has suggested that appropriate parent counseling may be effective in reversing underachievement. It seemed reasonable, therefore, to design a program, modeled on those that had been successful for high school students, for parents of our elementary students.

PARENT PROGRAM DESIGN

Special Considerations

It is important to remember that the parents of underachieving students probably feel a great deal of frustration. As the screening procedure was designed, their children, who are enrolled in an adaptive program for gifted underachievers, were highly successful when they entered school but gradually came to suffer academic, emotional, and/or social problems. Since the children were "okay" before school and are "not okay" now, it is tempting for parents to shift the entire responsibility for the problem to the school or to the child, who may be called lazy or intractable. Conversely, the school may find it easy to attribute all fault to the home causing the parents to feel guilty or also to blame the child.

In reality, it is quite likely that an intricate, interactive web of circumstances have compounded the child's difficulty and have alienated the parents and school. Unrealistic and conflicting demands easily create stress among the child, the school, and the parents (Seigel, 1986). An important challenge is to reestablish trust between the two agencies most significant in the child's life, home and school, in order to lessen the stress.

Philosophy

The primary position we took in our program was that parents are the ultimate educators of the child. The school's attempts to effect change, we believed, would have far more chance of success if parents were respected and viewed as people who were doing their best to raise their child effectively. We believed that they would be able to do an even better job if they had new alternatives to consider, were given a chance to evaluate the merit of those alternatives, and were given time to practice new behaviors.

A second position we adopted was that it was as important to listen to parents about their ideas, concerns, and needs as it was to listen to their children. It was just as important to share alternative approaches to help the parents solve daily problems as it was to help the students see various ways of solving their own social, emotional, and academic problems.

Implementation

Our initial contact with the parents occurred when a child was suggested as a candidate for the program. The letters to the parents about the screening procedures needed to convey warmth towards and respect for the parents. If a child was selected for the program, a pamphlet was sent to the parents. This pamphlet, found in Appendix E, defined underachievement among the gifted, described how the alternative program differed from the regular classroom program, offered examples of changes that occurred in students in similar programs, and encouraged the parents' attendance at the parent support group. A schedule of meetings and a listing of goals for the parent program was included.

Two-hour meetings were held weekly once the classes for the students began. The nine sessions included one hour of group instructional time conducted by the school psychologist and adaptive classroom teacher as a team. A second hour was set aside for informal discussion over refreshments, for raising and talking about typical problems that parents felt needed to be addressed with their children, and for individual conferences between parents and the school psychologist.

The parents who were involved felt the meetings were helpful. They wished to continue meeting, and we did so, eventually finding bimonthly meetings most convenient. The parents also decided to include the children on occasion. The consulting psychologist concurred, but recommended that a very structured situation, using carefully planned games such as those suggested in Robert Schachter's (1986) play therapy, be provided. Because this method is *therapy*, we strongly caution you not to use Schachter's methods unless a trained psychologist is present. Less effective, but useful in opening communication between generations, were commercially available games: Bridges, the Ungame, and Scruples were three we found that were fun and involved sharing thoughts and ideas.

In about one-third of the students' cases, both parents attended the evening sessions, another third had one parent in attendance, and the final third did not attend at all during the first year. At the close of the first semester in the program, students with both parents in attendance made the greatest affective and cognitive gains. The students with neither parent in attendance had made the fewest gains. Though the sample was too small to allow us to draw firm conclusions, and a multitude of other factors could have been operating to cause such results, the findings are intriguing.

THE CURRICULUM

In the following pages are included all the structured lessons that were used during the first year of the program with the parents of the children in the UAG class. The classes were called, "A Gift of Time and Understanding." The goals of this program were to help parents

1. Develop an understanding of some of the possible causes of underachievement in school

2. Examine their expectations for their child, to determine the appropriateness of such expectations
3. Explore their personal family structure and dynamics
4. Practice positive communication skills
5. Develop an understanding of the problems that require intervention and the sources of such help
6. Have the opportunity to discuss problems with the support group and develop self-help systems.

Each of these goals has been broken down into objectives. The lessons to help parents reach each of the objectives are provided. Strategies used by the teaching team in the UAG program are described, but they are certainly not the only ones that could be used. The materials used in the original classes, some of which were used by the instructors and some of which were available to the parents, are also cited.

LESSON PLANS
A Gift of Time and Understanding: A Program for Parents
Objectives, Strategies, and Resources

Goal 1: Parents will develop an understanding of some of the possible causes of underachievement in school.

Objectives: Parents will learn that
1. Social, behavioral, and academic problems can contribute to underachievement.
2. Some causes of social and behavioral problems include lack of recognition of uneven development leading to unrealistic expectations, a lack of social skills, perfectionism, difficulty accepting the limitations of others, and various emotional problems.
3. Some of the reasons children have academic problems include learning disabilities, creative/divergent personality attributes, poor work-study skills, boredom, and social/emotional behavior problems.

Possible Strategies:
• A break-the-ice game requiring physical movement (e.g., each person names a thing he thinks about a lot or that is important to him and writes it on a card held in view for the others; a ball of string is tossed to one participant; that person finds another person with a card connected in some way to hers; she tosses the ball to that person, who does likewise with another; the ball may not be tossed to the same person twice; when all have caught the ball once, it is rewound from the last to the first person; the catcher must state what he thinks the connection was; the thrower confirms or explains a

different connection [Clark, 1983b]). A discussion of the differences between people's ideas and of the feelings they have as they are put on the spot to "answer in class," can lead into a discussion of children's differences, including those things that cause them to underachieve.

• Presentation by the school psychologist on social and behavior problems common in underachievers.

• Presentation by the gifted and talented teacher, explaining the commonly observed academic problems that gifted underachievers evidence.

• Questions and answers follow.

Suggested Materials:
Clark, B. (1983a). *Growing up gifted.* Columbus, OH: Merrill.
Janos, P. M., Fung, H. & Robinson, N. (1985). Self-concept, self-esteem and peer relations among gifted children who feel different. *Gifted Child Quarterly, 29*(2), 78–81.
Seigel, P. (March 1986). An untitled paper presented at the Emotional Development of the Gifted: Promising Practices for Professionals and Parents conference. Center for the Study and Education of the Gifted, Teachers College, Columbia University.
Whitmore, J. R. (1980). *Giftedness, conflict, and underachievement.* Boston: Allyn and Bacon.

*   *   *

Goal 2: Parents will examine their expectations for their child to determine the appropriateness of those expectations.

Objectives: Parents will learn
1.   Human developmental stages and will identify in which stage each member of their family is at present.
2.   The "job" associated with each stage, according to Erikson.
3.   To draw a diagram representative of their child's physical, academic, emotional, and social development to help them visualize a realistic concept of their child.
4.   That they, as all parents, need to accept the figurative "death" of their ideal child and the reality of their actual child.
5.   Some of the emotional and social needs of the real child.

Possible Strategies:
• Presentation by the psychologist of developmental stages and passages.

• Activity led by the gifted coordinator: Diagramming a schematic of their child—the ideal and the real.

• Physical encoding: Role-playing the "burial" of the perfect child.
• Viewing the Council for Exceptional Children sound filmstrip #1, "The Emotional and Social Needs of Gifted Children," a two-filmstrip series highlighting the real issues gifted children face and the emotions such issues are likely to elicit (may be referred to later when dealing with the advocacy role of parents).

Suggested Materials:
   Outline drawings of "dream child"
   Schematic diagram for developing picture of real child
   Markers, pens, or pencils
   Box for "grave"
   Filmstrip from Council for Exceptional Children, "The Emotional and Social Needs of Gifted Children."

Bricklin, P. M. (1983). Working with the parents of learning-disabled/gifted children. In L. H. Fox, L. Brody, & D. Tobin (Eds.), *Learning disabled/gifted children*. (pp. 101–116). Baltimore, MD: University Park Press.
Davits, J. & Davits, L. (1979). *Making it: 40 & beyond: Surviving the mid-life crisis*. Minneapolis, MN: Winston Press.
Erickson, E. H. (1950). *Childhood and society*. New York: W. W. Norton.
Gesell, A. & Ilg, F. L. (1946). *The child from five to ten*. New York: Harper and Row.
Sheehy, G. (1976). *Passages: Predictable crises of adult life*. New York: E. P. Dutton.

*   *   *

Goal 3: Parents will explore their personal family structure and dynamics.

Objectives: Parents will learn to
1. Diagram their immediate and extended family constellations.
2. Explore the dynamics within the family, using sociograms.
3. Diagram the communication patterns within the family.
4. Examine family attitudes of other members of the family toward the child to know more about the emotional environment of the child.
5. Discuss types of parental roles (authoritarian, authoritative, and democratic) using the Socratic method and a continuum to learn:
       What beliefs can exist about the parental role
       What consequences exist for each belief system
       What their own parents believed
       What others in the group believe
       What they personally believe at this point in time
6. Understand the basic responsibilities of parenthood and be able to order them in terms of personal importance. Included for these children

should be the need for the parents to be the child's advocate and techniques for doing so effectively.

7. Distinguish between helping and doing for the child; between encouragement and praise (to develop internal motivation rather than external), and between positive and negative methods of prompting desired behavior in children.

Possible Strategies:

• Presentation by school social worker, school psychologist, or family therapist on family dynamics.

• Activity led by gifted coordinator: diagramming family constellation.

• Activity led by school social worker, school psychologist, or family therapist: Using sociogram technique to determine interactions, communication patterns, and power structure.

• Discussion led by psychologist: How to define attitudes of people and how these contribute to the emotional climate the child experiences.

• Presentation by social worker on three basic family types: authoritarian, authoritative, and democratic.

• Activity led by gifted coordinator: Use of continuum and Socratic method to explore values behind each family type and the consequences of each approach.

• Presentation by psychologist on responsibilities of parenthood. Values-clarification activity, that is, ranking each activity in order of importance to the individuals present. Sharing and discussing thoughts on differences with group.

• Presentation by psychologist on helping/doing for a child. Group classification activity, using sample behaviors and placing them in the proper category. Differences of opinion are discussed.

Suggested Materials:

Dreikurs, R. & Soltz, V. (1964). *Children: The challenge.* New York: Hawthorn Books.

Lerner, H. G. (1985). *The dance of anger: A woman's guide to changing the patterns of intimate relationships.* New York: Harper & Row.

Mace, N. J. & Rabins, P. B. (1981). *The 36-hour day: A family guide to caring for persons with Alzheimer's disease, related dementing illnesses, and memory loss in later life.* Baltimore, MD: Johns Hopkins University Press.

Montemayor, R. (1984). Changes in parent and peer relationships between childhood and adolescence: A research agenda for gifted adolescence. *Journal for the Education of the Gifted, 8*(1), 2–23.

Silverstone, B. & Hyman, H. K. (1976). *You and your aging parent: A guide to understanding emotional, physical, and financial needs.* New York: Pantheon Books.

Torman, W. (1976). *Family constellation.* New York: Springer.

Wagonseller, B. R. & McDowell, R. L. (1979). *You and your child: A common sense approach to successful parenting*. Champaign, IL: Research Press.

*   *   *

Goal 4: Parents will practice positive communication skills

Objectives: Parents will learn
1.   That communication involves both listening and talking.
2.   Ways to listen effectively.
3.   To rephrase complaints using "I" messages.
4.   To organize time to make space in their lives for communication about feelings and thoughts, not just "business" talk, with family members.
5.   The technique of the family meeting to consider family business.

Possible Strategies:
• Presentation by coordinator of programs for the gifted, explaining kinds of lessons children have on communication (using *Games Children Should Play*, etc.).
• Discussion of need for parents to understand the way their children will be trying to communicate with them; ways to reinforce their positive attempts; ways to respond.
• Lesson by coordinator, teaching parents effective listening, to include reflective listening and "I" statements as well as responses that encourage children to share feelings, but solve own problems.
• Discussion led by psychologist on the importance of scheduling time for family conversations.
• Lesson on time management and organization. Activity of listing "to do's" for tomorrow and arranging them in order of importance—to include time to talk to children and spouse.
• Videotape of students' class meeting as a way to deal with the "business" of class, including problems, responsibilities, and feelings. Translation by parents of this technique for family use to deal with family business; the technique will emphasize: (a) setting a regular, inviolate time; (b) an equal voice for all family members; (c) setting of ground-rules so that only items parents feel comfortable allowing the children to help decide are broached; (d) starting each meeting with something positive.

Suggested Materials:
Brownstone, J. E. & Dye, C. J. (1973). *Communication workshop for parents of adolescents: Leader's guide*. Champaign, IL: Research Press.
Brownstone, J. E. & Dye, C. J. (1973). *Communication workshop for parents of adolescents: Parents' review*. Champaign, IL: Research Press.

Cihak, M. K. & Heron, B. J. (1980). *Games children should play.* Santa Monica, CA: Goodyear.
Gaver, A. & Maxlish, E. (1980). *How to talk so kids will listen and listen so kids will talk.* New York: Avon.

*   *   *

Goal 5: Parents will develop an understanding of the problems requiring intervention and sources of help available to them.

Objectives: Parents will learn
1.   To distinguish between "phases," which can be expected at certain ages and serious problems needing intervention.
2.   The role the school is able to play in intervention.
3.   Community resources available to help deal with serious problems.

Possible Strategies:
• Review stages of life (Erik Erikson in Stevens, 1983).
• Introduce Gesell and Ilg, T. Berry Brazelton, and other resources that suggest normal developmental stages for children and adolescents.
• Presentations by resource people from the school's child-study team and local mental health center.

Suggested Resources:
Speakers from the Mental Health Center at the local hospital
Sound filmstrip: *Pre-teen stress,* Walt Disney films
Child-study team personnel

Gesell, A. & Ilg, F. L. (1946). *The child from five to ten.* New York: Harper and Row.
Stevens, R. (1983). *Eric Erikson: An introduction.* New York: St. Martin's.

*   *   *

Goal 6: Parents will have the opportunity to discuss problems with the support group and to develop self-help systems.

Objectives: Parents will have the opportunity to
1.   Broach personal and family problems within the support group under the leadership of a trained psychologist.
2.   Develop friendships and communication with other families having similar experiences with their children.
3.   Set up individual meetings with a trained psychologist.

4. Invite their children to structured game-night sessions so they and the children can practice their growing interpersonal skills under the guidance of a trained psychologist.

Suggested Strategies:
• Reserve a second hour each night of the parent-only instructional sessions for informal conversation.
• Schedule periodic sessions with children invited during the course of the parent instructional sessions. The children can be prepared for the sessions during the school day. Activities should be games and informal conversation.

Possible Resources:
GAMES: *Bridges* (available through the Church of Jesus Christ of Latter-Day Saints); *Ungame* (available in Toys "R" Us and through educational supply houses); *Scruples* (available in toy and department stores).

Fluegelman, A. (1981). *More new games! . . . and playful ideas from the New Games Foundation.* Garden City, NY: Doubleday.
Orlick, T. (1978). *The cooperative sports and games book: Challenge without competition.* New York: Pantheon Books.
Rohnke, K. (1977). *Cow's tails and cobras.* Hamilton, MA: Project Adventure.
Schachter, R. (1986, March). *Kinetic psychotherapy in the treatment of children.* A paper presented at the Emotional Development of the Gifted: Promising Practices for Professionals and Parents Conference. Center for the Study and Education of the Gifted, Teachers College, Columbia University.

PARENT AND STUDENT REACTIONS

The summary evaluation of the UAG program (Krantz, 1986) and the responses of the students and parents to a questionnaire about the impact of the total program on the students involved (Supplee, 1987/1988) indicated that the student behavior and achievement did improve. In the final evaluation, conducted by the school district that first implemented the UAG program (Supplee, 1986), it was assumed that the changes in students were due to the school-sponsored program. This assumption was based on responses by parents to the interview questions in the Krantz study, to the questionnaire used in the Supplee study (1987/1988), and to anecdotes used as testimony by parents at a Board of Education meeting, where a decision to continue the program using local rather than grant funds was being made.

Responses by parents to the questionnaire and interviews in the two studies cited revealed that there were no concurrent changes in the families of these students that could have caused the observed changes in student behavior and achievement except those that could be traced to the school program. The parents of children who were enrolled in the adaptive class reported feeling more satisfied with their school system than were the parents of those children who had similar problems and were not enrolled.

The students' responses to the questions about family support in the Supplee study (1987/1988) revealed that student perceptions of family support for the school changed over time. The change was greatest for the students having both parents participate in the parent meetings, least in those students having neither parent participate in the parent meetings. Before students entered the adaptive program, their responses about parental support varied widely. After enrollment in the program, students felt their families

1. Perceived the school's expectations as fair and right for the students
2. Showed great interest in school
3. Felt that the students were getting a good education
4. Were mostly satisfied with the students' grades
5. Felt that homework put some, but not undue, pressure on the students.

Parents are a critical element in effecting the kind of change that gifted underachievers need in their lives. Prior to the UAG program, many parents did recognize that their children were having difficulty but until the adaptive program began, did not know specifically what the problems were or how to make changes that would help their children. A link between home and school was established. The school provided an education for parents as well as for their children. The compounding effect of a better understanding of how to deal with and help their children, the happiness and reduction of stress that followed, and the actual achievement gains they saw in their children, made parents champions for the cause.

SUMMARY

This chapter reviewed the mixed findings from earlier research on parent counseling to help gifted students reverse their underachievement. The design of the parent program used in conjunction with the school program for UAG students was described. Key to the success of this program was remembering to reestablish trust between the parents of the youngsters and the school. Two fundamental tenets led to the reestablishment of that trust: viewing parents as the ultimate educators of their children; and listening to the needs, ideas, and concerns of the parents, just as the children were listened to and heard.

Actual lesson plans for others interested in implementing the program in the same way were provided. Suggested resources for both instructors and parents were cited. Finally, the evaluation results, which suggest that this aspect of UAG was crucial to the rapid reversal of self-destructive behaviors in the students, were given.

CHAPTER 10

Endings and Beginnings

The gifted underachiever's program developed over time as we met the identified children, learned their individual needs, found new materials that appealed to them, and talked with their parents and regular teachers. Two things remained constant in our class: the affective curriculum and the whole-group reading classes. However, the system of scheduling classes changed in the regular school, and thus in the UAG program as well.

OTHER SUBJECTS: TAILORING STUDENTS' PROGRAMS

After the first year of the UAG program, the children enrolled in the adaptive class still met during the first two periods of the day but, because of changes in scheduling in the school as a whole, missed a variety of subjects, not just math and reading. Seventh and eighth graders missed either science or social studies for the entire year during one period of the school day, and art, music, physical education, and health over the four quarters during the other period they were in UAG. Fifth and sixth graders missed reading and language arts, which included writing, spelling, handwriting, and grammar instruction. Third and fourth graders continued to miss math and reading, as had been the case for all students during the first year of operation.

In learning to meet the needs of the students, the teachers learned to compact nearly every discipline taught in school at nearly every grade. Based on their experience, some guidelines are offered.

Science

If students were scheduled to miss a laboratory science, the most reasonable adaptation was to rework their basic schedule so they had science at a time other than the two periods they were scheduled for UAG. While the UAG teachers were capable and qualified to teach science, the classroom was inappropriate. In the adaptive room, there were simply no laboratory facilities to do the job well at the upper grades. Students were able to work on outside projects that correlated with their science classwork, but no direct instruction in science occurred. That remained the province of the science teacher.

Special Subjects: Physical Education, Family Life, Music, Art

Physical education is mandated for 150 minutes per week in New Jersey. As there was no alternative time to schedule their physical education program as there had been in science, the UAG students were required to be excused from UAG for this class. Problems were avoided by scheduling the affective curriculum lessons and the students' individualized mini-lessons around their scheduled gym classes.

The family-living portion of the health course is also a mandated subject in the state but had no required number of minutes. In this case, the curriculum was compacted. Students were pre-tested on the objectives in the curriculum guide. Instruction was designed to teach only those objectives the students had not yet mastered. Many of the assignments made in this subject were appropriate independent study topics, so not only were students learning family-life content, they were also learning work-study skills that would serve them in good stead in many disciplines.

In music and art, facilities and time were limited. The children were not excused for regular instruction in music and art. The UAG children were often gifted in these areas and needed a differentiated curriculum to meet their needs. Their regular curricula in art and music were replaced with creative activities that also helped them manage stress in their lives. This replacement was a trade-off. The art and music teacher were understandably not happy about our students missing their classes. However, they were more than helpful once they realized the students were not being totally deprived of experiences in the arts. It became evident that, in many cases, the students' experiences in the arts in the UAG class were more integrated, more in tune with their special gifts, than the general curriculum could be. In time, the special teachers in these areas became highly supportive co-workers. The instrumental music instructor listened to two pieces that Jamal improvised and offered to work with him individually to help him learn to write the innovative rhythms and melody patterns he created. The art teacher generously shared materials and ideas, as the children explored the various masters and the media those artists used. By teaching about the arts within the affective curriculum and providing exploratory activities in the centers in the classroom, we bought time for the other things these students needed to learn.

Health

As part of the affective curriculum, strategies to improve mental health were taught nearly every day. The close link between mental and physical health was stressed. While the students did not receive instruction in first aid and safety, nutrition, and substance abuse, this omission was rationalized on the basis that this specialized curriculum was the equivalent of an individualized program tailored to our students' specific needs. Building students' self-esteem and the ability to learn on one's own, which could include what was needed to have a healthy life, was likely to have long-lasting effects. Good self-esteem and good decision-making skills would allow students to make better choices about nutrition, addictive substances, and sexual behavior.

Social Studies

The core curriculum of social studies was compacted and adjusted to be more appropriate for gifted learners. Basic themes that crossed grade levels, for example, the ways different societies meet the basic social needs of people, served as the basis for the mini-lessons. Students related that theme to the geographical region or the historical period organizing instruction at their particular grade level. Sixth-grade students discovered how Central American nations, now and in the past, met people's social needs; seventh-grade students learned how such needs were met in ancient Greece and Rome; eighth-grade students related the theme to the early days of our nation. Their basic text was a beginner's guide; frequent library work supplemented their texts. A culminating activity, such as interviewing each student in "Sixty Minutes" style, while the student played the role of a leader in the nation or time period under study, served to synthesize what the students had learned. Other themes studied included revolution, the development of culture, and the work of social scientists.

STUDIES OF THE UAG PROGRAM

Evaluations of Grant-Supported Program Development

The adaptive program developed in three stages and was evaluated at each stage. Due to the small numbers of students involved at the time, and with no statistics to support inferences, it is clear that the main impact of the program is better assessed through the clinical descriptions and the case studies of the students presented in this text.

For readers interested in the entire evaluation reports, *Reaching the*

Gifted Underachiever: 1984–85 Grant Program Summative Evaluation and *Reaching the Gifted Underachiever 1985–86 Grant Program Summative Evaluation* are available through the New Jersey State Department of Education or directly from Green Township Schools, Box 14, Greendell, NJ 07839. The 1984–1985 report describes the development process of the identification instruments and a skeletal curriculum based on program goals. The report also details student outcomes in terms of self-esteem, attitudes towards school, improvement in socialization skills, and growth in academic achievement during the first five months of program operation. The 1985–1986 report discusses the following four questions that were posed and studied the second year:

1. What were true program effects as opposed to Pygmalion and/or Hawthorne effects?
2. Was the program teacher specific?
3. Could the program be run continuously with students entering and leaving at random times?
4. Could the program be disseminated easily?

Evaluation by the Center for the Study and Education of the Gifted

The Center for the Study and Education of the Gifted at Teachers College, Columbia University, conducted an ethnographic study on the program during its early stages (Krantz, 1986). Every student in the program, the parents of every student, every teacher in the school, and every school administrator was interviewed to determine whether the adaptive class was identifying the right children and whether the program had the effect on the students' academic and affective needs that it set out to have. The report also made recommendations for improvements. Copies of this evaluation report are also available from Green Township Schools or from the Center for the Study and Education of the Gifted.

ETHNOGRAPHIC STUDY OF DIFFERENCES IN STUDENTS' ACHIEVEMENT

The final study became my dissertation. Despite the measurable success of the adaptive program in the early reports, questions remained. Hidden by mean gains in achievement tests and impressive self-esteem scores was the fact that some students did far better than others. Attention needed to be paid to what was *not* revealed by these evaluations. *Listen to the Children* (Supplee,

1987/1988) was an exploratory case study, designed to bring about a better understanding of the similarities and differences in the children enrolled in the program for gifted underachievers. It attempted to answer the question What were the most important differences in the students and factors in the adaptive class that helped reverse underachievement by students?

Method

The design of the study required that twelve students be selected. Four of those students were to be "successful," meaning that they were enrolled in the adaptive program, had returned to the mainstream, and were achieving well in that setting. Four others were to be grouped as "not yet" students; these students were enrolled in the program and had not yet achieved the program goals. The last group, the "not included" students, were selected from those who were screened for, but never included in, the program because they appeared to be less in need.

The study followed an embedded, multi-case design (Yin, 1984). I first studied the four individual students who had successfully met the program goals. Each case was analyzed to determine if patterns existed in that student's characteristics. Each case was also analyzed to see what that student perceived as features of curricula, class climate, instructional procedures, and family support that were helpful in making him or her more successful in school. The four successful cases were then compared to one another. This analysis yielded patterns of student characteristics. The same procedure was followed to search for patterns in students' perceptions regarding the important features of curricula, class climate, instruction, and family support.

Individual case studies were then conducted on students who had not yet successfully met all the program goals. A cross-case analysis looked for patterns in these four "not yet" cases across the same factors. Results of this analysis were compared to those of the "success" group. Finally a third set of four individual cases was conducted, using the "not included" students. Again a cross-case analysis was made. Patterns found in the "not included" group were compared to those of the students in the first two groups. Inferences were then made about the similarities and differences among the groups.

Interviews were conducted with all three groups over a three-day period. Students and their parents also completed questionnaires to elicit further information. Formal school records and anecdotal records kept by the UAG classroom teachers were also used to confirm conclusions suggested by the interview and questionnaire data.

Construct validity, external validity, and internal validity were checked. Construct validity is supported through triangulation of the data. A chain of evidence can be followed by reading the single cases available from the researcher and the tabulated data in the appendixes of the study (Supplee, 1987/1988). The reader can follow derivation of the answers from the initial research question to the final conclusions. External validity was established by basing the study on respected work in the field of underachievement among the gifted. Internal validity, though not required to be addressed in an exploratory study, was attempted through pattern-matching techniques and through replication logic (the more replications that exist from case to case, the more strongly inferences are supported). In this study, only conclusions supported by at least three of the four students in each group are reported. Theoretical replication was also attempted. The data obtained from the "not included" group supported propositions about why included students were successful.

Reliability was informed through

1. Use of a case-study protocol
2. Development of an annotated bibliography, itemizing the database documents available to other researchers
3. Descriptions that are as operational as possible of the way in which the material in the case-study database was gathered
4. Operational descriptions of the analysis of the data so that procedures may be carefully replicated by future researchers.

What Made a Difference

Differences in the values of the students regarding their abilities; their academic weaknesses, including learning disabilities; and their preferred learning styles appear to be the reasons some students were more successful than others. The students' growth through the zone of proximal development and ability to transfer their learning in each area of cognitive and affective learning dictated the rate of their return to the mainstream.

Students' self-perceptions. Prior to entrance into the adaptive program, students in each group perceived an equal number of negative traits in themselves. Students who were in the "successful" and "not yet" groups, however, saw themselves with fewer positive traits than did students in the "not included" group.

All of the students enrolled in the adaptive class appeared to change their perceptions of themselves quickly after beginning to participate. Two cases in the "not yet" group were enrolled for only two months. Their responses, which were similar to those of the students enrolled for a much longer time, indicate how rapidly students changed. Anecdotal records and pre- and post-test results on the *Coopersmith Self-Esteem Inventory* (1981) support the conclusion that it is possible to observe an increase in positive and a lessening of negative traits in students within the first two months of their participation.

The degree to which self-perceptions enter into school achievement has been the subject of much research. The weight of evidence suggests there is a persistent interaction between the two variables (Purkey, 1970). Self-perceptions affect achievement; achievement affects self-perceptions. The study of self-perceptions, both past and present, offers some fairly consistent findings. Based on the contributions of Rogers, Allport, and others reported in Beane and Lipka (1986) these findings can be summarized as

1. The concept of self has a central place in personality, acting as a source of unity and guide to behavior.
2. Self-perceptions blend into a general sense of self (self-concept).
3. Self-perceptions tend to seek stability, consistency, and enhancement.
4. Self-perceptions may be based on roles played by the individual as well as attributes she believes she possesses.
5. Self-perceptions arise mainly in a social context, influenced largely by feedback from "significant others."

Prior to his enrollment in school, the student's self-perceptions most reasonably result from family, the first "significant others" in the children's lives. Children, then, come to school with a preestablished sense of who they are, what they can do, and how they should act. This sense of self may be healthy or unhealthy. The school, through its institutional features (climate, rules, grouping, grading, professional behavior, etc.), makes a persistent effort to become another "significant other" in the life of the children. The institutional features become the "hidden curriculum" (Jackson, 1968) of the school, teaching values and enhancing or discouraging positive self-perceptions, depending on the variability of the learners' performances within that setting and the support students receive in assimilating the cultural conventions operating there.

The self-concept the child brings to school may be either acceptable or unacceptable in that socializing institution. Regardless of the child's initial self-concept, the school then affects the child's self-perceptions. What distinguishes the underachieving gifted children in this study is that they have internalized a magnified sense of the negative messages they have received from home, school, or both sources, without internalizing strong, corresponding positive messages to provide balance before enrolling in the UAG class. Even though all students evidenced growth in their sense of self-esteem after enrolling it may be that the degree of parental support evident to the children and demonstrated by the parents' participation in the UAG parent program affects the students' achievement to a greater extent.

Whether students value their intelligence. Other possible reasons for the differences in student success were explored. One of those was the students' conception of intelligence, originally studied by Dweck and Bempechat (1980). Dweck and Bempechat found that "entity theorists" were those who believed that intelligence was a fixed commodity with which one could show off. They expended little focused effort in learning, expected teachers to guide them constantly, and reached poor mastery. If the theory is correct, what should have been demonstrable was that less successful students would have the belief that all that was needed to be highly intelligent was inborn talent. But this is not what resulted: None of the students in any of the groups of cases attributed genius or high intelligence to inborn capabilities only. No one appeared to believe that intelligence was something to show off. Yet some were still poorer achievers than others. Neither did these cases appear to be "incremental theorists"; that is, students who believed that intelligence was a resource with which to learn new things, who expended much effort in self-guided activities in school, and who made good progress. All students in all groups believed that effort and/or a person's attitude was important in becoming a genius or highly intelligent. These data do not bear out the earlier research (Dweck & Bempechat, 1980; Zelman, 1985).

Differences did exist in the appreciation of high intelligence among the students in the group. Valuing high intelligence, rather than having a particular conception of intelligence that includes effort on the person's part, may provide clues to increased achievement in these students. The results of the study suggest that *how* students valued the intelligence they have more accurately predicted their success in the program and may, in the long run, more accurately predict whether they reach their potential as adults. Only students in the "not included" group remarked, without prompting on the part of the researcher, on their lack of desire for, or lack of motivation for, being highly intelligent. One girl stated that she was not willing to pay the social price she felt was inherent in high intelligence. One boy implied he would be highly intelligent only if his parents said he should be.

The students' sense of control over their lives. It may be the appropriateness of the match between the tasks expected of the children and their perceived ability to reach those expectations, as well as the degree of support they perceived in the school environment, that affects their achievement. Research by Weiner (1976, 1979, 1983) and Dweck (1975) proposed that students' perceptions of the causes for their success were important determinants of their future success. These researchers believed children could be grouped into two categories, those who felt they were helpless in effecting success and those who were mastery oriented. Mastery-oriented students felt they were able to control whether they were successful or not in a given task. Modifications in the students' perceptions were suspected of producing a change in their actions.

In this study, students were asked to perform a series of tasks that were challenging, but within their capabilities. Two tasks were academic in nature, a reading task and a mathematical task. A drawing task was included to check students' perceptions on a non-academic task that demanded some creativity. A problem-solving task, the solution of which depended largely on luck, was included to check the validity of student responses. The students' increasing sense of mastery in mathematics, discussed in Chapter 7, clearly demonstrated a change from "not included" to "not yet" to "success" students. The researcher questioned students about the differences that might have led to the increased sense of mastery. The students' descriptions of the teachers' proceeding from "instructors" to "coaches" to "well-wishers" were remarkably similar to the description given by Duffy, Roehler, and Mason (1984), when they describe instruction that takes place within the zone of proximal development. Duffy et al. (1984) noted that the process of becoming independent problem solvers is a process of gradual internalization. First, the adult, or adult-like person (the instructor), controls and guides the child's activity. Gradually, the adult and child share the responsibilities, with the child taking the lead and the adult (the coach) guiding the responses and providing correctives where the child has erred. Finally, the adult (the well-wisher) gives the child full range of responsibilities and provides support.

No equally clear pattern emerged for the reading task. Helplessness scores were similar for the "success" and the "not included" group, and increased dramatically for the "not yet" group. This would not be expected if the adaptive program positively affected students' sense of mastery. Here, knowledge of the individual cases was important.

One student in the "not yet" group was a successful reader. The other three were identified as perceptually impaired, evidencing reading/language disabilities. No one in the "success" group was so diagnosed. Only one of the "not included" students was identified as perceptually impaired. It is quite likely that the disabilities experienced by the "not yet" students confused the results and interfered with an adequate assessment of the students' increasing or decreasing sense of mastery in reading.

Prior research (Dweck, 1975) implied that students' overall orientation could be placed on a continuum from more helplessness to more mastery. No attempt was made to distinguish between life-type tasks and school-type tasks nor to distinguish between different types of academic tasks. The data from this research confirm that students' perceptions of the reasons for success do differ. They may be affected by the adaptive program, but in this study, the differences appeared to depend on the task, not on a general personality orientation of the student.

Learning disabilities. A second look at the learning disabled students in the UAG class is indicated. At least four, and perhaps five, of the twelve case-study students (33%–42%) were learning disabled, whereas the percentage of learning disabled in the general population ranges from 1 percent to 15 percent, depending on the source used (Lerner, J., 1985). While not occurring in every gifted underachiever, learning disabilities do exist in some, and a disproportionate number of those in the "not yet" group were identified as disabled. They appear to be least affected by the adaptive program as it exists. Students with disabilities in reading may rightfully feel helpless if they have not learned appropriate strategies to deal with the problem. It may be that, in addition to, not in place of, the more positive social climate of the adaptive classroom, the learning disabled/gifted child needs to be identified, and needs an individual, prescriptive program such as that provided for Ned, and recommended by Tannenbaum (1983) based on his analysis of Whitmore's (1980) success.

Given the large number of students in the "not yet" group who were affected, it is crucial to screen for learning disabilities among the referred students. Because of the students' giftedness, this possible diagnosis is easily overlooked, even by trained learning specialists. A gifted child who scores in the average range on screening instruments used to detect learning disabilities is as disabled as a child with average or slightly above average ability whose disability places him or her clearly below the norm. If students' disabilities are not recognized and if services are not provided, social and emotional consequences emerge.

Learning styles. Two of the tasks used to determine the students' ability to use metacognitive processing point out interesting differences in the students and hint at differentiated approaches to processing information. One of the designed tasks in the study looked at secondary ignorance. The other was used to determine students' degree of confidence in their ability to perform a task.

Secondary ignorance is the space between realizing that something is unknown and learning it. The secondary-ignorance tasks in this study were designed to allow the researcher to know when students recognized that they needed to know more. Students were asked to create directions for a simple game. Student responses were tape-recorded. Their recording was replayed and students were asked to decide if the directions were complete. Students' verbal responses were recorded. They were then asked to play their game, explicitly following their recordings. Students were asked again to decide if their directions had been complete.

The results on this task indicated a wide spread in students' abilities to correctly assess the completeness of the directions they heard. There were differences, as well, in the abilities of students to determine whether the directions were complete when they actually followed them step-by-step. These differences did not appear to be attributable to age or maturity.

A closer look at the secondary-ignorance task reveals that it may have been checking secondary ignorance only in an auditory-processing task. Future research should construct parallel visual tasks that check secondary ignorance. A learn-to-draw task might prove useful, especially if used in conjunction with the auditory test. Secondary ignorance in students might be more accurately assessed. The secondary-ignorance subtest may lend weight to the observation that some underachieving gifted students have difficulty with oral language–processing. Four of the twelve case-study students had difficulty performing this task. The four did not all fall into the same group ("success," "not yet," or "not included"), but did include the one student who was formally identified with this problem.

The confidence task, in contrast to the secondary-ignorance task, was one that relied on good visual memory and visual discrimination in students. Students were asked to look at a series of twenty sketches. They told the researcher whether the picture was "new," meaning they had never seen it before, or "old," meaning it had a duplicate in the series that they had seen already. Students then told the researcher whether or not they were certain of their answers. Every case-study student had a minimum score of 95% on the identification task, with a maximum confidence rate of 90%.

The exceptionally consistent and correct results on this task raise interesting questions. Was the task too easy, thus not discriminating among the students' abilities adequately? Or were these students more efficient processors of visual information than auditory information? It would be important to construct a corresponding auditory task that checks confidence.

Other data can be presented that support the idea of more efficient visual processing by these students. One is a mismatch between the students' predictions of the most successful study strategies and those they actually used for successful study. In another task conducted with the case-study students, they were asked to predict the outcome of strategic activities. After watching a videotape of a student modeling four different study strategies (rehearsing, looking, labeling, and categorizing), the students stated which one they thought would be most effective. Students were then given two minutes to learn and remember the images on twelve different picture cards. They were told to use whatever method they wished in order to learn them.

Most students predicted that categorizing and rehearsing would be the most effective study strategies, but *used* labeling and looking to study their own pictures. Only one low score (7 of 12 correct) resulted; this was the one student who used rehearsing. Other students had between 10 and 12 correct using visual strategies. Six of the eight students (75%) in the "success" and "not yet" groups chose to use a method requiring visualization when confronted with a memory task. One student described how she categorized the pictures and then visualized placement of these categories on the table to help her recall. Another student described how he visualized the pictures by putting them into a four-by-three matrix. He then thought of unusual connections between the pictures in the column, for example, a "birdwatch phone" that could be used to tell other birdwatchers things. It may be that the students intuitively selected a strategy that better matched their strengths than those they had been taught will "work."

The learned-helplessness task described earlier also supported students' stronger visual abilities. The drawing portion of the task asked students to visualize, and then draw, a kite in flight. All of the students performed the task successfully. Most students attributed their success to ability and effort, attributions that indicate mastery orientation. Anecdotal records also support exceptional visual ability translated into drawing ability. One student lavishly illustrated his journal with drawings; another had illustrations, which he drew in class from memory, published in *Shoe Tree* magazine; a third approached all his work in writing workshop by drawing his stories before writing about them.

By no means should a person assume that only one of the factors discussed here could itself be *the* cause of the differences between the students' rate of change in the UAG class. Such an assumption would set research on the subject of gifted underachievers back about fifty years. Just as interactions occur between self-perceptions and achievement, and interactions occur between the two social institutions that are "significant others" in the life of the child, so are there likely to be interactions between these suggested differences. These interactions are made more complex by the child's role. Children's self-perceptions affect their responses to significant others. Their self-perceptions also affect how they value intelligence, the degree of control they feel in situations, and how they deal with their disabilities and learning-style differences. Variability of learners' performances are also a function of the tasks at hand, the settings in which learning occurs, and the amount of support provided by significant others (Gavelek, 1984). An impenetrable web of cause-and-effect relationships develops; no one part can change without bringing about changes in others.

OBSERVATIONS THAT DESERVE FURTHER STUDY

No educational innovation is static. As each new student enrolled, as each original student moved back into the mainstream, as each new teacher assumed responsibility for the class, things were done slightly differently and more was learned in the process. It is important for anyone involved with these children to continue to record what is tried, how it worked, and how it was evaluated, especially in other contexts. By continuing to add to what is known, someday all "starfish" may have the chance to regenerate, to become the stars they are.

Continued Identification and Follow-up

As the first UAG students returned to the mainstream, spaces opened up in the adaptive classroom. The file of candidates not accepted into the class on the first round supplied a list of new students from which to draw. It was important, however, to let the faculty know they could continue to refer students for consideration. In the original class, the decision was made to remind teachers semi-annually that new nominees would be accepted. The first reminder came in November. As the routine screening for gifted students occurred each year at this time in third grade, new students who had some of the characteristics of gifted underachievers were discovered. These students were considered as space opened in the resource room. People were reminded a second time in March, around report card time. All new referrals were compared to those students already in the files to check for relative neediness. As space was available, the likeliest candidates were phased in as quickly as possible.

Questions remain. Is this the most appropriate method of screening for the program? What effect does it have on students who are screened once and then passed over, while a new student is offered a spot? Does the procedure help to entrench the program? Does it continue to sensitize teachers to the special needs of these students, thus helping all three groups: the "graduates," those who are screened but not admitted, and new students who are identified?

The Non-Achiever in a Group of Non-Achievers

The one student who decided not to achieve anywhere, not even in a class for underachievers, raised an issue deserving serious thought. As she was ready to graduate, time cured the problem for the teachers, although not the student. Thought should be given ahead of time to the way in which this dilemma will be handled. No one adaptation is going to be right for every student, no matter how carefully screened and placed the students are. The best thinking that can be offered at this time, but which is open to revision, is that schools should continue to serve the child as best they possibly can. Maybe the student in question only needs more time before opening up to trust others and grow to potential. If the child becomes so disruptive that learning conditions are unproductive for the other students, then a different placement for the child should be considered.

Parental Request

Several pairs of siblings were in the UAG class over time. In one case, due to a parental request, one of the two siblings was removed from the program. When the second child was admitted to UAG, exceptional rivalry between the sisters became immediately evident. Instinctively the teacher felt that the children needed to be together under the supervision of a teacher so they could work through their problems and learn how to relate to each other better. The parent, though, felt an unhealthy situation was developing at home because of their intense rivalry. Though the program goals had not been reached, the first sibling was withdrawn. She had made quite remarkable gains both cognitively and affectively, and she was able to maintain many of them over three months, the length of time she remained in our public school system. At that point, her parents placed her in a private boarding school, which she still attends.

Why siblings would be recommended for the UAG class is not difficult to guess. Whether siblings should be placed together is a topic worthy of study.

Exiting the Group—The Breaking-Away Syndrome

To decide if a student was ready to be pushed from the nest, the teachers returned to the goals and objectives for the program and matched the changes observable in the student to those goals and objectives. It seemed that students were ready cognitively to leave the group before they were ready emotionally.

In most cases, students' affective development occurred in two stages. During the first period of growth, students learned to function effectively within the small group. Within a year, at most, all the students were successful in the adaptive classroom. They were also more successful in their regular classes, but not always to the same degree as in the special program.

How was one to know when to encourage them to leave? In the beginning stages of the program, the teachers looked for cues from the outside world. When classroom teachers began to comment often on how well a student was doing, it seemed to be time to begin to talk to the student about returning to the mainstream. Transitions were provided. The child's strongest academic area (of those taught in the UAG class) was identified, and the child was asked to bring samples of the work done in regular classes to our class. These were used for instruction, usually not in cognitive concepts, but rather for individual school survival skills lessons. We posed questions: "How would you manage an assignment like this if you were in this class, and what would you do when you finished? What problems would you face? How would you handle those problems? Why don't you pretend you are there now and see how you do?"

There was one absolute rule: No child would be forced to return before he or she felt ready. When a child felt ready, once she could deal comfortably with regular assignments, could devise ways to enrich the assignment for herself and could deal with the routine nature of assignments effectively, the teacher suggested returning for that one class. During the other period, the child returned to UAG. When this first step was successful, the routine was repeated for the other subject and homework assignments were reintroduced. The child dealt with difficulties through school-survival skills mini-lessons. Eventually, the students asked to return full-time and the class planned a grand, graduation-to-the-real-world send-off.

What no one expected, and what the teachers were therefore not prepared for, was the "breaking away" syndrome. The first students who left the program were those who graduated and went on to high school at the end of the first five months. It was grand and exciting for them, particularly since each student won at least one award at graduation. The ending point for them, with a beginning in clear view, was well-defined. It was the students who were returning to the regular classes within their own school who needed to break away. Anyone who has sent children off to college or out into the world on their own will undoubtedly recognize the behaviors of the students, but the teachers were taken by surprise. In order to get ready emotionally to leave, the children went through a period of outright hostility and rebellion. They returned to pre-program behaviors, and the teachers wondered if all their efforts had gone to waste. The students seemed to be saying, "See, this whole thing is a bunch of hogwash. I don't need this or you, and it hasn't done me any good to be here. Look how rotten I can be."

When the first child exhibited this rebellion, we were confused and frustrated. When the second child did, we raised pattern-alert antennae. By the time the third child rebelled, the teachers realized that this hostility was probably an important sign of readiness. Marty was the first student to break away from the program before he graduated. Now he acknowledges that he had to cut himself off from the group in this manner. It was hard to leave: These were his friends; this was his safe place. He had to convince himself that it wasn't important for him to be there any longer, that it wasn't so wonderful as he thought.

The question that should be answered is whether another way to smooth the transition can be found. Maybe the break is necessary, but maybe not.

PREPARED CHANCE

Tannenbaum (1983) recognized the importance of chance in the development of talent or the bringing of talent to fruition. He felt it was so important that he included it as one of the five conditions necessary for giftedness to occur. He believed the most difficult problem in dealing with chance factors was that they were unpredictable and always created an element of the unknown when forecasting fulfillment of promise.

Bandura (1982) also stated that chance encounters played a prominent role in shaping the course of human lives. Recalling Tannenbaum's (1983) third condition, Bandura believed certain entry skills, that is, personal resources, were needed to gain acceptance in a group. Then the resources, interests, and skills of the people in that group determined the future circles, with further interest and skills, in which they might move. Chance, Bandura believed, was most likely to affect life courses when individuals came to like the people they met or the satisfactions they gained from them. Lasting bonds were the vehicle for personal changes that could have long-term effects. Further, he stated, to exercise personal control required tools, both emotional and social supports.

Deliberate attention to the affect is one way to prepare children for their chance, their acceptance into the social circles that may further their development. The affective curriculum also begins to develop their "showcasing" skills, those skills that allow them to sell their talents to others. Perhaps these can be defined as "entrepreneurial" skills. A third part, and one that many programs for the gifted have accepted as part of their responsibility, is helping students find the arenas for their areas of interest. For children, it might mean involving them in exhibitions, contests, and the like to have them achieve notice. Without fail, it should also mean teaching them to be aware of certain niceties, such as learning to say, "Thank you," to those who have helped. Gifted underachievers as well as achievers deserve this kind of help to bring their talents to fruition.

FROM STARFISH TO STARS

Our starfish, with limbs torn off, were a sad set of specimens when first they came to UAG, yet were beautiful because of the tenacity with which they hung onto life and were determined to improve. Slowly they regenerated, and the larger systems surrounding them grew to support them as well. The starfish became more and more like stars when provided with the conditions needed for their giftedness to emerge.

As this book draws to a close, the students who passed through the program at one time or another during the past few years are presented again. These vignettes are, for the most part, based on self-report or the reports of parents, and share all the limitations of self-reports. But the consistency with which most of them believe they maintained the gains they made in the UAG class is encouraging—especially when we consider their starting-points.

• Marcia is currently in junior high school. Her report card shows all A's and B's in the top classes. She is also active in sports and is on the student council. Her parents are more than pleased with her success.

• Karen was withdrawn from the program when her sister was identified as a candidate for the program. Karen finished out that year (three months), with no loss of achievement in a regular classroom in the same school. She transferred to a private boarding school for the next academic year. There she experienced some difficulty adjusting to the new living arrangements and new, higher expectations. She came close that first year to failing algebra. She did not fail, however, and is currently achieving at an average level. She has friends and seems happy with herself.

• David is in high school, proving that he did not have to follow in his brother's footsteps and become a dropout. His achievement is not great, but he has kept his future options open by staying in school.

• Douglas is earning mostly A's and B's with an occasional C in high school. He is also preparing to run his third marathon this coming spring; when he entered UAG, this achievement would have been impossible, given his lack of self-esteem and nonexistent task commitment, as well as his accident-prone behavior.

• Helen has faded into the world of the average. She is still in elementary school, but has not successfully reached her potential. On a positive note, she is not failing, as she was when we first received her as a student.

• Jamal, too, is still in elementary school. His social and emotional development remain delayed. But his creative writing ability and his artistic talents have earned him distinction. He has received schoolwide awards at the end of each year, including "Most Improved Student," "Most Creative Student," and the like.

• Mike also has remaining social and emotional difficulties, but he is achieving very well in the cognitive areas. His parents withdrew him from public school after the last change of teachers in the UAG. His current placement in a private school permits him to accelerate academically. The small class size there is similar to the support group in UAG and he functions relatively well within it. Larger social groups are still a problem for Mike, but he is active in sports and appears to be a good team player.

• Ned is on his way to a career in the world of entertainment. He made arrangements to interview several of his idols, the stars of "Saturday Night Live." From them, he learned that the road to fame is tough, but rewarding, and worth the effort of sticking to it until you make it. To them, he gave insights into the mind of a junior high school youth determined to make the choices that will let him reach his goals. Ned is learning to balance his exceptional creativity with the practical necessity of learning to read. He is achieving satisfactorily in junior high school academics despite the learning disabilities that were identified after he enrolled in the UAG.

• Portia is the student we lost. She ran away from her home with her father during her first year of high school to try to find the mother who had deserted her two years earlier. At last report, she was living with her sister in Florida.

• Juliet has grown socially and academically. After attending several different high schools, she settled in our local public school. She chose her courses to develop her artistic abilities and is enrolled in college at present, studying business and art. She recently received an honorable mention in a national competition for a commercial art project.

• Marty is now in high school. He decided to attend the local vo-tech high, choosing to study computers so he could live within the dictates of his religion and enter a trade right after high school. The trade he chose is certainly academically challenging, and he is happy. At school, his achievement is exceptional, and he has won many friends through his lighthearted openness.

• Ginny is still in elementary school. She is achieving acceptably (B's and C's) and has developed a strong sense of self-esteem. No longer does she whisper and hide in a fantasy world. She is in charge of herself and often accepts a leadership role in small-group situations.

• Ricardo is currently in high school. The last time he spoke to me, his words were, "Guess what? I finally figured out that to get good grades here, I have to work!" When I asked him if he had decided to work, he answered, "One step at a time." Given that Ricardo was considered suicidal when he first enrolled in UAG, and that he now has a girlfriend, participates enthusiastically in school activities (contributing his particular talents in technical theater), is not failing, and demonstrates warmth and affection he tells quite a story of growth.

• Vicki is a junior high superstar. From the D's and F's she was earning when we met her, she is now consistently on the honor or high honor roll every marking period of the school year. Her flair for the dramatic is still evident and she writes and draws and paints prolifically.

• Cal graduated from high school last year. He had difficulty deciding what career he wanted to pursue, and thus whether to attend college or not. One option was to go into the business of making TV commercials with his family, and he certainly had the necessary artistic and creative talent. His other option was to study architecture. At last report, he was giving college a try, in the hope that his learning disability would not cause him too much difficulty. He knows if college does not turn out to be the proper choice for him he has other options. He feels good about himself.

The success of so many students brings a part of the poem "Stars" by Sara Teasdale to mind:

And a heaven full of stars
Over my head,
White and topaz
And misty-red;
Up the dome of heaven
Like a great hill,
I watch them marching
Stately and still,

And I know that I
Am honored to be
Witness
Of so much majesty.

("Stars," Sara Teasdale, 1920)

Marty and the others who returned "to the real world" are alive and well. Most are maintaining the gains they had made before leaving. They do have differences, like the topaz and misty-red in Sara Teasdale's poem. Some are shining brightly; others are yet a tiny flicker, harder to see because of the brightness of the others or the great distances between us. It has been an honor to be part of the change in their lives.

SUMMARY

Programs are never static. New students bring new needs, new years bring new scheduling challenges, new authors bring new materials. Some of the changes that occurred in the UAG program over the first few years were described.

The UAG program has been the subject of several studies, two by the New Jersey State Department of Education, which funded the pilot program, one by the Center for the Study and Education of the Gifted, at Teachers

College, Columbia University. The last was an ethnographic study that tried to determine the differences between the more successful students and less successful students. The latter study was presented in some detail. The things that made a difference were the students' sense of self, their valuing their intelligence, their sense of control over their lives, their learning disabilities, if any, and their preferred learning styles. Ideas for future research were also presented.

The importance of chance cannot be overemphasized. Chance encounters play a role in determining the course of all lives. The UAG program is designed to be a chance encounter, providing the students with opportunity. Vignettes of the students who passed through the program close out the text.

PART FOUR

RESOURCES

Screening Instruments

IDENTIFICATION MATRIX

Complete directions for using this matrix are found in Chapter 5.

								STUDENT NAME DATE GRADE SCHOOL H.R.
								IQ Group (G) or Individual (I)
								>1 S.D. drop in Reading Achievement tests over 3 years
								>1 S.D. drop in Math Achievement tests over 3 years
								>1 S.D. drop in Total Battery Achievement tests over 3 years
								Declining school grades
								Discrepancy of at least 1 S.D. between IQ/Achievement test/grades
								Self nomination
								Peer nomination
								Parent nomination
								Teacher checklist
								Report card comments
								Outside activity/community nom.
								Creativity test score
								Interview using Richert protocol
								Product evaluation
								CST screening/recommendation

INTERVIEW PROTOCOL

(Modified form of protocol developed by E. Susanne Richert, EIRC, Sewell, NJ, 1983.)

1. On what do you spend most of your time outside of school when you can choose the activity?
2. What is the most unique or unusual activity in which you take part?
3. How much time do you spend on each activity or strong interest?
4. From whom or where did you learn about these activities or interests?
5. What have you done or produced as a result of your interest?
6. How would you evaluate the quality, effectiveness, or originality of your achievement?
7. What more would you like to know about your interest?
8. Would you like to talk with people who are experts on your interest? Read more about it?
9. If you had help getting the information, materials, or contacting experts, would you want to prepare a project, paper, model, slide tape, artwork, talk, etc. or use your new information for some real purpose, say, a problem you or someone else wants to solve?
10. What problems have you had in studying or working independently? In using your time? In finding information? In completing your project?
11. Would you like help in improving in these areas?
12. What is one thing you would change about school if you could?
13. Will you please, by (give student date), bring me one thing you have made or earned that is unique and that you are proud of?

Assessment of Interview, Product, and Product Improvement

	Not at All	Somewhat	Great Degree
1. Does the student initiate his/her own activities?	—	—	—
2. Is the student's interest intense enough so he/she has sought or will seek to learn more?	—	—	—
3. Does student show motivation to apply what he/she learns to produce something new?	—	—	—
4. Do activities, products, achievements show an original, creative approach?	—	—	—
5. Does student have problems initiating or completing independent activity?	—	—	—
6. Are there areas, like time management, needing attention?	—	—	—
7. Does student need assistance with study skills?	—	—	—

Appendix A

PARENT CHECKLIST FOR IDENTIFICATION*

Child's Name_____ Birth Date_____ Grade____
Parents' Name_____
Home Address_____
Phone_____ Today's Date_____

	High				Low
1. My child asks a lot of questions about a variety of subjects (may annoy with continual questions).	5	4	3	2	1
2. My child often prefers to work alone (may seem individualistic or idiosyncratic).	5	4	3	2	1
3. My child likes learning and/or creative, new experiences (may be bored by routine tasks and drill; may refuse to do rote homework).	5	4	3	2	1
4. My child stays with a project of his/her choosing until its completion (may rush through assigned tasks in careless or sloppy manner).	5	4	3	2	1
5. My child is observant and has a good memory for facts and details (may get bogged down in details).	5	4	3	2	1
6. My child can relate information gained in the past to newly acquired knowledge (may stubbornly cling to inaccurately made analogies).	5	4	3	2	1
7. My child asks "how" and "why" kind of questions (may be provocative, nonconforming or questioning of authority or parents).	5	4	3	2	1
8. My child has many original ideas to share (may tend to dominate others because of abilities).	5	4	3	2	1
9. My child likes to pretend; shows imagination (may appear to be "stretching the truth").	5	4	3	2	1
10. My child is able to plan and organize (may appear bossy).	5	4	3	2	1
11. My child has unusual insight into values and relationships (may perceive injustices and assertively oppose them).	5	4	3	2	1
12. My child has an extensive vocabulary for this age (may monopolize discussions).	5	4	3	2	1
13. My child often shows an interest in one subject exclusively (may be difficult to involve in topics *not* of interest).	5	4	3	2	1
14. My child evaluates facts, arguments, and persons critically (may be self-critical, impatient with or critical of others, including parents and teachers).	5	4	3	2	1
15. My child has a number of interests or hobbies that	5	4	3	2	1

*Modified from work by E. Susanne Richert, EIRC, Sewell, NJ, 1983.

keep him/her busy (may lead to disorderly surroundings).

16. My child tries to *excel* in anything he/she does (may   5   4   3   2   1
    give up if he/she cannot excel).

17. My child persists in the face of unexpected difficul-   5   4   3   2   1
    ties and tries to solve his/her own problems (may
    adamantly refuse adult help or guidance).

18. My child has a sense of humor that is advanced for   5   4   3   2   1
    this age (may joke or pun at inappropriate times).

Specific examples explaining "5" ratings (Please list number preceding item):

My child shows an unusual ability in (please comment on both academic and non-academic areas):

LETTERS TO PARENTS REGARDING SCREENING

Dear_____
    I had the chance to talk today with _____, who is being considered for our special program for gifted, underachieving students. My purpose during the meeting was to determine the strength of outside interests and activities. This information, an evaluation of a product of your child's choice, a test of creative thinking, and a survey of regularly available school information will be used to narrow the group being considered for the program to about half its present number. When all the interviews are completed, you will receive a letter explaining whether your child will be recommended for further screening.
    If you have any questions, either now or when you receive the next letter, please feel free to call me. I will be very happy to talk to you.

                                  Sincerely,

Dear_____
    The second stage of screening for our gifted, underachieving students is complete. In a pilot program such as this, choices need to be made. The students selected for the program showed a greater need than _____. However, by reaching this point in the screening, our staff has been made more aware of the very special qualities your child has. Such knowledge makes it easier for our fine professionals to meet your child's needs.
    While your child will not be participating in the program for gifted underachiev-

ers, we are inviting him/her to participate in our Type III time. This option offers a student the chance to pursue specific interests or talents under my guidance. It is the students' responsibility to propose and plan a challenging project and to carry out the work. The teacher's role is that of a resource person, helping to procure supplies, teach unusual skills, contact mentors, etc.

Thank you for your help. It has been a real pleasure getting to know your child better. I hope we can work together in the future to continue to make school the exciting, gratifying place it can be.

If you have any questions, please feel free to call.

Yours truly,

PERMISSION FROM PARENTS TO PARTICIPATE

I give permission for my child _____, to be enrolled in the pilot program for gifted underachievers.

I understand that an individualized educational plan will be written for my child that will detail specific goals he/she is to reach this year and that I will have the opportunity to approve these goals.

_____

Parent's Signature

_____

Date

LETTER REGARDING PARENT PROGRAM

Dear _____,

A meeting of the parents and guardians whose children are enrolled in the underachieving gifted program will be held on _____ from _____ P.M. to _____ P.M. Topics to be discussed include:

1. Goals of the program
2. Management of the IEP
3. Parent–student counseling
4. Evaluation of students and program

A question-and-answer period will follow.

We request that at least one parent from each family attend the meeting if at all possible. Please RSVP by _____.

Thank you,

REMINDER TO STAFF ABOUT NEW NOMINATIONS

To: Fellow staff members
From:
Re: Underachieving gifted program/new student recommendations
Date:
Deadline:

Just a reminder to keep your eyes open for the children who might benefit from our program for gifted underachievers. These may be children who were nominated last year, but not included due to lack of space. Or, they may be students who are just now starting to exhibit the characteristics of gifted underachievers.

Please review the attached checklist. If a child comes to mind, please complete the checklist for that child. Also, please check the permanent record file for that child and provide the objective and subjective data requested on the referral form attached. Additional forms may be copied or are available in my room.

Thank you for your continuing help. Without you and your thoughtful questions and help, we would not be able to work on the cutting edge of excellent educational programs. I deeply appreciate you all.

REFERRAL FORM FOR NEW NOMINATIONS

STUDENT NAME _____ HOMEROOM _____ DATE OF BIRTH _____
DATE OF REFERRAL _____ TEACHER'S SIGNATURE _____

CHECKLIST TO IDENTIFY GIFTED UNDERACHIEVERS*

Observe and interact with the child over a period of time to determine if he or she possesses the following characteristics. If the student exhibits ten or more of the listed traits, including all that are bulleted, screening for the underachieving gifted program is highly recommended.

_____ • poor test performance
_____ • achieving at or below grade level expectations in one or all of the basic skills areas: reading and language arts, math, work-study skills
_____ • daily work frequently not complete or poorly done
_____ • superior comprehension and retention of concepts when interested
_____ • vast gap between qualitative level of oral and written work
_____ exceptionally large repertoire of factual knowledge
_____ vitality of imagination, creative
_____ persistent dissatisfaction with work accomplished, even in art
_____ seems to avoid trying new activities to prevent imperfect performance; evidences perfectionism, self-criticism
_____ shows initiative in pursuing self-selected projects at home

*Modified from work by J. R. Whitmore, 1980.

_____ • has a wide range of interests and possibly special expertise in an area of investigation and research
_____ • evidences low self-esteem in tendencies to withdraw or be aggressive in the classroom
_____ does not function comfortably or constructively in a group of any size
_____ shows acute sensitivity and perceptions related to self, others, and life in general
_____ tends to set unrealistic self-expectations, goals too high or too low
_____ dislikes practice work or drill for memorization and mastery
_____ easily distractible, unable to focus attention and concentrate on task
_____ has an indifferent or negative attitude toward school
_____ resists teacher efforts to motivate or discipline behavior in class
_____ has difficulty in peer relationships; maintains few friendships

PLEASE CHECK THE STUDENT'S PERMANENT RECORD FILE FOR THE FOLLOWING:
IQ: Name of Test:_____ Total score_____
Date Administered _____ Subscores, if available

Please list STANINE scores on achievement tests for the last three years in the following areas:

	Year:		
Reading (total comprehension)	_____	_____	_____
Math (total battery)	_____	_____	_____
Total battery (composite)	_____	_____	_____

Average grades: from the report card, please list the average grades in major subject areas for your grade and the previous three years.

	Year:			
Reading level _____	_____	_____	_____	_____
Math level _____	_____	_____	_____	_____
Social studies	_____	_____	_____	_____
Science	_____	_____	_____	_____
Other (please list)				

Teacher comments: Please search the cumulative file and report cards for comments similar to the following: "bright, capable, slow worker," "highly creative, poor work habits," "hard on self; uptight about academics, self-pressure evident," "absent a lot," "talks well, but doesn't apply self when working independently," "not working to potential," etc.

Please note such comments here:

APPENDIX B

Sources of Information on
Materials and Programs

MATERIALS AND PROGRAMS TO SUPPORT READING INSTRUCTION

For those readers who wish to know where to obtain the materials used in the UAG class, the following reference has been compiled:

Good Apple Publishers, P.O. Box 299, 1204 Buchanan Street, Carthage, IL 62321-0299, telephone 800-435-7234
   Distributes *Reading: A Novel Approach* (Szabos, 1984).
Children's Express, 20 Charles Street, New York, NY 10014.
   Produces a nationally syndicated column. All the writing is done by students up to the age of 13, with high school students working as editors and managers. Students not living in New York may write as correspondents in a press club.
Learning to Read Through the Arts Programs, Inc. Solomon R. Guggenheim Museum (1071 Fifth Avenue, New York, NY 10028, telephone 212-360-3561).
   This model was developed in association with the museum. *PALS: A Guide for Teachers and Students*, edited by Barbara Rabson and Renata Warshaw, is a carefully designed program that has been field tested and reports exceptional reading gains.
The Writing Project, Teachers College, Columbia University (525 West 120th Street, New York, NY 10027)
   The Writing Project offers summer courses for teachers each year for credit or noncredit. Teachers have hands-on experience working with fellow teachers to develop their expertise in implementing a writer's workshop in their classrooms. Teachers also participate in the writing process, learning firsthand how it feels to be a student-author, in a process-centered classroom. Teachers participating in the summer workshops are invited to return for several weekends the year following the course for refresher workshop Saturdays. Keynote participants often include well-known children's authors and important leaders in the Writing Project.

SOURCES OF HELPFUL MATH MATERIALS

There are many intriguing manipulative materials available commercially. Several companies produce and distribute these materials. We recommend that you write for their catalogs. Some companies we have found to be particularly helpful and prompt are:

Creative Publications, Ordering Department, 5040 West 111th Street, Oak Lawn, IL 60453, 800-624-0822

Delta Education, Box M, Math Department, Nashua, NH 03061-6012, 800-258-1302 Editorial/Marketing Offices, 788 Palomar Avenue, Sunnyvale, CA 94086, 408-720-1400

ETA (Educational Teaching Aids), 199 Carpenter Avenue, Wheeling, IL 60090, 312-520-2500

Annotated Bibliography of Children's Literature

The following pages contain an annotated bibliography of some of our favorite children's stories. The American Library Association bibliographies suggest many more and are regularly updated. Another helpful reference is a small pamphlet, "A Teacher's Guide to Using Books with Gifted Children" (Berler & Young, 1982). The pamphlet provides a synopsis of fifteen Yearling and Laurel-Leaf Books published by Dell. Topics for discussion, questions, and activities are suggested.

Adams, Barbara. (1979). *Like it is: Facts and feelings about handicaps from the kids who know.* New York: Walker.
   Excellent photographic and text essays about kids who happen to be different in one way. Good sharing of the affective needs of such children (grades 4–6).
Adler, C. S. (1979). *The magic of the glits.* New York: Macmillan.
   A dialogue that is bright, intelligent, and nonsexist reveals how a teenage boy must take care of a shy seven-year-old girl during his summer vacation. The conversations between mother and son are well written. Deals with overcoming fears, moving away, and giving friends space to be themselves.
Adoff, Arnold, comp. (1968). *I am the darker brother.* New York: Macmillan.
   An excellent assortment of poems dealing with the black experience, but expressing feelings any minority, including the gifted, may have about not fitting into the larger society in which they live.
Arrick, Fran. (1983). *God's radar.* Scarsdale, NY: Bradbury.
   Deals with a conflict in religious beliefs when a student moves to the Bible Belt but is not of that religious persuasion. Touches on censorship of books (grades 7–9).
Asher, Sandy. (1983). *Things are seldom what they seem.* New York: Delacorte.
   Excellent characterization of gifted "weirdo," and kids who deal with the problem of a pedophile teacher's effects on students. Good resolution to the situation, but one line in story implies that sex among teens is acceptable. Read before recommending to a child (grades 7–9).
Asimov, Isaac, ed. (1984). *Young mutants.* New York: Harper and Row.
   One story, "The Children's Room," is recommended; language in the other sto-

ries could be considered offensive by some families. The recommended story is about seeing things differently and parents' willingness to accept this.

Baer, Frank. (1983). *Max's gang*. Boston: Little, Brown.

Translated from German, Max's Gang is a fascinating contrast to stories about the plight of Jews during Hitler's reign. This story details life for young German children who were sent to schools out of Germany to protect them, and the struggles they endured to return to Germany at the end of the war. Suffering, deprivation, hunger, and pain as well as people who were and were not willing to help are portrayed. Excellent takeoff point for discussion of author's point of view and critical thinking experiences (grades 7–9).

Balis, Andres. (1984). *P. J.* Boston: Houghton Mifflin.

Story of a perfectionist "teacher's pet" who gets into trouble to prove she's not perfect. How she deals with the horrendous problems she creates for herself provides good grounds for discussion (grades 4–6).

Baroh, Virginia Olsen, comp. (1969). *Here I am!* New York: E. P. Dutton.

Poems written by young people from many minority groups.

Chaikin, Miriam. (1983). *How Yossi beat the evil urge.* New York: Harper and Row.

See description in text, Chapter 6 (grades 2–4).

Chambers, Aidan. (1983). *The present takers.* New York: Harper and Row.

Book deals with peer threats and ganging up (grades 7–9).

Clavell, James. (1981). *The children's story.* New York: Delacorte Press.

A story about the malleability of children's minds and the ease with which belief systems can be changed in children. Very thought-provoking, even for adults.

Cleary, Beverly. (1983). *Dear Mr. Henshaw.* New York: Morrow, William.

Describes life from a child's point of view since his parents' divorce. Uses letters to an author.

Clifton, Lucille and DiGrazia, Thomas. (1980). *My friend Jacob.* New York: E. P. Dutton.

A young boy's relationship with an older, retarded friend reveals that friends can help each other in many ways (primary grades).

Cunningham, Julia. (1980). *A mouse called Junction.* New York: Pantheon.

A young mouse leaves his overprotected environment in search of experiences and learns that caring about others is more important than material goods (grades K–3).

Hansen, Joyce. (1980). *The gift-giver.* Boston: Houghton/Clarion.

Children in inner-city neighborhoods are no strangers to peer pressure, as this story of 10-year-old Doris shows. Amir, her new friend, doesn't follow the crowd, and his example helps Doris grow in self-confidence and in her understanding of others (intermediate grades through adult).

Hermes, Patricia. (1980). *What if they knew?* New York: Dell.

A young girl tries to hide her epilepsy from her friends for fear of rejection. She learns that real friends don't care if she is somehow different from the rest (intermediate grades to adult).

Kenny, K. and Krull, H. (1980). *Sometimes my mom drinks too much.* Milwaukee, WI: Raintree.

Young Maureen learns that her mother's alcoholism is no reflection on her own worth as a person. An important topic presented in a simple, direct way. Children will realize they are not alone in facing this family problem (grades 1–6).

Morgenroth, Barbara. (1979). *Tramps like us.* New York: Atheneum.
Problem novel about two kids who are misunderstood by their affluent parents and don't fit in with the school crowd, distinguished by the fact that Vanessa and her friend Daryl are intelligent, sensitive rebels who can reject the system without losing their sense of self-worth. Another one to read before suggesting to students, but worthwhile for older students (late junior high or high school age).

Oneal, Zibby. (1981). *The language of goldfish.* New York: Viking.
Carrie Stokes clings to the world of childhood in which a remembered goldfish pond is a magical place. Growing up becomes for her a painful journey to the edge of suicide and back again. Good for discussion of how growing up is harder for some people than others, conflict in dealing with changes, people who excel in art and math, and being different (grades 7–9).

Reiss, Johanna. (1972). *The Upstairs Room.* New York: Harper-Row.
A good story to contrast and compare with the *Diary of Anne Frank*. Two sisters spent two years hiding during World War II, but under very different conditions (grades 5–8).

Shreve, Judith S. (1980). *Living with a parent who drinks too much.* New York: Greenwillow.
A practical guide for both child and teacher, this book offers specific suggestions to make life more meaningful to a child living with an alcoholic; also cites ways for a child to seek additional help (intermediate grades and adult).

Sobol, Harriet Langsam. (1979). *My other-mother, My other-father.* New York: Macmillan.
A realistic presentation of a contemporary problem: children struggling through the emotional and logistical maze of divorce and remarriage. This honest appraisal of what it means to be a stepchild is well done, pertinent, and relevant (primary and intermediate grades).

Stein, Sara Bonnett. (1984). *On divorce.* New York: Walker.
A unique blend of vivid, full-page photographs and text help to create a shared experience between child and adult. The text allows the adult to deal with the child's natural curiosity about this subject (primary grades).

Stevenson, James (1980). *Howard.* New York: Greenwillow Books.
A duck, toad, pigeon, and some mice team up to survive the winter in New York City. The message of mutual support applies to the human condition as well (primary grades).

Talbot, Tony. (1980). *Dear Greta Garbo.* New York: Putnam.
Story of a young person's search for identity and independence amid the traumas of family life. A story about growing up that ends on a positive note.

Tolan, Stephanie S. (1980). *The liberation of Tansy Warner.* New York: Charles Scribner's Sons.
Teenage Tansy feels she is to blame when her mother abandons the family. This novel follows her emotional development as she grows in assertiveness and learns to confront her feelings (intermediate grades and adult).

VanLeeuwen, Jean. (1979). *Seems like this road goes on forever.* New York: Dial.

Feeling unloved by her stern, preoccupied parents, Mary Alice commits a series of self-destructive acts that lead to her hospitalization. Unable to speak, with the help of a skilled therapist, she recalls her past hurts, comes to understand them, and chooses a new direction (intermediate grades and adult).

Walker, Mary Alexander. (1980). *Maggot*. New York: Atheneum.

A unique combination of circumstances brings three lonely people together. Their sometimes tumultuous friendship helps them to learn about themselves and each other and to survive in what they perceive to be an unaccepting society (grades 5–9).

Zolotow, Charlotte. (1978). *Someone new*. New York: Harper and Row.

A thoughtful and provocative story about a child who discovers he is changing, and comes to realize what growing up means (primary grades).

Mathematics Curriculum Content Objectives

MEASUREMENT

Below are listed what the learner will be able to do:

Level 1

Linear: Measure using inches, feet, meters.
Weight: Understand concept of heaviness of a kilogram, pound.
Capacity: Use cup, pint, quart, liter as units of liquid measure.
Time: Tell time by hour, half-hour, quarter-hour.
Identify day of the week on a calendar.
Money: Know value of and use penny, nickel, dime, and mixed group of coins.
Counting Measure: Use concept of pair, dozen.

Level 2

Linear: Measure using centimeter.
Estimate number of centimeters, meters, inches, feet, yards.
Weight: Classify objects as greater than, less than a pound, kilogram.
Capacity: Use equivalent measures (C., pt., qt., gal., ml., l.).
Time: Identify day of the week, week of the month, and month of a year using a calendar.
Temperature: Read temperature in degrees F., C.
Money: Know value of and use quarter, half-dollar, dollar, group of coins containing these.
Select coins to match a value.
Counting Measure: Use concept of pair, half-dozen, dozen.

Level 3

Linear: Use square in., ft. to measure an area.
Measure and record in simplest form to nearest in., ft., yd., and metric units.
Estimate square area in standard and metric units.

Weight: Determine weight to nearest pound, gram, kilogram using various types of scales.

Capacity: Measure liquids accurately in C., pt., qt., gal., ml., and l.

Estimate approximate volume of liquids in standard and metric units.

Time: Tell time to nearest five minutes.

Understand A.M. and P.M. notation.

Record time in seconds, minutes, and hours using appropriate notation.

Temperature: Record temperatures using degrees F. and C.

Level 4

Linear: Measure and record in simplest form to nearest quarter inch, foot, yard, mile.

Find equivalent measures (in. to ft., ft. to yd., in. to yd., ft. to mile).

Measure and record length in simplest metric unit.

Weight: Weigh and record in simplest standard form (oz., lb., T.).

Find equivalent standard measures (oz. to lb., lb. to T.).

Weigh and record in simplest metric unit (g. and kg.).

Capacity: Measure and record in simplest standard measure (C., pt., qt., gal.).

Find equivalent standard measures of capacity.

Measure and record in simplest metric measure of capacity (ml., l.).

Recognize dry measure terms (pint, quart, peck, bushel).

Time: Tell time to nearest second using a stopwatch and second hand.

Record time to nearest second using proper notation.

Convert given length of time to mixed units (e.g., 68 hrs. to 2 days and 20 hours).

Find the sum of two periods of time; express answer in simplest terms.

Multiply periods of time and express in simplest terms.

Temperature: Understand freezing and boiling points of water in degrees F. and C. to use as a relative guide to hotness and coldness on each scale.

Money: Determine a correct amount of change.

Round money to nearest dime and dollar.

Level 5

Linear: Read scaled ruler to nearest $\frac{1}{16}$ in.

Convert, using approximations, between standard and metric measures of length (km. to miles; meters to in., etc.).

Weight: Convert, using approximation, between standard and metric measures of weight (kg. to lb., lb. to g., etc.).

Capacity: Convert, using approximations, between standard and metric measures of capacity (qt. to l., oz. to ml.).

Measure using dry measures.

Time: Determine elapsed time between two given times.

Temperature Graph daily fluctuations in temperature.

Money: Determine unit cost when given total cost and number of identical items.

Determine number of items that can be purchased when given total amount to be spent, item cost.

Scale: Given a scale of miles, estimate distance between points.
  Make a scale drawing.

Level 6

Linear: Measure line segments to nearest millimeter.
Weight: Weigh objects to nearest ounce.
  Weigh nearest gram (using double arm balance, and if available, triple beam balance).
Capacity: Measure liquids to nearest oz., C., pt., ml., l., etc.
Time: Determine time to nearest second accurately using standard clock.
Temperature: Determine increase and decrease in temperature in degrees F. and C.
Money: Given any combination of coins and paper, determine value.
Scale: Given length of a line and a scale, determine length represented.

Level 7 / 8

Linear: Perform basic operations in standard and metric systems, expressing answer in simplest terms.
Weight: Perform basic operations in standard and metric systems, expressing answer in simplest terms.
  Distinguish between mass and weight (e.g. by calculating mass and weight of self on different planets).
Capacity: Perform basic operations in standard and metric systems, expressing answer in simplest terms.
Time: Convert units of time.
  Convert standard time to military time (24-hour clock, as used by computer clocks).

GEOMETRY

Level 1

Plane Shapes: Identify square, circle, triangle, rectangle.
Point/Line/Segment: Identify symbol for point, line segment.

Level 2

Plane Shapes: Identify interior, exterior of circle, square, triangle, rectangle.
  Identify sides, corners (angles) and square corners of geometric shapes.
Point/Line/Segment: Construct line segments, and points defining line segments.

Level 3

Plane Shapes: Identify parallelograms, circles, rectangles, squares from descriptions of figures.
  Identify triangle and right triangle from descriptions.

Point/Line/Segment: Label segments, lines, rays, using appropriate mathematical symbols.

Solids: Identify cube, cone, cylinder, pyramid, and name attributes.

Measurement: Find perimeter of squares and rectangles.

Find area of two-dimensional shapes in square units.

Find volume of three-dimensional shapes in terms of cubic units.

Geometric Relationships: Understand relationships between plane shapes by using paper-folding activities in Paper and Scissor Polygons (Creative Publications).

Level 4

Plane Shapes: Identify quadrilaterals, hexagons, octagons.

Point/Line/Segment: Identify angles as obtuse, right, acute.

Identify segments as perpendicular or parallel.

Solids: Identify edges, faces, vertices of solid figures.

Measurement: Find area of any closed regular polygon.

Find surface area of rectangular solid.

Find volume of a rectangular solid.

Circles: Identify radius and diameter.

Geometric Relationships: Investigate and discover the properties of geometric figures and other formal concepts through the use of Mira.

Level 5

Plane Shapes: Construct different types of quadrilaterals.

Categorize square, rectangle, parallelogram, "other" quadrilaterals.

Identify triangles as isosceles, equilateral, and scalene.

Point/Line/Segment: Draw point, line, segment, ray, endpoint.

Identify intersection.

Use protractor to find degrees of a given angle.

Compare angles using greater than, less than, equal to.

Solids: Identify rectangular, triangular prisms, and sphere.

Measurement: Find area of a rectangle when presented with height and base.

Find perimeter of a triangle, parallelogram, rectangle, and square, using standard and metric measures.

Circles: Construct a circle using a compass.

Label circumference, diameter, radius.

Transformation/Congruence/Symmetry: Construct a reflection, rotation.

Identify congruent figures and congruent sides of two geometric figures.

Tesselations: Construct kaleidoscopes to generate a wide variety of geometric figures, tesselating patterns.

Level 6

Plane Shapes: Understand concept of plane.

Identify and name all regular polygons (3–10 sides).

Describe attributes of triangles: isosceles, scalene, and equilateral.

Point/Line/Segment: Construct perpendicular and parallel lines.
    Classify angles as acute or obtuse by number of degrees.
    Recognize angles as adjacent or vertical.
Measurement: Determine perimeter of any polygon.
    Given formula $C = \pi(d)$ find circumference $(\pi = \dfrac{22}{7})$
    Determine volume of rectangular prism and cube when given length of sides.
Circles: Identify center, chord.
Transformation/Congruence/Symmetry: Determine if a figure has a line of symmetry.
Tesselations: Discover the geometric concepts governing regular and nonregular tesse-
    lations.

Level 7 / 8

Plane Shapes: Name an intersection on a plane.
    Identify sides and vertices of a given polygon.
    Identify trapezoid, rhombus.
Point/Line/Segment: Construct an intersection of two lines.
    Label angles by identifying the vertex and sides of the angle.
    Describe skew lines.
    Recognize straight angles.
    Identify pairs of complementary, supplementary angles.
    Find measures of complement, supplement of given angles.
    Name vertical and adjacent angles in the geometric figure.
    Use knowledge of vertical, supplementary, complementary angles to find missing
    measures.
Measurement: Find volume of prism, cone, cylinder, sphere.
Transformation/Congruence/Symmetry: Draw line of reflection, rotation.
Construction: Use available tools (compass, protractor, straightedge, computer) to con-
    struct:
    Bisector of a given angle
    Perpendicular bisector of a segment
    Copy of a segment
    Perpendicular from a point on a line
    Perpendicular to a line from a point not on the line
    Pair of parallel lines
    Regular polygons using circles, central angles
Tesselations: Create Escher-type drawings.

PROBLEM-SOLVING AIDS

Level 1

Understanding a Problem: Say what plan they want to use to solve the problem.
    Write a number sentence to represent a picture.
    Solve a picture sentence.

Estimation: Estimate the answer to a problem before solving it.
Making Charts and Graphs: Read a pictograph.
    Read a picture chart.

Level 2

Understanding a Problem: Decide whether a problem needs an estimate answer or an exact answer.
    Describe how they solve the problem
    Identify missing and extraneous information in given problem.
    Write a number sentence to represent a concrete model used.
Estimation: Estimate the answer to a problem using front end estimation.
Making Charts and Graphs: Construct charts using information from the study of measurement.

Level 3

Understanding a Problem: Frame word problems orally to represent life situations that involve addition and subtraction, multiplication and division.
    Discuss alternate ways to solve the same problem
    Discuss extensions of a problem they solved.
    Write number sentences to represent pictured sets.
    Write number sentences to represent movement on a number line.
Estimation: Estimate sums and differences using rounding.
Making Charts and Graphs: Locate information in a table.
    Obtain information from pictographs, bar graphs, and line graphs.

Level 4

Understanding a Problem: See relationships between problems they have solved.
    Develop a "library" of model problems to use in solving future problems.
    Solve multi-step problems.
    Express a word phrase in mathematical notation.
Estimation: Estimate cost by rounding items to nearest dollar or dime.
    Estimate answers to problems using compatible numbers.
Charts and Graphs: Complete a table showing various units applying a single rate.
    Determine charge given a series of items to be purchased, tax rate table, and amount tendered.
    Determine shipping cost of a series of items given point of origin, destination, and rate table.
    Collect data and construct a table revealing information obtained.
    Make inference based on tables.

Level 5

Understanding a Problem: Given alternate methods to solve the same problem, tell why the one they chose is best in that situation and when another method would be better.

Given average speed, gas mileage, and cost of gas, determine traveling time and trip cost.

Determine correctness of telephone bill given rate table, type and number of calls, tax.

Estimation: Estimate answers to problems with special considerations.

Estimate whether enough money is available to purchase item given amount available and exact item costs.

Making Charts and Graphs: Interpret bar, broken-line, and circle graphs to answer relevant questions.

Construct graphs using ordered pairs after solving number sentences with two variables.

Averages/Probability: Find the average of several class grades.

Identify the chance of selecting a given item from a set of objects given the set's composition.

Level 6

Understanding a Problem: Solve a problem by working backwards, making a diagram.

Solve a nonroutine problem with only one number.

Represent a life problem with a number sentence using whole numbers, decimals, and mixed numbers.

Solve wage problems given hourly rate and hours worked.

Solve take-home pay given earnings and deductions.

Estimation: Check calculator correctness by using estimation.

Making Charts and Graphs: Construct line, bar, and pictographs given table of values.

Averages/Probability: Interpret batting averages as examples of probability.

Average a list of numbers.

Level 7 / 8

Understanding a Problem: Define discount, rate of discount (%), marked price, and sale price.

Compute sale price, discount, and rate of discount when two of the three elements are given.

Determine increase and decrease in stock market quotations.

Define commission and rate of commission.

Compute commission, rate of commission, and sale price when two of the three elements are present.

Compute total earnings when basic salary, rate of overtime, and hours of overtime are given.

Define principal interest, and rate of interest.

Compute simple interest when rate and principal are known.

Determine cost of a loan over time when principal and rate are known.

Estimation: Determine which form of estimation is best for a given problem.

Routinely apply estimation to solve problems.

Making Charts and Graphs: Read an amortization table.

Graph positive and negative integers and 0 on a number line.

Graph a given sentence with two variables.

Name coordinates of a given point.

Graph ordered pairs.

Interpret and construct 100% bar and circle graphs to depict statistical data.

Averages/Probability: Find the mean of a set of whole numbers.

NUMBERS/NUMERATION

Level 1

Sets: Use term *set* to mean a group.

Identify an empty set.

Recognize the number of elements in a set.

Compare the number of elements in a set.

Match objects in two sets.

Recognize numeral representations of number of objects in a set up to 10.

Counting: Read, count, and order number symbols through 100.

Count by 1's to 100.

Count by 2's to 12.

Symbols: Use = , <, > to compare two numbers less than 10.

Number Words: Read and write numbers through 10.

Read, count, and order number symbols through 100.

Place Value: Identify sets of 10.

Ordinals: Identify ordinals through tenth.

Odd and Even: Identify odd and even numbers from 1 to 40.

Fractions: Understand one-half of a set, one-half of a whole.

Understand one-fourth of a set, one-fourth of a whole.

Level 2

Sets: Recognize numeral representing a number of objects in a set to 100.

Order sets from large to small.

Counting: Count by 2's, 5's, and 10's to 100.

Symbols: Select <, >, = to compare numbers less than 100.

Number Words: Recognize name and number words through 100.

Place Value: Recognize 100 as ten 10's.

Record 100 in three places.

Compare numbers using place value.

Ordinals: Identify ordinals through twentieth.
   Identify, read, and write words *first* and *second*.
Fractions: Understand one-third of a set, one-third of a whole.
   Compare fractional parts of a whole (½, ¼, ⅓).

Level 3

Counting: Identify the next number after a word with 9 in the ones place.
   Count by 2's, 3's, 4's, 5's, and 10's to 300
   Complete sequences involving intervals of 2, 5, 10, or 100.
Symbols: Use $<$, $>$ to complete inequalities.
Number Words: Recognize, name, and read number words for numerals up to 1000.
   Write standard numeral when given its name up to million.
   Read dollars and cents to $1000.00.
Place Value: Group objects by thousands.
   Name place value of numerals up to millions.
   Round to nearest ten.
Ordinals: Identify, name, and write ordinals through thirty-first.
   Differentiate between cardinal and ordinal numbers.
Fractions: Identify equivalent fractions (e.g., ½ = ¼), using shaded parts of a whole.
Properties: Recognize commutative property of $+$ and $\times$.
   Recognize associative property of $+$ and $\times$.
   Know zero rule for addition.
   Know distributive property for multiplication.

Level 4

Counting: Count by 6's, 7's, 8's, 9's, ½'s and ¼'s.
Symbols: Use N or another variable to represent a number in an equation ($+$ and $-$).
Place Value: Identify a digit in a named place position through one millions place.
   Read and write number symbols to one million.
   Identify in expanded notation numerals through 9,999,999.
Ordinals: Recognize, name, and read ordinals through 99th.
Fractions: Identify numerator and denominator of a fraction.
   Identify any shaded part of a whole and write representative fraction.
   Identify and write representative fraction for any subset of a set.
   Compare fractions with picture representation using $<$, $>$, or $=$.
   Identify equivalent fractions using number lines (8ths).

Level 5

Counting: Count by common decimal fractions.
   Count by 10's, 200's, etc.
Place Value: Identify the one millions place value column.
   Read aloud any given numeral to 999,999,999.

Write any numeral through 999,999,999 when numeral is presented orally.
Write six-digit number in corresponding number words.
Write a four-digit numeral in expanded notation.
Write standard numeral when presented with numeral in expanded form (up to four digits).
Round a numeral up to four digits to the nearest tens, hundreds, thousands.
Fractions: Identify fractional part of a whole and the corresponding fractions ($\frac{1}{10}$, $\frac{1}{8}$, $\frac{1}{6}$, $\frac{1}{5}$, etc.).
Given two fractions, correctly identify the larger.
Powers: Find the square when presented with a base number.

Level 6

Counting: Identify the next number when presented with a sequence of numbers.
Place Value: Identify a number shown on a Russian or Chinese abacus.
Write up to seven-digit numeral in expanded notation.
Write up to five-digit numeral in expanded notation, using powers of ten.
Write standard form for numeral presented in expanded notation.
Round numerals up to six digits to nearest tens, hundreds, thousands.
Ordinals: Identify a number as an ordinal or cardinal number.
Fractions: Identify equivalent fractions.
State that fractions represent either part of a whole or part of a set.
Identify the least common denominator (LCD) for 3 fractions.
Identify the reciprocal of a common fraction or whole number.
Powers: Write exponential notation for a product such as $10 \times 10 \times 10$.

Level 7 / 8

Place Value: Determine place value for each digit in a decimal fraction.
Write word names for decimal numbers.
Fractions: Identify simplified fractions.
Identify equivalent fractions.
Compare fractions.
Find the average of two fractions and/or mixed numerals.
Properties: Illustrate the commutative and associative properties of $+$ and $\times$.
State the property of zero for addition.
State the property of one for multiplication.
State and illustrate the distributive property of multiplication over addition.
Powers: Identify meaning of a negative exponent.
Write exponential notation given a fractional numeral.
Write scientific notation given a standard numeral.
Expand numerals using positive and negative exponents.
Find the product of numbers with exponents by adding the exponents.
Find the quotient of numbers with exponents by subtracting exponents.
Find the powers of powers (e.g., five to the sixth power squared).

BASIC OPERATIONS

Level 1

Addition: Join two sets and give the total number of members.
   Understand that addition is joining of sets.
   Add 2 one-digit numerals in both vertical and horizontal form.
   Know basic facts through 10.
   Know that the sum of two addends is not affected by order (commutative property).
   Know that the sum of more than 2 addends is not affected by grouping (associative property).
Subtraction: Know that subtraction is the inverse of addition.
   Know facts through 10.
   Determine a missing addend through 10.

Level 2

Addition: Add one digit and two digit numerals with regrouping to tens.
   Calculate sum of repeating number (e.g. 3 fours, $4 + 4 + 4$; 5 twos, $2 + 2 + 2 + 2 + 2$).
   Basic addition facts through 20.
   Find the sum of two 3-digit numerals with regrouping.
   Find the sum of three addends with regrouping.
   Add zero to a number.
Subtraction: Know facts through 18.
   Subtract zero from a number.
   Determine missing addend through 18.
Multiplication: Know facts through 5.
   Associate multiplication fact with its related addition fact.

Level 3

Addition: Add 4 or more digits with regrouping.
Subtraction: Subtract three-digit numerals with regrouping.
   Subtract with up to three zeros in top numerals.
   Find missing addend by subtraction.
Multiplication: Know facts through nine-times-table.
   Multiply one-digit multiplier by four-digit multiplicand with regrouping.
   Multiply two-digit multiplier by three-digit multiplicand.
Division: Demonstrate that division can mean separating into equal sets or repeated subtraction.
   Recognize that division is the inverse of multiplication.
   Write multiplication and division number families.
   Divide with one-digit divisor, three-digit dividend.
   Check division by multiplication.

Level 4

Addition: Group digits to "sums of tens" in column addition.
Find sum of two fractional numbers with like denominators.
Find sum of two mixed numbers having fractions with like denominators.
Subtraction: Find difference when presented with two fractions having like denominators.
Multiplication: Multiply four-digit multiplicand by two-digit multiplier.
Create a set of equivalent fractions by multiplying numerator and denominator by the same number.
Identify equivalent improper fraction for whole number.
Division: Show that division is repeated subtraction (one-digit divisor and four-digit dividend).
Divide using standard division algorithm (one-digit divisor).
Divide by a multiple of 10 and a three-digit dividend.
Divide using a 2-digit divisor and 3- or 4-digit dividend.
Check division by multiplying.
Identify equivalent mixed numeral by dividing an improper fraction.

Level 5

Addition: Find sums of up to five addends involving up to five-digit numerals.
Find the sum of two common fractions with like or unlike denominators.
Add two or more mixed numerals.
Change two or more mixed numerals to improper fractions and find the sum.
Find the sum of a whole number and a common fraction.
Add decimals to the hundredths place.
Subtraction: Find the difference between two fractions with like denominators.
Find the difference between two mixed numerals with unlike denominators, no regrouping.
Find the difference between two mixed numerals with regrouping.
Subtract decimals with regrouping.
When given monetary values (dimes, nickels, etc.), convert to decimal form and subtract.
Multiplication: Multiply four-digit multiplicand by three-digit multiplier.
Find equivalent fractions.
Change a mixed numeral to an improper fraction.
List multiples of given numbers.
Find the least common denominator for more than two given fractions.
Multiply a decimal by a single given numeral.
Division: Find quotient for a five-digit dividend and three-digit divisor.
Convert an improper fraction to a mixed numeral.
Divide a decimal by a single-digit divisor.

Level 6

Addition: Add any positive or negative rational number.
  Add any fractional or mixed numeral.
  Add any decimal number.
Subtraction: Subtract any positive or negative rational number.
  Subtract any fractional or mixed numerals.
  Subtract any decimal number.
Multiplication: Multiply two common fractions.
  Multiply two mixed numerals.
  Multiply whole numbers and mixed numerals.
  Multiply two decimals.
Division: Divide up to a seven-digit dividend by up to a four-digit divisor.
  Divide two common fractions.
  Divide a whole number by a decimal.
  Divide a decimal by a decimal.

Answers to Parents' Questions

This booklet is distributed to parents when their children are recommended for the program for gifted underachievers.

WHAT PARENTS OFTEN ASK ABOUT
THE SPECIAL CLASS FOR GIFTED UNDERACHIEVERS

Your child has been recommended for our special program for gifted children who are underachieving in school. Many parents have asked questions about this program when they first learn of it. The following are the most frequently asked questions and the answers we offer. Please read them. If you have additional questions, our coordinator of gifted programs will be most happy to try to answer them for you. Please feel free to call.

1. What Is a Gifted Underachiever?

Gifted underachievers are children who seem to have high potential. They may have a high IQ score, or their achievement test scores may be high. They may have a special creative spark noticed by their teachers or you, their parents.

But, for some reason, these children are not doing so well as could be expected in school. Some may be failing some or all subjects. Others may be doing merely average work, which is below expectation based on our predictors of school success.

* * *

2. Why Doesn't the School Just Let Them Be Average?

Some children are content being average. More frequently, children with high IQ's or high achievement test scores and failing grades know they should be doing better—often without anyone saying so in words. For some reason, and the reasons are varied, they simply can't. This causes their sense of self-esteem to drop, leading to more difficulty and frequently more failure. So allowing them to be "average" doesn't last; without help, these children frequently fall below average.

We have found that many of the children served in the past are learning disabled, or have been undereducated, or have lacked motivation. These problems can be helped. But special techniques are necessary.

* * *

3. Then Why Not Put Them in the Regular Remedial Classes If They Are Failing?

It would seem that the existing programs might suffice. Our resource-room teachers are good teachers who have helped nongifted children with their special needs. Why not also the gifted?

Normal resource rooms function with a rationale that works effectively for children with normal ability. Repetition and highly structured approaches have been shown both in research and practice to help typical students with learning problems of various types.

But gifted children are not typical learners. Research and practice have also shown that repetition and high structure are precisely the two conditions most counterproductive for gifted students. These children learn exceptionally well in a classroom using varied, novel approaches that capitalize on the high reasoning ability and creativity the students have.

Placing these children in the regular resource room would tax that teacher's ability to help either group of students effectively. It would hurt, not help, the students normally placed there, the gifted students who have learning problems, and the teacher responsible for their education.

4. What Goes on in the Special Class?

The special program designed for these children has two major parts.

One part deals with cognitive skills. We help by finding out what specific skills the children are missing and help them to learn those skills. We use methods that are appropriate for the gifted. We concentrate on the basic skills areas of reading, language, and math, but enrich their instruction by building it around their special interests. As soon as the children are ready, we accelerate their learning.

We also teach "school-survival skills." These are things that most good students pick up without direct teaching. Somehow, these students do not. They include such skills as how to ask for teachers' help, how to budget their work time, how to remember assignments and so on.

The second part of the program deals with affective—social and emotional—skills. We teach "pro-social" skills, such as how to start and end a conversation with a new friend, how to say no to someone who is causing a distraction without alienating them, and how to solve disagreements.

Common problems the children share are discussed and dealt with in small-group discussions. Children learn ways to deal with stress, to communicate better with others who are older or the same age, and to make good decisions for themselves.

Other important affective activities include building trust in others through co-operative games and sports, learning to make and enforce fairly the group's decisions, which affect themselves and others, and learning to live up to their responsibilities to others.

*   *   *

5. What Do They Miss by Being in the Special Class?

The children attend class for the first two periods of the school day. Most children leave their regular reading and math classes to receive instruction in these skills in the special class. The teacher of the special class assumes all responsibility for academic growth in these subjects.

Seventh- and eighth-grade students miss either a social studies or a science class and a "specials" class of art, music, or health. The teacher of the special class and the regular classroom teacher of the missed subjects plan together to be sure the children are not penalized by missing the class. The special teacher and classroom teacher together determine the child's grades.

*   *   *

6. What is Their Schedule Like in the Special Class?

During these two periods, small-group meetings about 20 minutes long are set aside for school-survival skills, pro-social skills, stress-reduction skills, cooperative sports and games, and class meetings. One such meeting is held daily.

The remaining 80 minutes of class time is split into ten-minute blocks. Mini-lessons, teaching a child or small group of children one concept or skill they need to learn, are scheduled in each ten-minute block. These are usually the reading, language, math, or social studies/science lessons students miss.

While the children are not working directly with the teacher, they are expected to complete the "must do" assignments. Each day they must write in their journal. They also complete a reading and a math assignment based on the most recent instruction or a review of a previously learned concept. These assignments are checked by the teacher before the next lesson is planned.

There are also "may do" centers. These provide enrichment and a chance to practice new social skills. They include art activities, computer programs, practical life activities (such as snack preparations and kitchen clean-up), independent reading and creative writing, as well as independent studies. Students are encouraged to bring work, especially long-term assignments, from their regular classes to work on during this time. Our goal is to teach them to deal with choice and to manage their time effectively.

*   *   *

7. How Does the Teacher Know What to Teach My Child?

An individual educational plan is prepared for each child, based on the regular school curriculum as well as the special curriculum designed for this program. The child's plan will include major goals based on his or her strengths and weaknesses in the academic and affective areas the program covers.

Children are tested on an individual achievement test to determine the appropriate instructional level. They are then pre-tested on skills normally taught at that level. Only those skills that give them difficulty are included in the plan. There is no need to reteach something the child already knows well.

*   *   *

8. Will My Child Still Get a Report Card?

Yes. This is a direct result of a request by the students. They will be graded on achievement, but *not* compared to their regular classmates. Instead, at the start of the marking period, the student and the teacher set reasonable goals for the student in each subject area. These goals are taken from the individual plan and are listed in the student's notebook. Instruction is planned to help students meet the stated goals. While adjustments can be made during the marking period, at the close the student and the teacher decide whether those goals have or have not been achieved.

"A" means all goals have been achieved at an excellent level. "B" means most goals have been achieved at a very good level. "C" means about three-fourths of the goals have been completed at an acceptable level. "D" and "F" are not used. Instead, "NG" will be assigned if work falls below an appropriate level for this class. This is a signal that a parent–student–teacher conference is needed.

Besides regular report cards, a narrative report will be sent with every student. This will define the specific gains, based on teacher observations, made by the student toward educational goals. When "NG" is assigned, the narrative will describe for you what *has* been achieved by the student.

At least twice yearly, during the regularly scheduled parent conferences, we will ask to meet with you so we can discuss your child's progress face-to-face. Please feel free to schedule more frequent personal or phone conferences if you feel the need.

*   *   *

9. What Should I Tell My Child about the Program?

When you agree to place your child in this program, the teacher will meet with the child and explain what is included in this booklet to him or her. Most of the children we have worked with felt good about "going to the gifted class." Occasionally, a child does not understand what we have said and sees it as a threat or punishment. Please schedule a parent–teacher–student conference if you know this is the case with your child.

We recommend to parents that they tell children this is a special class to help them with their special talents in a special way. It will also help them learn to solve some of their problems. It should be enjoyable and it should make them feel good about themselves.

Children enrolled in the early classes have said they liked the special class because

> "There's lots to choose from."
> "There's no boring review."
> "You feel like you want to do the work, not because you have to."
> "You're not always in the wrong when you don't do what the others do."
> "The teacher cares about you."
> "You learn to get rid of tension."
> "Suddenly I like school; I'm never absent."

10. What Changes Have Taken Place in Past Students?

In January of 1986, an evaluator from the Center for the Study and Education of the Gifted, Teachers College, Columbia University, came to Green Township. She interviewed students, parents, and teachers to learn if this program had really made a difference in the lives of children. She also checked achievement test scores and school grades and scores on a test of self-esteem. This is what she found.

On the Iowa Test of Basic Skills, reading gains were more than 1.5 months for each month students were enrolled. On the Woodcock–Johnson Assessment Battery, an individual achievement test, the average gain in reading skills was *two years and three months* in the five-month period!

In language arts, again on the Woodcock–Johnson, the average gain in language skills was *one year and five months* in a five-month period.

Math gains were also positive. Average gain was 5.9 months in the five-month period. This is still slightly above average, although not so impressive as the reading and language gains. Research shows that this difference in gains is typical for programs of this sort. It may be due to the selection of test items for a math achievement test rather than to lower gains by the children.

A self-esteem inventory indicated the program was influential in substantially improving attitude toward school and a general sense of well-being in the students.

Parents interviewed offered the following perceptions of changes in their children. These examples have been selected from a sample of thirty.

> "She improved her ability to start homework and finish it without my nagging."
> "He has the ability now to sit through tests without messing it up. It's incredible. He's a different person."
> "He would have been lost in a crowd without the UAG."
> "He's happier than we've ever seen him."
> "She is more tolerant of others in the family."
> "He improved his attendance."

"A complete turnaround, she is less excitable and anxious, and more loving to all of us."

Teachers were more tempered, but offered the following from among thirty quotes appearing in the evaluation:
"I hated to fail some of them, but [earlier] they literally didn't do a thing or turn in work. Now, there's some change."
"You can see Ned is already relaxed and different."
"They're learning some controls."
"Work done is unbelievably good, compared to before UAG."

*   *   *

11. How Can I Learn More to Really Help My Child?

A parent support group meets regularly in the evening so that working parents can attend. The special classroom teacher, the school psychologist, and occasional community resource people share tips with parents. They try to help parents better understand their children and their children's needs.

The goals of this program are to help parents

Develop an understanding of some of the possible causes of underachievement in school.

Examine their expectations for their child to determine if they are appropriate expectations.

Explore privately their personal family structures and the dynamics in it.

Practice the same positive communication skills their children are learning so they know how to respond to new behavior.

Develop an understanding of which problems children have that are passing "phases" and which require outside help.

Have the opportunity to discuss problems with the support group and to develop self-help systems.

A schedule of this year's meetings is included for your convenience. Each meeting includes an hour of instruction and activities followed by some informal time for questions and socialization. Please plan to come. We need each of you for a good group.

References

Bagley, M., & Hess, K. (1982). *200 ways of using creative imagery in the classroom.* Woodcliff Lake, NJ: New Dimensions of the 80's.

Baldridge, J. V., & Deal, T. (Eds.) (1983). *The dynamics of organizational change in education.* Berkeley, CA: McCutchen.

Bandura, A. (1982). The psychology of chance encounters and life paths. *American Psychologist, 37*(7), 747–755.

Basile, L. J. (1980). *The special education plan and record book.* New York: Teachers College Press.

Baum, S. (1984). Meeting the needs of learning disabled gifted students. *Roeper Review, 7,* 16–19.

Baum, S., & Kirschenbaum, R. (1984). Recognizing special talents in learning disabled students. *Teaching Exceptional Children, 16,* 92–98.

Beane, J. A. & Lipka, R. P. (1986). *Self-concept, self-esteem, and the curriculum.* New York: Teachers College Press.

Beating the odds: Professor finds unlikely achievers control their own fate. (1985–86, Fall/Winter). *TC Today, 14*(1), p. 3.

Berler, J., & Young, S. (Eds.). (1982). *A teacher's guide to using books with gifted children.* New York: Dell.

Bloom, B. (Ed.) (1956). *Taxonomy of educational objectives. Handbook I: Cognitive domain.* New York: David McKay.

Borg, W. R., & Gall, M. E. (1983). *Educational research: An introduction.* New York: Longman.

Borland, J., & Jacobs, H. H. (1986, June). Borland–Jacobs interdisciplinary model. In H. H. Jacobs (Chair), *Interdisciplinary curriculum design.* Course conducted at Teachers College, Columbia University, New York, NY.

Bricklin, P. M. (1983). Working with the parents of learning-disabled/gifted children. In L. H. Fox, L. Brody, & D. Tobin (Eds.), *Learning-disabled/gifted children* (pp. 243–260). Baltimore, MD: University Park Press.

Brown, A. L., & Ferrara, R. A. (1985). Diagnosing zones of proximal development. In J. Wertsch (Ed.), *Culture, communication, and cognition: Vygotskian perspectives* (pp. 273–305). New York: Cambridge University Press.

Brownstone, J. E., & Dye, C. J. (1973). *Communication workshop for parents of adolescents: Leader's guide.* Champaign, IL: Research Press.

Calkins, L. M. (1986). *The art of teaching writing.* Portsmouth, NH: Heinemann Educational Books.

Chaikin, M. (1983). *How Yossi beat the evil urge.* New York: Harper & Row.

Cihak, M. K., & Heron, B. J. (1980). *Games children should play.* Santa Monica, CA: Goodyear.

Clark, B. (1983a). *Growing up gifted.* Columbus, OH: Charles E. Merrill.

Clark, B. (1983b, November). *Integrative education strategies for optimizing learning using brain based curriculum.* Paper presented at the National Association for Gifted Children Convention, Philadelphia, PA.

Clark, B. (1986). *Optimizing learning: The integrative education model in the classroom.* Columbus, OH: Merrill.

Clemens, F. W., & Mullis, H. T. (1981, December). *Helping the gifted child cope with stress.* Paper presented at the Council for Exceptional Children/Talented and Gifted Conference, Orlando, FL.

Commission on Standards for School Mathematics of the National Council of Teachers of Mathematics. (1989). *Curriculum and evaluation standards for school mathematics.* Reston, VA: The Council.

Conference Board of The Impact of Computing Technology on School Mathematics (1985). *Recommendations on curriculum, instruction, and teacher education.* Report of the Conference supported in part by the National Science Foundation.

Coopersmith, S. (1981). *Coopersmith self-esteem inventory.* Palo Alto, CA: Consulting Psychologists Press.

Cushenberry, D. C., & Howell, H. (1974). *Reading and the gifted child.* Springfield, IL: Charles C. Thomas.

Daniels, N., & Cox, J. (1988). *Flexible pacing for able learners.* Reston, VA: Council for Exceptional Children.

Daniels, P. R. (1983). *Teaching the gifted/learning disabled child.* Rockville, MD: Aspen Systems Corporation.

Daurio, S. P. (1979). Educational enrichment versus acceleration: A review of the literature. In W. C. George, S. J. Cohn, & J. D. Stanley (Eds.), *Education of the gifted: Acceleration and enrichment* (pp. 13–63). Baltimore, MD: Johns Hopkins University Press.

Davits, J., & Davits, L. (1979). *Making it: 40 & beyond: Surviving the mid-life crisis.* Minneapolis, MN: Winston Press.

Diener, C., & Dweck, C. (1980). An analysis of learned helplessness: II. The processing of success. *Journal of Personality and Social Psychology, 39,* 940–952.

Dreikurs, R., & Soltz, V. (1964). *Children: The challenge.* New York: Hawthorn Books.

Duffy, G. G., Roehler, L. R., & Mason, J. (1984). *Comprehension and instruction: Perspectives and suggestions.* New York: Longman.

Duffy, G. G., Roehler, L. R., Meloth, M. S., Vavrus, L. B., Book, C., Putnam, J., & Wesselman, R. (1986). Relationships between explicit verbal explanations during reading skill instructions and student awareness and achievement: A study of reading teacher effects. *Reading Research Quarterly, 21*(3), 237–252.

Dweck, C. (1975). The role of expectations and attributions in the alleviation of learned helplessness. *Journal of Personality and Social Psychology, 31,* 674–685.

Dweck, C., & Bempechat, J. (1980). Children's theories of intelligence: Consequences for learning. In S. G. Paris, G. M. Olson, & H. W. Stevenson (Eds.), *Learning and motivation in the classroom* (pp. 239–256). Hillsdale, NJ: Lawrence Erlbaum.

Eberle, R. F. (1977). *Scamper: Games for imagination development.* Buffalo, NY: D.O.K. Publishers.

Education Consolidation and Improvement Act of 1981, Section 582, Title 97–35.

Education for All Handicapped Children Act of 1975, Title 94–142.

Erickson, E. H. (1950). *Childhood and society.* New York: W. W. Norton.

Feuerstein, R. (1979). *The dynamic assessment of retarded performers.* Baltimore, MD: University Park Press.

Fluegelman, A. (1981). *More new games! and playful ideas from the New Games Foundation.* Garden City, NY: Doubleday.

Fox, L. H., & Brody, L. (1983). Models for identifying giftedness: Issues related to the learning-disabled child. In L. H. Fox, L. Brody, & D. Tobin (Eds.), *Learning-disabled/gifted children* (pp. 101–116). Baltimore: University Park Press.

Fox, L. H., Brody, L., & Tobin, D. (Eds.) (1983). *Learning disabled/gifted children.* Baltimore: University Park Press.

Frasier, M., & McCannon, C. (1981). Using bibliotherapy with gifted children. *Gifted Child Quarterly, 25*(2), 81–85.

Gallagher, J. (1975). *Teaching the gifted child.* Boston: Allyn and Bacon, Inc.

Gardner, H. (1983). *Frames of mind: The theory of multiple intelligences.* New York: Basic Books.

Gavelek, J. R. (1984). The social contexts of literacy and schooling: A developmental perspective. In T. L. Raphael & R. E. Reynolds (Eds.), *The contexts of school based literacy* (pp. 3–26). New York: Random House.

Gaver, A., & Maxlish, E. (1980). *How to talk so kids will listen and listen so kids will talk.* New York: Avon Books.

George, W. C., Cohn, S. J., & Stanley, J. D. (Eds.). (1979). *Education of the gifted: Acceleration and enrichment.* Baltimore, MD: Johns Hopkins University Press.

Gesell, A., & Ilg, F. L. (1946). *The child from five to ten.* New York: Harper and Row.

Good, T., & Grouws, D. (1988, February). *The Missouri math model.* Paper presented at an in-service meeting, Roxbury Township Schools, Succasunna, NJ.

Gross, N., Giaquinta, J. B., & Bernstein, M. (1971). *Implementing organizational innovations: A sociological analysis of planned change.* New York: Basic Books.

Grouws, D. A. (1988). Teaching tomorrow's skills responsibly. *Arithmetic Teacher, 35*(2), 6.

Guilford, J. P. (1967). *The nature of human intelligence.* New York: McGraw-Hill.

Harnadek, A. (1984). *Mind benders: warm up, A, B, C.* Pacific Grove, CA: Midwest Publications.

Heinemann, A. (1977). Underachievers among the gifted and talented. In *Star power: Providing for the gifted and talented. (Module 6).* Austin, TX: Education Service Center.

Hendricks, G., & Roberts, T. (1977). *The second centering book.* Englewood Cliffs, NJ: Prentice-Hall.

Herzfeld, G., & Powell, R. (1986). *Coping for kids: A complete stress control program for students ages 8–18.* West Nyack, NY: Center for Applied Research in Education.

Jackson, P. (1968). *Life in classrooms.* New York: Holt, Rinehart, and Winston.

Jacobs, H. H. (1986, June). The Socratic method. In H. H. Jacobs (Chair), *Interdis-*

ciplinary curriculum design, Course conducted at Teachers College, Columbia University, New York, NY.

Janos, P. M., Fung, H., & Robinson, N. (1985). Self-concept, self-esteem and peer relations among gifted children who feel different. *Gifted Child Quarterly, 29*(2), 78–81.

Kennedy, L. M. (1986). A rationale. *Arithmetic Teacher, 33*(6), 6–7.

Kookogey, A. K., & Stern, J. L. (1985). *SPARKS.* Rahway, NJ: Rahway Public Schools.

Krantz, B. (1986). *Evaluation report for the Greentownship [sic] (Sussex County) elementary school.* New York: Center for the Study and Education of the Gifted, Teachers College, Columbia University.

Kratwohl, D., Bloom, B., & Masia, B. (1964). *Taxonomy of educational objectives. Handbook II: Affective domain.* New York: David McKay.

Labuda, M. (Ed.). (1974). *Creative reading for gifted learners: A design for excellence.* Newark, DE: International Reading Association.

Lerner, H. G. (1985). *The dance of anger: A woman's guide to the changing patterns of intimate relationships.* New York: Harper & Row.

Lerner, J. (1985). *Learning disabilities: Theories, diagnosis, and teaching strategies.* Boston: Houghton Mifflin.

Lewin, K. (1958). Group decision and social change. In Macoby et al. (Eds.), *Readings in social psychology* (pp. 459–473). New York: Holt, Rinehart and Winston.

Lieberman, A., & Miller, A. (1979). *Staff development: New demands, new realities, new perspectives.* New York: Teachers College Press.

Mace, N. J., & Rabins, P. B. (1981). *The 36-hour day: A family guide to caring for persons with Alzheimer's disease, related dementing illnesses, and memory loss in later life.* Baltimore, MD: Johns Hopkins University Press.

Mangieri, J. N., & Madigan, F. (1984). Reading for gifted students: What schools are doing. *Roeper Review, 7*(2), 68–70.

Martin, C. E. (1984). Why some gifted children do not like to read. *Roeper Review, 7*(2), 72–75.

Martin, K. (1988). Toward improved instruction for mathematically able students. In N. Daniels & J. Cox (Eds.), *Flexible pacing for able learners* (pp. 85–95). Reston, VA: Council for Exceptional Children.

McCowan, R. D. (1968). Group counseling with underachievers and their parents. *School Counselor, 16,* 30–35.

McGinnis, E. & Goldstein, A. P. (1984). *Skillstreaming the elementary school child: A guide for teaching pro-social skills.* Champaign, IL: Research Press.

Miller, L., & Wolf, T. (1978). Staff development for school change: Theory and practice. In A. Lieberman & L. Miller (Eds.), *Staff development* (pp. 144–160). New York: Teachers College Press.

Mink, O. B. (1964). Multiple counseling with underachieving junior high school pupils of bright-normal and higher ability. *Journal of Educational Research, 58,* 31–34.

Montemayor, R. (1984). Changes in parent and peer relationships between childhood and adolescence: A research agenda for gifted adolescence. *Journal for the Education of the Gifted, 8*(1), 2–23.

National Council of Supervisors of Mathematics. (1988). *Basic mathematics skills for the 21st century*. Minneapolis, MN: National Council of Supervisors of Mathematics. Draft position paper.

National Council of Teachers of Mathematics. (1987). *Providing opportunities for the mathematically gifted*. Reston, VA: The Council.

National Institute of Education. (1984). *Becoming a nation of readers: The report of the Commission on Reading*. Champaign, IL: Center for the Study of Reading.

Nichols, R. C. (1965). The inheritance of general and specific ability. *NMSC Research Report, 1*(1). Evanston, IL: National Merit Scholarship Corporation.

Ohlsen, M., & Gazda, G. (1965). Counseling underachieving bright pupils. *Education, 86*, 78–81.

Ojemann, G. (1985, April). *The neurobiology of extraordinary intellectual giftedness*. Paper presented at the meeting of the Foundation for Brain Research, New York City.

Orlick, T. (1978). *The cooperative sports and games book: Challenge without competition*. New York: Pantheon Books.

Palincsar, A. S., & Brown, A. L. (1984). Reciprocal teaching of comprehension-fostering and comprehension-monitoring activities. *Cognition and Instruction, 1*(2), 117–175.

Parnes, S. J. (1972). *Creativity: Unlocking human potential*. Buffalo: D.O.K. Publishers.

Passow, A. H. (1985). Intellectual development of the gifted. In F. R. Link (Ed.), *Essays on the intellect* (pp. 23–44). Alexandria, VA: Association for Supervision and Curriculum Development.

Perkins, J. A., & Wicas, E. A. (1971). Group counseling bright underachievers and their mothers. *Journal of Counseling Psychology, 18*, 273–278.

Peterson, K. (1977). *Bridge to Terabithia*. New York: Harper & Row.

Phenix, P. (1964). *Realms of meaning*. New York: McGraw-Hill.

Pirozzo, R. (1982). Gifted underachievers. *Roeper Review, 4*(4), 18–21.

Purkey, W. W. (1970). *Self-concept and school achievement*. Englewood Cliffs, NJ: Prentice-Hall.

Raph, J. B., & Tannenbaum, A. J. (1961). *Underachievement: Review of Literature*. Mimeo. Talented Youth Project, Horace Mann–Lincoln Institute of School Experimentation. New York: Teachers College, Columbia University.

Raph, J. B., Goldberg, M. L., & Passow, A. H. (1966). *Bright underachievers*. New York: Teachers College Press.

Renzulli, J. (1977). *The enrichment triad model: A guide for developing defensible programs for the gifted and talented*. Mansfield Center, CT: Creative Learning.

Renzulli, J. (1978). What makes giftedness? Reexamining a definition. *Phi Delta Kappan, 60*, 180–184, 261.

Richert, E. S. (1982). *National report on identification*. Sewell, NJ: Educational Improvement Center South.

Richert, E. S. (1983, April). *Personality patterns of the gifted*. Paper presented at the annual meeting of the Sussex County Association for the Gifted, Sparta, NJ.

Rimm, S. (1983, November), *Gifted underachievers*. Paper presented at the National Association for Gifted Children Convention, Philadelphia, PA.

Rohnke, K. (1977). *Cow's tails and cobras*. Hamilton, MA: Project Adventure.

Rosner, S. L., & Seymour, J. (1983). The gifted child with a learning disability: Clinical evidence. In L. H. Fox, L. Brody, & D. Tobin (Eds.), *Learning disabled/ gifted children* (pp. 77–97). Baltimore, MD: University Park Press.

Rupley, W. H. (1984). Reading teacher effectiveness: Implications for teaching the gifted. *Roeper Review, 7*(2), 70–72.

Sarason, S. B. (1971). *The culture of the school and the problem of change*. Boston: Allyn and Bacon.

Schachter, R. S. (1986). *Kinetic psychotherapy in the treatment of children*. Paper presented at the Emotional Development of the Gifted: Promising Practices for Professionals and Parents, a conference sponsored by the Center for the Study and Education of the Gifted, Teachers College, Columbia University, New York, NY.

Seigel, P. (1986, March). An untitled paper presented at the Emotional Development of the Gifted: Promising Practices for Professionals and Parents, a conference sponsored by the Center for the Study and Education of the Gifted, Teachers College, Columbia University, New York, NY.

Senf, G. M. (1983). The nature and identification of learning disabilities and their relationship to the gifted child. In L. H. Fox, L. Brody, & D. Tobin (Eds.), *Learning disabled/gifted children* (pp. 37–49). Baltimore, MD: University Park Press.

Sheehy, G. (1976). *Passages: Predictable crises of adult life*. New York: E. P. Dutton.

Silverstone, B., & Hyman, H. K. (1976). *You and your aging parent: A guide to understanding emotional, physical, and financial needs*. New York: Pantheon Books.

Smith, L. M., & Keith, P. M. (1971). *Anatomy of an educational innovation: An organizational analysis of an elementary school*. New York: John Wiley and Sons.

Sternberg, R. (1984, May). *A triarchic theory of intellectual giftedness*. Paper presented at the Symposium on Cognition and Giftedness, Teachers College, Columbia University, New York.

Stevens, R. (1983). *Erik Erikson: An introduction*. New York: St. Martin's.

Supplee, P. L. (1986). *Reaching the gifted underachiever: 1985–86 grant program summative evaluation*. Trenton, NJ: New Jersey State Department of Education.

Supplee, P. L. (1987/1988). Listen to the children: An analysis of a program to reverse underachievement among the gifted (Doctoral dissertation, Teachers College, Columbia University, 1987). *Dissertation Abstracts International, 48*(7), 1738-A.

Supplee, P. L. (1989). Children at risk: The gifted underachiever. *Roeper Review, 11*(3), 163–166.

Suydam, M. N. (1986). Manipulative materials and achievement. *Arithmetic Teacher, 33*(6), 10.

Szabos, J. (1984). *Reading: A novel approach*. Carthage, IL: Good Apple.

Tannenbaum, A. J. (1983). *Gifted children: Psychological and educational perspectives*. New York: Macmillan.

Tannenbaum, A. J., & Baldwin, L. J. (1983). Giftedness and learning disability: A paradoxical combination. In L. H. Fox, L. Brody, & D. Tobin (Eds.), *Learning disabled/gifted children* (pp. 11–36). Baltimore, MD: University Park Press.

Teasdale, S. (1920). "Stars." *Flame and shadow*. New York: Macmillan.

Terman, L. M. (1924). The physical and mental traits of gifted children. In G. M.

Whipple (Ed.), *Report of the society's committee on the education of gifted children.* The Twenty-Third Yearbook of the National Society for the Study of Education (pp. 155–167). Bloomington, IL: Public School Publishing.

Thompson, L. J. (1971). Language disabilities in men of eminence. *Journal of Learning Disabilities, 4*, 34–45.

Thorndike, R. L. (1963). *The concepts of over- and underachievement.* New York: Bureau of Publications, Teachers College, Columbia University.

Thornton, C. A., & Wilmot, B. (1986). Special learners. *Arithmetic Teacher, 33*(6), 38–41.

Torman, W. (1976). *Family constellation.* New York: Springer.

Udall, A. J., & Maker, C. J. (1983). A pilot program for elementary-age learning-disabled/gifted students. In L. H. Fox, L. Brody, & D. Tobin (Eds.), *Learning-disabled/gifted children* (pp. 223–242). Baltimore: University Park Press.

Vail, P. L. (1987). *Smart kids with school problems: Things to know and ways to help.* New York: E. P. Dutton.

Wagonseller, B. R., & McDowell, R. L. (1979). *You and your child: A common sense approach to successful parenting.* Champaign, IL: Research Press.

Weick, K. (1978). Educational organizations as loosely coupled systems. In J. V. Baldridge & T. Deal (Eds.), *The dynamics of organizational change in education* (pp. 15–37). Berkeley, CA: McCutchen.

Weiner, B. (1976). An attributional approach for educational psychology. In L. Shulman (Ed.), *Review of research in education* (pp. 179–209). Itasca, IL: Peacock.

Weiner, B. (1979). A theory of motivation for some classroom experiences. *Journal of Educational Psychology, 71*(1), 3–25.

Weiner, B. (1983). Speculations regarding the role of affect in achievement-change programs guided by attributional principles. In J. M. Levine & M. C. Wang (Eds.), *Teacher and student perceptions: Implications for learning* (pp. 57–73). Hillsdale, N.J.: Erlbaum.

Wellington, C. B., & Wellington, J. (1965). *The underachievers: Challenges and guidelines.* Chicago: Rand McNally.

Wertsch, J. V. (1979). From social interaction to higher psychological processes: A clarification and application of Vygotsky's theory. *Human Development, 22*, 1–22.

Wertsch, J. V., McNamee, G. D., McLane, J. B., & Budwig, N. A. (1980). The adult–child dyad as a problem-solving system. *Child Development, 51*, 1215–1221.

Whitmore, J. R. (1980). *Giftedness, conflict, and underachievement.* Boston: Allyn and Bacon.

Winkler, R. C., Teigland, J. J., Munger, P. F., & Kranzler, G. D. (1965). The effects of selected counseling and remedial techniques on underachieving elementary school students. *Journal of Counseling Psychology, 12*, 384–387.

Witty, P. A. (1958). Who are the gifted? In N. B. Henry (Ed.), *Education of the gifted.* The Fifty-Seventh Yearbook of the National Society for the Study of Education, Part II (pp. 41–63). Chicago: University of Chicago Press.

Woodcock, R. W., & Johnson, M. B. (1977). *Woodcock–Johnson Assessment Battery, Part II.* Allen, TX: DLM Teaching Resources.

Wozniak, R. H. (1980). Theory, practice, and the "zone of proximal development" in

Soviet psychoeducational research. *Contemporary Educational Psychology, 5*(2), 175–183.

Yin, R. K. (1984). *Case study research: Design and methods.* Beverly Hills, CA: Sage Publications.

Zelman, S. (1985). *Individual differences and the computer learning environment: Motivational constraints to learning LOGO.* Paper presented at the annual meeting of the American Educational Research Association, Chicago.

Index

About the Author

Patricia Lambert Supplee, an experienced teacher who has taught at all levels from preschool through college, is also a consultant in gifted education. She was awarded the John C. Gowan Graduate Student Scholarship Award for her work on the underachieving gifted student. Dr. Supplee has contributed articles to *Roeper Review, Teachers College Record,* and the *Gifted Children Newsletter* and has written a number of curricula designed for gifted students from kindergarten through eighth grade. She received her Ed.D. degree from Teachers College, Columbia University, and has been an adjunct professor at Rutgers University. Currently, Dr. Supplee is an elementary principal in Stanhope, New Jersey. She and her husband live with their two gifted children in Andover, New Jersey.